The Rightful Place of Science:
New Tools for
Science Policy

Volume I

The Rightful Place of Science:

New Tools for Science Policy

Volume I

Edited by
Daniel Sarewitz

Foreword by
Michael M. Crow

Consortium for Science, Policy & Outcomes
Tempe, AZ, and Washington, DC

THE RIGHTFUL PLACE OF SCIENCE:
New Tools for Science Policy
Volume I

The Rightful Place of Science series explores the complex inter-actions among science, technology, politics, and the human condition.

For information on The Rightful Place of Science series, write to: Consortium for Science, Policy & Outcomes
P.O. Box 875603, Tempe, AZ 85287-5603
Or visit: http://www.cspo.org

Other volumes in this series:

Pielke Jr., R. 2018. *The Rightful Place of Science: Disasters & Climate Change*, 2nd ed. Tempe, AZ: Consortium for Science, Policy & Outcomes.

Miller, C. A., and Muñoz-Erickson, T. A. 2018. *The Rightful Place of Science: Designing Knowledge*. Tempe, AZ: Consortium for Science, Policy & Outcomes.

Model citation for this volume:

Sarewitz, D., ed. 2018. *The Rightful Place of Science: New Tools for Science Policy*, vol. I. Tempe, AZ: Consortium for Science, Policy & Outcomes.

ISBN: 0999587757

ISBN-13: 978-0999587751

FIRST EDITION, OCTOBER 2018

CONTENTS

VOLUME I

FOREWORD

I think of myself as a knowledge enterprise architect. I have spent the past forty years building institutions, especially but not exclusively within the university sector, that create and circulate knowledge to help solve society's problems and open up new opportunities for humanity to thrive. In this effort, I have been privileged to work with many extraordinary scientists driven by a passion for discovery. And I have also at times felt hampered by the lack of both fresh ideas and decision tools that could help guide the design of programs, policies, and institutions that maximize the societal benefit of scientific and technological advance.

That we have lacked such tools is perhaps unsurprising. Coming out of World War II, the United States had no economic competitors. We could benefit from a vibrant and creative industrial sector, a dozen or more preeminent research universities, and a social consensus around the need to out-compete the Soviet Union militarily, economically, politically, and culturally. The system of science that emerged from these conditions was practically guaranteed to succeed. And succeed it did, dominating the world of science and fueling an incredibly broad array of innovations—in everything from agriculture to aeronautics, and from geospatial data to genomics—that are today the economic and technological bedrock of a globalizing society.

From the knowledge enterprise design perspective, this success was significantly predicated upon a single principle: the more money spent on science, the more benefit that would accrue to society. The United States took this principle seriously, with public expenditures on university science alone rising by more than forty times (after adjusting for inflation) from the 1950s to the present day.

But along the way—as other nations learned to compete with us economically and technologically; as new challenges to human well-being emerged; as the research system grew in size and complexity; and as science itself took on an ever-expanding range of topics and problems and roles in society—the idea that the social value of science was determined solely by the amount of money spent on it revealed itself to be ridiculously incomplete. Starting in the 1960s, a rather small group of scientists, social scientists, philosophers, and decision makers in government, industry, and academia began to explore and debate principles and policies for assuring the social value of science. Their work did a good job uncovering and articulating many of the key variables, tensions, and dynamics at play.

Yet I think it's fair to say that little in the way of usable methods and tools emerged in the succeeding decades that could guide people, like me, who were seeking to design and improve the performance of knowledge enterprises.

In the late 1990s, as I took on the role of executive vice provost at Columbia University, it was apparent that the challenges that society would face in the twenty-first century demanded new types of knowledge enterprises for which we lacked even the most basic design principles and tools. In response, I created a small research and policy group in 1999 called the Center for Science, Policy & Outcomes (CSPO), whose main task was to develop theories, methods, and tools that could help guide the design and operation of knowledge enterprises in evolving toward the needs of a rapidly transforming world.

CSPO expanded significantly to become the Consortium for Science, Policy & Outcomes when it moved to Arizona State University, shortly after I took on that university's presidency in 2002. CSPO pursued its mission by articulating three fundamental questions about enterprise and policy design for science and innovation, and then implementing multiyear research programs to develop preliminary theories, methods, and tools aimed at addressing these questions.

The questions were:

1. How can science agendas be developed and pursued to ensure that they best meet the needs of decision makers?

2. How can science agendas and programs be assessed in terms of their capacity to achieve desired public values?

3. How can scientific and technological advance at the frontiers of innovation be steered to maximize social benefit and minimize problems?

The resulting research programs were (respectively):

1. RSD: Reconciling the Supply of and Demand for Science.

2. PVM: Public Value Mapping.

3. RTTA: Real-Time Technology Assessment, which evolved into a larger program of Anticipatory Governance of Emerging Technologies.

These programs were compelling enough to attract significant, multiyear support from a number of funders, including the V. Kann Rasmussen Foundation, the U.S. National Science Foundation, and the Rockefeller Foundation.

This volume—the first of two—brings together an illustrative sampling of the articles and reports produced by the first two programs, including basic theory and method development for each question, as well as case studies that can show how the theory and method are applied to real-world problems. The second volume, focused on governing emerging technologies, will do the same for the third question.

I have said that the work is preliminary, because the task at hand is immense, and needs to be taken up broadly across the community of scholars and practitioners who are interested in improving the social value of science in today's world. Of course, much remains to be done to further develop, test, refine, and improve these foundational efforts. But for anyone in a position to influence the design and evolution of knowledge enterprises, especially in academia and government, but in the private sector as well, this collection provides the closest thing we have today to a definitive guidebook.

Michael M. Crow
President, Arizona State University
September 2018

PART I. PRODUCING USABLE SCIENCE FOR BETTER DECISION MAKING

How can science agendas be developed and pursued to ensure that they best meet the needs of decision makers?

The idea that policies and public policy decisions should be "evidence-based" seems obvious, but the kinds of scientific information that decision makers can use may be very different from what scientific research programs are equipped to provide. The context of decision making may typically be a more important determinant of the value of science than the originality or accuracy of research results. The challenge for knowledge enterprise design is typically not one of "communicating science," but of institutional arrangements that can reconcile the processes of knowledge creation and use. Knowledge users turn out to be critical actors in the creation of usable science. These four chapters provide conceptual frameworks and practical guidance for fostering complementarities between the capabilities of science and the knowledge needs of decision makers.

1

THE NEGLECTED HEART OF SCIENCE POLICY: RECONCILING SUPPLY OF AND DEMAND FOR SCIENCE[*]

Daniel Sarewitz and Roger Pielke Jr.

Introduction to the Problem

Most scientific research, whether funded by public or private moneys, is intended to support, advance, or achieve a goal that is extrinsic to science itself. While some research is not expected by anyone to have a result other than the advance of scientific knowledge, such work is an extremely small portion of the overall science portfolio. Funding for research generally considered to be "basic" by those who perform it is usually justified by the expectation that the results will contribute to a particular desired outcome. For example, much of the research supported by the U.S. National Institutes of Health (NIH) is considered "basic" by medical researchers, in that it explores fundamental phenomena of human biology, but robust public support for

[*] Reprinted from D. Sarewitz and R. A. Pielke Jr., "The Neglected Heart of Science Policy: Reconciling Supply of and Demand for Science," *Environmental Science & Policy* 10, no 1 (2007): 5-16, with permission from Elsevier.

NIH is explicitly tied to the expectation (and legislative mandate) that research results should end up improving human health.

In pursuing a particular societal goal or set of goals, how do we know if a given research portfolio is more potentially effective than another portfolio? This question would seem to lie at the heart of science policy, yet it is almost never asked, much less studied systematically. Given the complexity of the science enterprise, of the processes of resource allocation, knowledge creation, and knowledge application, it would be very surprising indeed if the capacity of the existing enterprise to advance desired outcomes could not be significantly improved upon. For example, it is broadly accepted that current global priorities in biomedical research are very poorly aligned with global health priorities, a problem commonly termed the "10/90 problem," in reference to the observation that only about 10 percent of the global biomedical research budget is allocated to diseases accounting for about 90 percent of the worlds' health problems.[1]

Moreover, doing research always raises the question: "What research?" Looking again at biomedicine, scientists and other science policy decision makers heatedly debate the question of how much emphasis should be placed on exploring the molecular genetic origins of disease, versus environmental, behavioral, nutritional, cultural, and other origins.[2] Similar tensions flare up in debates over the appropriate balance between treatment (e.g., drugs) and prevention (e.g., vaccinations). Genetics and treatment often win out, not necessarily because they are known to be the best routes to advancing human health, but because they lie at the confluence of advanced technology, high prestige science, market incentives, and even ideology (e.g., genetic determinism[3]).

Indeed, just "doing research" on a problem of societal importance says nothing directly about whether or under

4

what conditions the research can effectively contribute to addressing that problem.[4] A major commitment to AIDS research starting in the late 1980s led in fairly short time to antiretroviral drugs that are, thus far, quite effective in the treatment of AIDS patients. Yet 90 percent of AIDS sufferers have no reasonable prospect of ever receiving this treatment, largely because they (or the societies in which they live) cannot afford it. The potential for science to contribute to societal goals depends critically on factors well beyond science.

Given how little attention is paid to understanding the relationship between alternative possible research portfolios and stipulated societal outcomes, there is no a priori reason to expect that existing research portfolios are more effective than other possible research portfolios at contributing to the achievement of desired societal outcomes. This being the case, the key question — the neglected heart of science policy — is how one might approach the problem of rigorously assessing the relationship between a research portfolio (or a set of alternative portfolios) and the societal outcomes that the portfolio is supposed to advance.

Some would argue that this problem is inherently intractable. Because the connections between research and societal outcomes cannot be accurately predicted in detail, the argument would go, predicting the differing outcomes of an array of hypothetical or counterfactual research portfolios is impossible. We think such arguments (which are common in science policy debates) are wrong-headed and wrong. Wrong-headed because science policy decisions are constantly being justified on the basis of putative linkages between research investments and desired outcomes. If such justifications cannot be supported analytically or logically, then they should not be asserted in the first place. Wrong because contingency, complexity and non-linearity (i.e., in the relations between science policy decisions and societal outcomes) are obstacles to accurate predictions, but they need not prevent improved decision-making,[5] where "improved" means more likely to achieve desired outcomes.

Our approach in this paper is to conceptualize science in terms of a "supply" of knowledge and information, societal outcomes in terms of a "demand" function that seeks to apply knowledge and information to achieve specific societal goals, and the relationship between the two as "reconciled," in part, through science policy decision processes. In the next section we develop this conceptualization, drawing briefly from many areas of science policy scholarship. The core of our argument is that "better" science portfolios (that is, portfolios plausibly viewed as more likely to advance desired societal outcomes, however defined) would be achieved if they reflected an understanding of the supply of science, the demand for science, and the complex, dynamic relationship between the two. We will provide a general method for pursuing such knowledge, using the specific example of climate change science to illustrate how research on science policy could be organized to support improved decisions about the organization of science itself.

Understanding and Mediating the Supply of and Demand for Science in Science Policy

We borrow from economics the concepts of "supply" and "demand" to discuss the relationship of scientific results and their use for several reasons.[6] First, the analogy is straightforward. Decisions about science (i.e., science policy decisions) determine the composition and size of research portfolios that "supply" scientific results. People in various institutional and social settings who look to scientific information as an input to their decisions constitute a "demand" function for scientific results. Of course, the demand function can be complicated by many factors, e.g., sometimes a decision maker may not be aware of the existence of useful information or may misuse, or be prevented from using, potentially useful information. In other cases, necessary useful information may not exist or may not be accessible. But our key point is that there is reasonable conceptual clarity in distinguishing between people, institutions, and processes concerned with the supply of science, and those concerned with its use. Indeed, conventional notions of science policy exclusively embody decisions related to the former.

Nonetheless, a second reason for characterizing scientific research in terms of supply and demand is to recognize that, just as in economics, in the case of science, supply and demand are closely interrelated. Science policy decisions are not made in a vacuum but with some consideration or promise of societal needs and priorities. Thus there is a feedback between the (perceived) demand for science and the (perceived) characteristics of supply. People with spinal cord injuries or diabetes, influenced by the rhetoric of scientists studying embryonic stem cells, in turn create an enhanced demand for such research. However, whether embryonic stem cell research is itself the "right" path to achieving the desired goals (in this case, presumably cures for the injuries or diseases) is not necessarily apparent. Numerous alternative paths may be available.[7]

At the same time, we recognize the power and importance of scholarship over the past several decades that reveals the complex manner in which science and society co-evolve, or are co-produced.[8] The insights from such work dictate that categories such as "supply" and "demand" cannot be understood as conceptually discrete or fully coherent. Moreover, both supply of and demand for information emerge from complex networks of individuals and institutions with diverse incentives, capabilities, roles, and cultures. Yet in the face of such complexity, decisions about resource allocation, institutional design, program organization, and information dissemination have been and are still being made. That is, while notions of "supply" and "demand" may embody considerable complexity, they also represent something real and recognizable: on the one hand, people conducting research that has been justified in terms of particular societal outcomes, and on the other, people making decisions aimed at contributing to those outcomes.

Some think the supply function is inherently optimized so long as scientists are freely pursuing knowledge with minimal external interference. This position, most rigorously espoused by the Hungarian-British polymath Michael Polanyi, views the scientific community as an autonomous, self-regulating market organized to identify and pursue the most efficient lines of knowledge generation.[9] Any "attempt at guiding scientific research toward a purpose other than its own is an attempt to deflect it from the advancement of science."[10] From this perspective, the supply of scientific knowledge is best generated without any connection or attention to demand for particular types of knowledge.

The apparent logical and practical weakness of this perspective — that knowledge, efficiently pursued, may or may not be knowledge that has any utility in the world — has been answered in two ways. First, basic knowledge is conceived as accumulating in a metaphorical reservoir from which society can draw to solve its multifarious problems. The reservoir is filled most rapidly and effectively through the advance of science independent of considerations of application. Second, application of basic knowledge to real world problems is often serendipitous, so there is no way to predict the connection between a given line of research and a given social goal. Chemistry (or, one supposes, solid earth geophysics or cosmology) is as likely to help cure a certain disease as is molecular genetics. Numerous anecdotes are offered up to illustrate the significance of serendipity in connecting inquiry to utility.[11]

Of course no one really advocates this model in its extreme form. Certainly, if the time scale is long enough (decades and beyond), fundamental advances in knowledge often have broad application beyond anything that could be anticipated, but on the time scales that motivate support for research, strategic investments in basic understanding are invariably conceived in the context of related areas of potential application. This reality has given rise to a weaker version of the science-as-a-self-regulating-market argument, where the need to make strategic investment choices among disciplines and research topics is tacitly acknowledged, but scientists and science advocates still argue that they are best positioned to contribute to social goals if they are given autonomy to pursue knowledge in directions guided by the logic of nature, not the exigencies of social need.[12]

The idea that the creation of scientific knowledge is a process largely independent from the application of that knowledge within society has had enormous political value for scientists, because it allows them to make the dual claims that (1) fundamental research divorced from any consideration of application is the most important type of research,[13] and (2) such research can best contribute to society if it is insulated from such practical considerations, thus ensuring that scientists not only have putative freedom of inquiry, but also that they have control over public resources devoted to science. The continued influence of this perspective was asserted by Alan Leshner,[14] Chief Executive Officer of the American Association for the Advancement of Science: "Historically science and technology have changed society, society now is likely to want to change science and technology, or at least to help shape their course. For many scientists, any such overlay of values on the conduct of science is anathema to our core principles and our historic success."

Empirical studies of the complex connections between research and societal application give little support to the foregoing conceptions. One of the richest areas of scholarship in this realm has focused on the origins of technological innovation, where case studies and longitudinal surveys have revealed networks of continual feedbacks among a large variety of actors, including academic scientists, industrial scientists, research administrators, corporate executives, policymakers, and consumers. The resulting picture is complex and yields no single, straightforward model for how knowledge and application interact; yet one feature that invariably characterizes successful innovation is ongoing communication between the producers and users of knowledge. Moreover, historical studies of innovation typically show precisely the opposite of what one would expect from the autonomous science argument. Emerging technological frontiers often precede deep knowledge of the underlying fundamental science. It is precisely the demand for better theoretical foundations among those worried about applications that has driven the growth of fundamental science in many areas.[15] As economist Richard R. Nelson writes: "for the most part science is valuable as an input to technological change these days because much of scientific research is in fields that are oriented to providing knowledge that is of use in particular areas."[16]

If this seems spectacularly circular, then that is precisely the point: science agendas are closely aligned with areas of technological application because certain areas of science demonstrate themselves to be of particular value to some groups of users. This is a very different view of the world than one in which science advances independently of subsequent applications. Research on the relations between industry and universities, for example, strongly demonstrates that the priorities of academic basic science have long been aligned with the needs of industry.[17] Such alignment is not a result of serendipity, but of the development of networks that allow close and ongoing communication among the multiple sectors involved in technological innovation. Thus, fundamental research relevant to innovation does indeed go on in universities where scientists have considerable autonomy to pursue basic knowledge, but the priorities and directions of this fundamental work are strongly influenced by collaboration with scientists, engineers, and managers working closer to the actual point of product development and application (and they, in turn, are influenced by a variety of end-users or consumers). In the useful term introduced by political scientist Donald Stokes, this type of fundamental science is "use-inspired," and it is central to the successful functioning of modern, high technology economies.[18] More generally, the production of knowledge in the broader context of applications has been termed Mode 2 science by Michael Gibbons and his colleagues, to distinguish it from the traditional insistence on "pure" science as the ultimate source of social value.[19]

Two attributes of this discussion bear emphasis. The first is that, in contrast to the canonical portrayal of fundamental science contributing to application because it is free to advance in isolation from consideration of application, studies of technological innovation have often shown exactly the opposite—that it is the awareness of potential application and utility that ensure the contribution of fundamental research to innovation. Second, in contrast to the portrayal of scientific advance as something that is unpredictable and therefore beyond planning or control through influences beyond the scientific enterprise, the history of post-World War II science and technology policy is one of strategic decisions about investments in particular areas of science and engineering in support of specific areas of societal application, such as communications, computing, advanced materials, aviation and avionics, weapons systems, and biotechnology. From the creation of agricultural research stations in the mid-19th century, to the advent of the transistor shortly after World War II, to the continued advance of human biotechnologies today, strategic decisions to focus public sector resources in particular areas of science have consciously and successfully linked research portfolios to technological advance and such societal outcomes as economic growth, agricultural productivity, and military power.

Such outcomes are themselves highly complex, of course. In the past several decades, other lines of scholarship[20] have illuminated how the multifarious societal consequences of scientific and technological advance bear clear evidence of a dynamic relationship between the producers and users of knowledge and innovation, and that this relationship itself is strongly conditioned by broader contextual factors.

For example, the natural, cultural, and political attributes of the United States in the nineteenth century gave rise to an organization of agricultural science closely tied to the practice of farming and the needs of farmers (and strongly resisted, at first, by scientists seeking to preserve their autonomy), including the development of institutional innovations — the agricultural research station and extension services — to bring supply and demand sides together.[21] The inextricable linkages between science, technology, and the geopolitics of the Cold War drove the institutional symbiosis of universities, corporations, and the military that dominated the demand–supply relation in U.S. science for half a century and motivated President Eisenhower's famous warning about the overweening power of the "military-industrial complex."[22] Feminism and the growing political power of the women's movement in the U.S.

eventually led to an understanding that a health research system run by males was often biased toward males in its priorities, practices, and results. Such insights, which were at the time controversial but are now widely accepted, led to significant changes both in the conduct of science and its application in ways that benefit women.[23] Similarly, the political empowerment arising from the gay rights movement in the United States ultimately influenced the course of AIDS research in ways that directly benefited AIDS sufferers in the U.S., for example through more rapid clinical testing and approval of treatments.[24] Based on these successes, "disease lobbies" in the United States have become a significant factor in shaping biomedical research priorities.

Such examples illustrate that the supply of science is often responsive to the presence of a well-articulated demand function. Put somewhat more bluntly, scientific research trajectories are often decisively influenced through the application of political pressure by groups with a stake in the outcomes of research and the power and resources necessary to make their voices heard. Obviously, this does not mean that science can produce whatever is asked of it. Moreover, groups lobbying for one type of research or another may or may not actually understand how best to advance their interests. For example, it might be the case that health care delivery reform or changes in behavior would return greater benefits to some disease lobbies than more funding for a particular type of research.

More significantly, there is no reason to think that the influence of particular political interest groups (whether they be disease lobbies or pharmaceutical corporations) on the supply of science will yield outcomes that are broadly beneficial to society; they may, on the contrary, lead to the preferential capture of benefits by certain groups.[25] For instance, the very fact that most health research is carried out in affluent societies and responds to the health needs of affluent people has resulted in an increasingly wide gap between science agendas and global health priorities. Scientific opportunities that are likely to yield the greatest return in terms of social benefit (e.g., through vaccine development) are widely neglected. Nonetheless, politics provides a key mechanism for mediating the relationship between — for reconciling — supply of and demand for science via the science policy decision processes that so strongly determine the character of the supply function.

The philosopher Philip Kitcher has identified an ideal, which he terms "well-ordered science,"[26] that describes an optimal relationship between supply and demand (though he does not articulate it using these terms), achieved through an ideal process of representative deliberation:

> *For perfectly well-ordered science we require that there be institutions governing the practice of inquiry within society that invariably lead to investigations that coincide in three respects with the judgments of ideal deliberators, representatives of the distribution of [relevant] viewpoints within society. First, at the stage of agenda-setting, the assignment of resources to projects is exactly the one that would be chosen through the process of ideal deliberation.... Second, in the pursuit of the investigations, the strategies adopted are those which are maximally efficient among the set that accords with the moral constraints the ideal deliberators would collectively choose. Third, in the translation of results of inquiry into applications, the policy followed is just the one that would be recommended by ideal deliberators....[27]*

Well-ordered science, like all ideals (democracy, justice, freedom), sets a standard that cannot be met but toward which aspirations can be aimed: science that is maximally responsive to the needs and values of those who may have a stake in the outcomes of the research; the best possible reconciliation of supply and demand. This philosophical ideal adds a normative overlay to what has been demonstrated empirically. Not only are the supply of and demand for science related to each other through a process of politically mediated feedbacks, but in a democracy it is desirable that this feedback process be maximally responsive to the negotiated common interests of relevant stakeholders, rather than captured by particular special interests. Indeed, as Kitcher asserts: "the current neglect of the interests of a vast number of people represents a severe departure from well-ordered science."[28]

Kitcher's notion of "well-ordered science" is procedural; it describes a well-informed process of defining research agendas and practices that reflects the priorities and norms of relevant stakeholders (including, of course, scientists involved in the research). In the real world, intermediary institutions—sometimes called boundary organizations—may enhance the pursuit of well-ordered science by mediating communication between supply and demand functions for particular areas of societal concern.[29] Again, this is not a matter of asking scientists to "cure cancer" or "end war," it is a process of reconciling the capabilities and aspirations of knowledge producers and knowledge users.

Even if the procedural ideal were achieved, it would not guarantee the achievement of a particular stipulated social outcome. Many of the goals of science—curing a given disease, for example—may be difficult to attain for a variety of reasons, ranging from intrinsic scientific difficulty to cultural or institutional complexities. But the key point is that departures from well-ordered science are inherently less likely to achieve such outcomes, because research agendas will not reflect the priorities, needs and capabilities of the broadest group of constituents that could potentially make use of the resulting knowledge and innovation.

Supply of and Demand for Science in Decision-Making

Our discussion so far has aimed at building a conceptual foundation for assessing the relations between supply of and demand for science as input to the science policy decisions that help reconcile those relations. We have shown: (1) that the notion of supply and demand functions for science helps to clarify the dynamic role of science in society; (2) that supply of and demand for science are reconciled in various ways, with various degrees of success (depending in part on who defines "success"); (3) an ideal reconciliation of supply and demand would match the capabilities of science with the needs of those who could most benefit from it. We now apply these insights to what logically ought to be the most obvious — and tractable — problem of supply–demand relations in science: the use of science to support decision-making in public affairs.

In areas as diverse as national innovation strategies, technological risk, and environmental protection, science is increasingly called upon to provide information that can improve decision-making in public affairs.[30] This growing role for science in part reflects the increasing capacity of scientific methods and tools to study complex systems ranging from genes to climate. But it also reflects the rapidity of societal evolution that results from the increasing power and global reach of science and technology. That is, science is called upon as a tool to monitor and assess the changes that science itself helps to induce.[31] The expectation that science can help inform human decisions about societal change has been especially strong in the area of the environment, and we focus our discussion on the problem of climate change.

Research on decision-making has long recognized that there is no simple connection between "more information" and "better decisions,"[32] and that, to the extent "more information" does not solve a problem, the fault cannot simply be located with the decision maker (i.e., in the demand function). More information may not lead to better decisions for many reasons, e.g., the information is not relevant to user needs; it is not appropriate for the decision context; it is not sufficiently reliable or trusted; it conflicts with users' values or interests; it is unavailable at the time it would be useful; it is poorly communicated. Also, of course, the idea of "better decisions" depends on who stands to benefit from which decisions. Some types of information may support decisions that benefit some people but adversely affect others.

Apparently commonsensical ideas, for example, that climate forecasts would be valuable to people who make decisions related to climate behavior (e.g., water managers, emergency managers, agricultural planners) turn out to be very complex, as such factors as institutional structures, prior practice, socioeconomic conditions, and political stakes and power distributions, strongly influence the types of information that decision makers need and use, and the array of stakeholders that might benefit from such decisions.[33]

Scholars striving to understand the behavior of scientific information in complex decision contexts (especially those related to the environment and sustainability) have converged on the recognition that the utility of information depends on the dynamics of the decision context and its broader social setting.[34] Utility is not immanent in the knowledge itself. For example, Michael Gibbons describes the transition from a gold standard of "reliable" knowledge as determined by scientists themselves, to "socially robust" knowledge that, first, "is valid not only inside but also outside the laboratory. Second, this validity is achieved through involving an extended group of experts, including lay 'experts.' And third, because 'society' has participated in its genesis, such knowledge is less likely to be contested than that which is merely reliable."[35]

Arriving at a similar set of insights, David W. Cash and his colleagues have shown that information capable of improving decisions about the management of complex environmental systems must have the three attributes of credibility, salience, and legitimacy, attributes which can only emerge from close and continual interactions among knowledge producers and users.[36] Roger Pielke and colleagues similarly recognized that effective integration of science and decision-making required a tight coupling among research, communication, and use.[37] Political scientist David Guston pointed to the value of boundary organizations at the interface between science and decision-making for helping to ensure that such integration can occur.[38] The philosophers of science Silvio Funtowicz and Jerome R. Ravetz coined the term "post-normal science" to describe the complex organization of knowledge production necessary to address problems of decision-making, in contrast to older notions of autonomous—"normal"—scientific practice.[39]

Despite these conceptual advances—derived, in part, from studying relative successes in such areas as international agricultural research and weather forecasting—the overall picture is neither clear nor encouraging. While the rich world spends billions annually on research aimed at supporting environmental policy, there is not much evidence that significantly enhanced decision-making capabilities or environmental outcomes have resulted.[40] To suggest that "politics" has prevented progress on such issues is merely to restate the problem. Indeed, the recent spate of media and public attention focused on the problem of the "politicization of science" in the United States reflects the persistent notion that the contribution of science to decisions is mostly a process of delivering facts to users, and that failure to attend to facts reflects problems in the demand function (i.e., "politics").[41] This debate is oblivious to the sorts of insights summarized above, which teach us that science is always politicized, and that the real-world challenge is to cultivate an inclusive and non-pathological process of politicization[42] that allows a democratically appropriate—well-ordered—reconciliation of supply of and demand for information or knowledge. Put somewhat differently, understanding the politics embodied in the supply and demand functions is a key analytical task in support of their improved reconciliation via science policy decisions.

While there are many complex reasons why it is difficult to generate "socially robust knowledge," scholarly attention has focused principally on the dynamics of interactions between knowledge producers and decision makers, and on the need for institutional innovation to enhance such interactions, as briefly summarized above. Very little consideration has been given, however, to science policy — that is, to the decision processes that strongly determine the priorities, institutional settings, and metrics of success for the supply of scientific research.[43] Correspondingly, very little consideration has been given to the types of information or knowledge that science policy decision makers could call upon to improve the reconciliation of supply and demand.

The neglect of science policy is especially problematic because the science policy decisions that strongly determine research portfolios, particularly at the macro level, are likely to be made by people, and in institutions, that are distant from the interfaces between research and its potential use. Indeed, the complex interactions among knowledge producers, knowledge users, and intermediaries that characterize post-normal science often takes place within a context of scientific research agendas whose main characteristics have already been determined through science policy decisions. To further complicate matters, the very process of establishing such characteristics helps to empower some potential users (who may benefit from the structure of the supply function) while marginalizing others. These problems are particularly acute for large scale, long-term research efforts, such as global climate change science.

Origins of the Climate Change Supply Function

In 2003, seven leading U.S. climate scientists wrote (in response to an article by the authors of this paper[44]):

The basic driver in climate science, as in other areas of scientific research, is the pursuit of knowledge and understanding. Furthermore, the desire of climate scientists to reduce uncertainties does not … arise primarily from the view that such reductions will be of direct benefit to policymakers. Rather, the quantification of uncertainties over time is important because it measures our level of understanding and the progress made in advancing that understanding.[45]

This argument restates the traditional logic for public support of science, discussed at the beginning of our paper: that the exploration of nature, motivated by the desire for understanding, is the best route to beneficial social outcomes. It is consistent with (though more extreme than) the original rationale for the U.S. Global Change Research Program (USGCRP), under whose aegis more than $25 billion were spent on climate research between 1989 and 2003. While the USGCRP was intended by policymakers to provide "usable knowledge" for decision makers, its structure and internal logic reflected the belief that the best route to such usable knowledge was via research motivated predominantly by a desire to expand fundamental understanding. The USGCRP was also motivated by the belief that decision-making would be improved simply by providing additional scientific information (with a particular focus on predictive models) to those making decisions.[46]

To the extent that the USGCRP's science priorities were responsive to a particular decision context or demand function, this function was the international assessment and negotiation processes aimed at arriving at a global regime for stabilizing greenhouse gas emissions. To the extent that scientists who conduct climate research, and putative users of that science, were interacting, they were doing so mostly as part of the process of developing this regime. The key point here is that the science agenda (i.e., supply function) was linked to an extremely restricted expectation of what sorts of policies would be necessary to deal with climate change (i.e., global policies that governed greenhouse gas emissions), via simplistic but politically powerful notions about what would cause those policies to come about (i.e., increased scientific knowledge about climate change). In this highly restricted, supply-dominated context, the Intergovernmental Panel on Climate Change (IPCC) issued reports throughout the 1990s and early 2000s, written by teams of scientists that assessed the state of expanding knowledge about climate, while the U.S. National Research Council (NRC) issued reports, written by teams of scientists that analyzed research needs and priorities in the context of pursuing a comprehensive understanding of climate behavior. These expert-driven, supply-focused processes were the controlling political influences on the evolution of the climate research agenda.[47]

The fact that so many billions have been spent on climate research, not just in the United States but in other developed countries as well, in turn suggests that there is a demand function which is being served by this research (otherwise, why would policymakers keep spending the money?), although in fact very little is known about the structure and objectives of that demand function. To the extent that the IPCC can be viewed as a sort of boundary organization aimed at connecting the science to its use in society, then this demand function is mostly embodied in the international process for negotiating and implementing climate treaties under the U.N. Framework Convention on Climate Change, especially the Kyoto Protocol. Politicians and policymakers in the United States have, over the years, justified their support of the USGCRP largely in terms of the need to have better information before making decisions about climate, where "decisions about climate" has generally meant decisions about emissions reductions under the Framework Convention.

Yet the problem of climate change implicates a much broader array of potential decision makers in the climate change arena than those with a stake in international negotiations,[48] and would include farmers and foresters, local emergency managers and city planners, public health officials, utility operators and regulators, and insurance companies, among many others. Such constituencies, which define a diverse demand function, have little impact on the evolving agenda for climate research, which has been driven almost exclusively by scientific organizations such as the IPCC and the NRC. In 2003 an exhaustive strategic planning process aimed at refining the USGCRP was dominated by scientific voices plus civil society groups advocating action on the Kyoto Protocol, with little input from actual decision makers who influence, are influenced by, and must respond to, climate change and climate impacts. The resulting *Strategic Plan for the U.S. Climate Change Science Program* contains comprehensive recommendations for continuing and expanding climate research, but little information about the needs and capabilities of the potential users of that information (though the report does highlight the importance of such users), and little analysis of how research is actually supposed to benefit various types of users.[49]

Meanwhile, relatively sparse but consistent research conducted under the category of "human dimensions of climate change" (mostly focused on annual to inter-annual climate variability) has shown that available information on climate is in some cases not deemed useful by decision makers,[50] in other cases benefits particular users at the expense of others,[51] and in yet other cases is misused and contributes to undesired outcomes,[52] and in all cases depends for its value on the types of institutions that are making the decisions.[53] Overall, however, the institutional structures and feedback processes that lead to increased understanding between supply and demand sectors (characteristic of Mode 2, post-normal, or well-ordered science, and documented as a key element of high technology innovation processes) are largely absent from the climate research enterprise, especially in the United States. The Potential Consequences of Climate Variability and Change did encompass a series of regional meetings involving, with various degrees of success, certain stakeholders, but this process has not been institutionalized; rather, it culminated in several reports whose purpose was "to synthesize, evaluate, and report on what we presently know about the potential consequences of climate variability and change for the U.S. in the 21st century."[54] The question of whether "what we presently know" is what we need to know to act effectively was not addressed.

Reconciling Supply and Demand in Climate Science: A Proposed Method

The insights derived from several decades of scholarship on the relationship between the production and use of knowledge in many domains of research and application suggest that the organization of climate science in the United States is unlikely to show a strong alignment between the supply of and demands for knowledge among a broad array of potential users. Adopting Kitcher's term, we here hypothesize that climate science is very far from being "well ordered." More importantly, we suggest both that this hypothesis is testable and that, given the scale of public investment and the potential environmental and socioeconomic stakes, the effectiveness of science policies could be greatly enhanced by testing it.

As long ago as 1992, a first (and, as far as we can know, last) step along these lines was taken in the Joint Climate Project to Address Decision Maker's Uncertainty.[55] The project sought to determine "what research can do to assist U.S. decision makers over the coming years and decades," it argued that "an ongoing process of systematic communication between the decision-making and the research communities is essential," and it concluded that "the process started in this project can serve as a foundation and model for the necessary continued efforts to bridge the gap between science and policy."[56]

More than a decade later, the scale of the climate research enterprise, in the United States as well as other affluent nations, has increased enormously, along with fundamental understanding of the climate system. At the same time we observe that there is little if any evidence that this growth of understanding can be connected to meaningful progress toward slowing the negative impacts of climate on society and the environment.[57] On the other hand, appreciation of the variety of decision makers and complexity of decision contexts relevant to climate change has greatly deepened. Understanding of this diversity should allow us to ask: what types of knowledge might contribute to decision-making that could improve the societal value of climate science? Next, we outline a methodology of science policy research for assessing and reconciling the supply and demand functions for climate science information.

Demand Side Assessment

Research on the human dimensions of climate, though modestly funded over the past decade or so, has made important strides in characterizing the diverse users of climate information (be they local fisherman and farmers or national political leaders); the mechanisms for distributing climate information; the impacts of climate information on users and their institutions. This literature provides the necessary foundations for constructing a general classification of user types, capabilities, attributes, and information sources. This classification can then be tested and refined, using standard techniques such as case studies, facilitated workshops, surveys and focus groups. Given the breadth of potentially relevant stakeholders, such a demand side assessment would need to proceed by focusing on particular challenges or sectors, such as carbon cycle management, agriculture, ecosystems management, and hazard mitigation.

Supply Side Assessment

Perhaps surprisingly, the detailed characteristics of the supply side — the climate science community — are less well understood than those of the demand side. One reason for this of course is that over the past decade or so there has been some programmatic support for research on the users and uses of climate science, but no similar research on climate research itself. Potentially relevant climate science is conducted in diverse settings, including academic departments, autonomous research centers, government laboratories, and private sector laboratories, each of which is characterized by particular cultures, incentives, constraints, opportunities, and funding sources. Understanding the supply function demands a comprehensive picture of these types of institutions in terms that are analogous to knowledge of the demand side, looking at organizational, political, and cultural, as well as technical, capabilities. Such a picture should emerge from analysis of documents describing research activities of relevant organizations, from bibliometric and content analysis of research articles produced by these organizations, and from workshops, focus groups, and interviews. The result would be a taxonomy of suppliers, supply products, and research trajectories. As with the demand side assessment, the scale of the research enterprise suggests that this assessment process should build up a comprehensive picture by focusing sequentially on specific areas of research (such as carbon cycle science). This incremental approach also allows the assessment method to evolve and improve over time.

Comparative Overlay

Assessments of supply and demand sides of climate information can then form the basis of a straightforward evaluation of how climate science research opportunities and patterns of information production match up with demand side information needs, capabilities, and patterns of information use. In essence, the goal is to develop a classification, or "map," of the supply side and overlay it on a comparably scaled "map" of the demand side. A key issue in the analysis has to do with expectations and capabilities. Do climate decision makers have reasonable expectations of what the science can deliver, and can they use available or potentially available information? Are scientists generating information that is appropriate to the institutional and policy contexts in which decision makers are acting? Useful classifications of supply and demand functions will pay particular attention to such questions. The results of this exercise should be tested and refined via stakeholder workshops and focus groups.

The 2 x 2 matrix shown in Figure 1.1 schematically illustrates the process. We call this the "missed opportunity" matrix because the upper left and lower right quadrants indicate where opportunities to connect science and decision-making have been missed. Areas of positive reinforcement (lower left) indicate effective resource allocation where empowered users are benefiting from relevant science. As discussed above, this situation is most likely to emerge when information users and producers are connected by, and interact through, a variety of feedback mechanisms. Areas of negative interference may indicate both opportunities and inefficiencies. For example, if an assessment of demand reveals that certain classes of users could benefit from a type of information that is currently not available (upper left), then this is an opportunity — if provision of the information is scientifically, technologically, and institutionally feasible. Another possibility (lower right) would be that decision makers are not making use of existing information that could lead to improved decisions, as Bridget Callahan and her coauthors documented for some regional hydrological forecasts.[58] An important subset of the problem represented in this quadrant occurs when the interests of some groups, for political or socioeconomic reasons, are actually undermined because of the ability of other groups to make use of research results, as Maria Carmen Lemos and her fellow researchers demonstrated in a study of regional climate forecasts in northeast Brazil.[59] Finally (upper right), research might not be relevant to the capabilities and needs of prospective users, as Steve Rayner and his colleagues demonstrated in their study of water managers.[60]

Institutional Context

Decisions emerge within institutional contexts; such contexts, in turn, help to determine what types of information may be useful for decision-making. Supply and demand must ultimately be reconciled within science policy institutions, such as relevant government agencies, legislative committees, executive offices, non-governmental advisory groups, etc. Institutional attributes such as bureaucratic structure, budgeting, reporting requirements, and avenues of public input, combine with less tangible factors including the ideas and norms embedded within an institution, to drive decision-making about the conduct of research and the utility of results.[61] How do research managers justify their decisions? Are those justifications consistent with the decisions that they actually make? What ideas or values are implicit in the analyses and patterns of decisions that the institution exhibits? What incentives determine how information is valued? These sorts of questions can be addressed through analysis of internal and public documents, interviews, and public statements about why and how research portfolios are developed. Science policy researcher Elizabeth McNie has provided a more thorough discussion of what is known about how science policy institutions help mediate supply and demand.[62] This remains a key area for additional research, but is largely beyond the scope of our discussion here.

Figure 1.1: The Missed Opportunity Matrix for Reconciling Supply and Demand

		Demand: Can User Benefit from Research?	
		YES	NO
Supply: Is Relevant Information Produced?	NO	Research agendas may be inappropriate.	Research agendas and user needs poorly matched; users may be disenfranchised.
	YES	Empowered users taking advantage of well-deployed research capabilities.	Unsophisticated or marginalized users, institutional constraints, or other obstacles prevent information use.

Our analysis of the evolution of the climate science enterprise in the United States indicates that policy assumptions and political dynamics have largely kept the supply function insulated from the demand function except in the area of the international climate governance regime.[63] Some modest experiments, notably the RISA (regional integrated sciences and assessment) program of the National Oceano-graphic and Atmospheric Administration, have sought to connect scientists and research agendas to particular user needs at the local level, but these lie outside the mainstream of the climate science enterprise.

A research effort of the type sketched here can illuminate how well climate science supply and demand are aligned and who benefits from existing alignments. It can highlight current successes and failures in climate science policy, identify future opportunities for investment, and reveal institutional avenues for, and obstacles to, moving forward. Consistent with our perspective throughout this paper, the value of the method will in great part depend on how receptive science policymakers are to learning from the results of such research. We fully accept, of course, that knowledge generated about science policy is subject to the same pitfalls of irrelevance, insulation, neglect, mismatch, and misapplication that motivate our investigation in the first place. But our understanding of the current context for science policy decision-making gives us two reasons for optimism. First, the fundamental justification for the public investment in climate science is its value for decision-making. This justification, repeated countless times in countless documents and public statements, thus defines a baseline for assessing accountability and measuring performance via the type of approach we have described here. Second, and of equal importance, the very process of implementing the method we describe will begin to create communication, reflection, and learning among science policy decision makers and various users and potential users of scientific information hitherto unconnected to the science policy arena. In other words, the research method itself creates feedbacks between supply and demand that will expand the constituencies and networks engaged in science policy discourse, expand the decision options available to science policymakers, and thus expand the opportunities to make climate science more well-ordered. Undoubtedly, institutional innovation would need to be a part of this process as well, given the scale and scope of the climate science enterprise and the potential user community.

As a first step toward testing both this method (which should, of course, have broad applicability beyond climate change science) and the specific hypothesis that climate change science is far from well ordered, we convened two workshops to consider supply of and demand for science related to the global carbon cycle. Carbon cycle science is a high priority area of focus in climate change science, with annual public expenditures in the United States in excess of $200 million. Research priorities have been established largely in the manner described above, with little engagement between supply and demand sides.[64] Nevertheless, the investment in carbon cycle science is justified in terms of its value for a variety of information users in industry, agriculture, government, and other sectors.[65]

Our workshops brought together leading carbon cycle researchers, science policy decision makers, and users representing "carbon cycle management" decision contexts such as urban environmental planning, energy production, agriculture, and emissions trading. Perhaps not surprisingly, most users reported that they benefited little, if at all, from recent advances in carbon cycle science (the single exception being the user engaged in developing emissions trading schemes), and, importantly, that they would greatly welcome specific types of knowledge and information that could enhance their capacity to make effective "carbon management" decisions. The extent to which this poor reconciliation between supply and demand reflected the inability of users to take advantage of relevant available information (lower right quadrant in the matrix above), versus a failure to generate relevant and usable scientific information (upper left and right quadrants), awaits further analysis and a more rigorous implementation of our method (guided by what we learned during the workshop). But the larger point is that this level of reconnaissance supports the hypothesis that the science is not well ordered, as well as the prospect that a better reconciliation of supply and demand is both possible and desirable.

Enhancing Public Value in Public Science

In the public sector, science policy decision-making is mostly about how to allocate marginal increases in funding among existing research programs. At the same time, such allocation decisions are usually justified in terms of their value in pursuing societal outcomes extrinsic to science itself. In a world of limited science resources, then, it would seem more than sensible to bolster such justifications with better understanding of the implications of science policy decisions for societal outcomes. Nevertheless, consideration of how alternative research portfolios might better achieve stipulated societal outcomes is not a regular part of science policy discourse or decision processes.

There are several reasons for this, including:

1. The widespread belief that more science automatically translates into more social benefit;
2. The insulation of science policy decision processes from the contexts within which scientific knowledge is used;
3. The capture of science policy decision process by narrow political constituencies (drawn from either the supply or demand side);
4. The natural resistance of bureaucratic decision processes to changes inside the margins;
5. The absence of analytical frameworks and tools that can reveal connections among science policy decisions, the supply function for science, the demand function for science, and the effective pursuit of stipulated societal outcomes.

Much of our work (as well as that of a number of colleagues) in recent years has begun to consider how to develop such analytical frameworks and tools.[66] This work is stimulated by the possibility that scientific priorities and societal needs are poorly aligned in a number of critical areas. The challenge for scholarship, in our view, is (a) to identify particular cases where the promises upon which scientific funding are predicated are not being effectively met, and, more importantly, (b) to show that plausible alternative research portfolios might more effectively meet these promises. The challenge for science policy is to draw on such findings to enable better decisions about the allocation of limited resources.

In this paper we have outlined one way to conceptualize a desirable connection between science policy decisions, science, and social outcomes: via a reconciliation of the supply of and demand for science. We have offered a straightforward method for developing knowledge that could facilitate such a reconciliation, and an example—climate change research—illustrating the method's application. In doing so, our larger purpose is to challenge science policy researchers and science policy decision makers to seek ways to formalize and to make analytically tractable the neglected, researchable question that must lie at the heart of a meaningful science policy endeavor: how do we know if we are doing the right science?

Notes

[1] Global Forum for Health Research, *The 10/90 Report on Health Research 1999* (Geneva, Switzerland: World Health Organization, 1999).

[2] E.g., compare C. F. Curtis, "The case for deemphasizing genomics in malaria control," *Science* 290, no. 5496 (2000): 1508, with S. L. Hoffman, "Research (genomics) is crucial to attacking malaria," *Science* 290, no. 5496 (2000): 1509.

[3] R. C. Lewontin, *Biology as Ideology: The Doctrine of DNA* (New York, NY: HarperPerennial, 1993).

[4] B. Bozeman and D. Sarewitz, "Public value failures and science policy," *Science and Public Policy* 32, no. 2 (2005): 119-136; D. Sarewitz, G. Foladori, N. Invernizzi, and M. Garfinkel, "Science policy in its social context," *Philosophy Today* 48, no. 5 (2004): 67-83.

[5] E.g., H. D. Lasswell, *A Pre-View of Policy Sciences* (New York, NY: American Elsevier Publishing Company, 1971); C. Lindblom, "The science of 'muddling through,'" *Public Administration Review* 19 (1959): 79-88; D. Sarewitz, R. A. Pielke Jr., and R. Byerly Jr., eds. *Prediction: Science, Decision Making, and the Future of Nature* (Washington, DC: Island Press, 2000).

[6] Cf. K. Broad, "Bridging the supply and demand gap in climate forecast production and use," in M. H. Glantz, ed., *La Niña and Its Impacts: Facts and Speculation* (New York, NY: United Nations University Press, 2002), 246-252; D. Dalrymple, "Setting the agenda for science and technology in the public sector: the case of international agricultural research," *Science and Public Policy* 33, no. 4 (2006): 277-290.

[7] M. S. Garfinkel, D. Sarewitz, and A. Porter, "A societal outcomes map for health research and policy," *American Journal of Public Health* 96, no. 3 (2006): 441-446.

[8] E.g., S. Jasanoff, ed., *States of Knowledge: The Co-Production of Science and Social Order* (London, UK: Routledge, 2004).

[9] M. Polanyi, "The republic of science: its political and economic theory," *Minerva* 1 (1962): 54-74.

[10] M. Polanyi, "The republic of science: its political and economic theory," *Minerva* 1 (1962): 62.

[11] D. Sarewitz, *Frontiers of Illusion* (Philadelphia, PA: Temple University Press, 1996).

[12] Committee on Science Engineering and Public Policy, *Science, Technology and the Federal Government: National Goals for a New Era* (Washington, DC: National Academy of Sciences, 1993); R. A. Pielke Jr. and R. Byerly Jr., "Beyond basic and applied," *Physics Today* 51, no. 2 (1998): 42-46.

[13] A. Weinberg, "The axiology of science," *American Scientist* 58, no. 6 (1971): 612-617.

[14] A. I. Leshner, "Where science meets society," *Science* 309, no. 221 (2005): 8.

[15] E.g., N. Rosenberg, *Exploring the Black Box: Technology Economics and History* (Cambridge, UK: Cambridge University Press, 1994).

[16] R. R. Nelson, "The market economy, and the scientific commons," *Research Policy* 33 (2004): 455-471.

[17] E.g., M. M. Crow and C. Tucker, "The American research university system as America's de facto technology policy," *Science and Public Policy* 28, no. 1 (2001): 2-10; D. C. Mowery and N. Rosenberg, *Technology and the Pursuit of Economic Growth* (New York, NY: Cambridge University Press, 1989).

[18] D. Stokes, *Pasteur's Quadrant: Basic Science and Technological Innovation* (Washington, DC: Brookings Institution Press, 1997).

[19] M. Gibbons, C. Limoges, H. Nowotny, S. Schwartzman, P. Scott, and M. Trow, *The New Production of Knowledge* (London, UK: Sage Publications, 1994).

[20] E.g., S. Jasanoff, G. E. Markle, J. C. Petersen, and T. Pinch, eds. *Handbook of Science and Technology Studies* (Thousand Oaks, CA: Sage Publications, 2001)

[21] E.g., D. Cash, "In order to aid in diffusing useful and practical information: agricultural extension and boundary organizations," *Science, Technology, & Human Values* 26, no. 2 (2001): 431-453; C. Rosenberg, *No Other Gods: On Science and American Social Thought* (Baltimore, MD: John Hopkins University Press, 1997).

[22] D. D. Eisenhower, "Military-Industrial Complex Speech," Public Papers of the Presidents, 1035-1040 (1960).

[23] E.g., B. H. Lerner, *The Breast Cancer Wars: Hope, Fear and the Pursuit of a Cure in the Twentieth-Century America* (Oxford, UK: Oxford University Press, 2001); S. Morgen, *Into Our Own Hands: The Women's Health Movement in the United States 1969-1990* (New Brunswick, NJ: Rutgers University Press, 2002).

[24] S. Epstein, *Impure Science: Aids, Activism and the Politics of Knowledge* (Berkeley, CA: University of California Press, 1996).

[25] B. Bozeman and D. Sarewitz, "Public value failures and science policy," *Science and Public Policy* 32, no. 2 (2005): 119-136.

[26] P. Kitcher, *Science, Truth, and Democracy* (New York, NY: Oxford University Press, 2001).

[27] P. Kitcher, *Science, Truth, and Democracy* (New York, NY: Oxford University Press, 2001), 122-123.

[28] P. Kitcher, "What kinds of science should be done?" in *Living with the Genie: Essays on Technology and the Quest for Human Mastery*, A. Lightman, D. Sarewitz, and C. Desser, eds. (Washington, DC: Island Press, 2003), 218.

[29] For a comprehensive review, see E. C. McNie, "Reconciling the supply of scientific information with user demands: an analysis of the problem and review of the literature," *Environmental Science & Policy* 10 (2007): 17-38.

[30] House Committee on Science, *Unlocking Our Future Toward a New National Science Policy: A Report to Congress* (Sept. 24, 1998); United Nations Development Progamme (UNDP), *Human Development Report 2001: Making New Technologies Work for Human Development* (New York, NY: Oxford University Press, 2001).

[31] See U. Beck, *Risk Society: Towards a New Modernity* (London, UK: Sage Publications, 1992).

[32] W. C. Clark and G. Majone, "The critical appraisal of scientific inquiries with policy implications," *Science, Technology, & Human Values* 10, no. 3 (1985): 6-19; M. S. Feldman and J. G. March, "Information in organizations as signal and symbol," *Administrative Science Quarterly* 26 (1981): 171-186; D. Sarewitz, R. A. Pielke Jr., and R. Byerly Jr., eds., *Prediction: Science, Decision Making, and the Future of Nature* (Washington, DC: Island Press, 2000).

[33] E.g., K. Broad, "Bridging the supply and demand gap in climate forecast production and use," in M. H. Glantz, ed., *La Niña and Its Impacts: Facts and Speculation* (New York, NY: United Nations University Press, 2002), 246-252; M. Lahsen, "A Science-Policy Interface in the Global South: The Politics of Carbon Sinks and Science in Brazil," *Climatic Change* 97, no. 3 (2009): 339-372;

M. C. Lemos, T. Finan, R. Fox, D. Nelson, and J. Tucker, "The use of seasonal climate forecasting in policymaking: lessons from northeast Brazil," *Climatic Change* 55 (2002): 479-507; National Research Council (NRC), *Making Climate Forecasts Matter. Panel on the Human Dimensions of Seasonal-to-Interannual Climate Variability; Committee on the Human Dimensions of Global Change* (Washington, DC: National Academy Press, 1999); S. Rayner, D. Lach, H. Ingram, and M. Houck, "Weather Forecasts are for Wimps: Why Water Resource Managers Don't Use Climate Forecasts," Final Report to NOAA Office of Global Programs (2002).

[34] E.g., S. Jasanoff and B. Wynne, "Science and decision-making," in *Human Choice and Climate Change*, S. Rayner and E. L. Malone, eds. (Columbus, OH: Battelle Press, 1998), 1-88; R. A. Pielke Jr., D. Sarewitz, and R. Byerly Jr., "Decision making and the future of nature: Understanding and using predictions," in *Prediction: Science, Decision Making, and the Future of Nature*, D. Sarewitz, R. A. Pielke Jr., and R. Byerly Jr., eds. (Washington, DC: Island Press, 2000), 361-387.

[35] M. Gibbons, "Science's new social contract with society," *Nature* 402 (1999): C82.

[36] D. W. Cash, W. C. Clark, F. Alcock, N. M. Dickson, N. Eckley, D. H. Guston, J. Jager, and R. B. Mitchell, "Knowledge systems for sustainable development," *Proceedings of the National Academy of Sciences* 100, no. 14 (2003): 8086-8091.

[37] R. A. Pielke Jr., D. Sarewitz, and R. Byerly Jr., "Decision making and the future of nature: Understanding and using predictions," in *Prediction: Science, Decision Making, and the Future of Nature*, D. Sarewitz, R. A. Pielke Jr., and R. Byerly Jr., eds. (Washington, DC: Island Press, 2000), 361-387.

[38] D. H. Guston, "Stabilizing the boundary between politics and science: The role of the office of technology transfer as a boundary organization," *Social Studies of Science* (1999): 87-111.

[39] S. O. Funtowicz and J. R. Ravetz, "Three types of risk assessment and the emergence of post-normal science," in *Social Theories of Risk*, S. Krimsky and D. Golding, eds. (Westport, CT: Praeger, 1992).

40 D. W. Cash, W. C. Clark, F. Alcock, N. M. Dickson, N. Eckley, D. H. Guston, J. Jager, and R. B. Mitchell, "Knowledge systems for sustainable development," *Proceedings of the National Academy of Sciences* 100, no. 14 (2003): 8086-8091; K. N. Lee, "Appraising adaptive management," *Conservation Ecology* 3, no. 2 (1999): 3; Millennium Ecosystem Assessment, *Ecosystems and Human Well-Being: Health Synthesis* (Geneva, Switzerland: World Health Organization, 2005); D. Sarewitz, "How science makes environmental controversies worse," *Environmental Science & Policy* 7 (2004): 385-403.

41 E.g., M. Gough, *Politicizing Science* (Stanford, CA: Hoover Institution Press, 2003); C. Mooney, *The Republican War on Science* (New York, NY: Basic Books, 2005); Union of Concerned Scientists, *Scientific Integrity in Policymaking: An Investigation into the Bush Administration's Misuse of Science* (Cambridge, MA: Union of Concerned Scientists, 2004).

42 R. A. Pielke Jr., *The Honest Broker: Making Sense of Science in Policy and Politics* (New York, NY: Cambridge University Press, 2007); D. Sarewitz, "How science makes environmental controversies worse," *Environmental Science & Policy* 7 (2004): 385-403.

43 B. Bozeman and D. Sarewitz, "Public value failures and science policy," *Science and Public Policy* 32, no. 2 (2005): 119-136; J. H. Marburger, "Letters: Marburger makes his position clear," *Science* 307, no. 5709 (2005): 515.

44 R. A. Pielke Jr. and D. Sarewitz, "Wanted: scientific leadership on climate," *Issues in Science and Technology* (Winter 2003): 27-30.

45 T. Wigley, K. Caldeira, M. Hoffert, B. Santer, M. Schlesinger, S. Schneider, and K. Trenberth, "Letter," *Issues in Science and Technology* (Spring 2003).

46 R. A. Pielke Jr., "Usable information for policy: an appraisal of the U.S. Global Change Research Program," *Policy Science* 38 (1995): 39-77; R. A. Pielke Jr., "Who decides? Forecasts and responsibilities in the 1997 Red River flood," *American Behavioral Science Review* 7, no. 2 (1999): 83-101.

47 S. Agrawala, "Context and early origins of the Intergovernmental Panel on Climate Change," *Climatic Change* 39, no. 4 (1998): 605-620; S. Agrawala, "Structural and process history of

the Intergovernmental Panel on Climate Change," *Climatic Change* 39, no. 4 (1998): 621-642.

[48] E.g., see S. Rayner and E. L. Malone, eds. *Human Choice and Climate Change*, vol. 4. (Columbus, OH: Battelle Press, 1998); D. Sarewitz and R. A. Pielke Jr., "Breaking the global-warming gridlock," *Atlantic Monthly* 286, no. 1 (2000): 55-64.

[49] U.S. Climate Change Science Program, *Strategic Plan for the U.S. Climate Change Science Program*, Climate Change Science Program, Subcommittee on Global Change Research (2003).

[50] E.g., B. Callahan, E. Miles, D. Fluharty, "Policy implications of climate forecasts for water resources management in the Pacific Northwest," *Policy Science* 32, no. 3 (1999): 269-293; National Research Council, *Making Climate Forecasts Matter. Panel on the Human Dimensions of Seasonal-to-Interannual Climate Variability; Committee on the Human Dimensions of Global Change* (Washington, DC: National Academy Press, 1999); S. Rayner, D. Lach, H. Ingram, and M. Houck, "Weather Forecasts are for Wimps: Why Water Resource Managers Don't Use Climate Forecasts," Final Report to NOAA Office of Global Programs (2002).

[51] E.g., K. Broad, "Bridging the supply and demand gap in climate forecast production and use," in M. H. Glantz, ed., *La Niña and Its Impacts: Facts and Speculation* (New York, NY: United Nations University Press, 2002), 246-252; M. C. Lemos, T. Finan, R. Fox, D. Nelson, and J. Tucker, "The use of seasonal climate forecasting in policymaking: lessons from northeast Brazil," *Climatic Change* 55 (2002): 479-507.

[52] E.g., K. Broad, "Bridging the supply and demand gap in climate forecast production and use," in M. H. Glantz, ed., *La Niña and Its Impacts: Facts and Speculation* (New York, NY: United Nations University Press, 2002), 246-252; R. A. Pielke Jr., "Who decides? Forecasts and responsibilities in the 1997 Red River flood," *American Behavioral Science Review* 7, no. 2 (1999): 83-101.

[53] D. W. Cash, W. C. Clark, F. Alcock, N. M. Dickson, N. Eckley, D. H. Guston, J. Jager, and R. B. Mitchell, "Knowledge systems for sustainable development," *Proceedings of the National Academy of Sciences* 100, no. 14 (2003): 8086-8091.

[54] National Assessment Synthesis Team, *The Potential Consequences of Climate Variability and Change* (Washington, DC: U.S. Global Change Research Program, 2001).

[55] J. C. Bernabo, *Joint Climate to Project to Address Decision Makers' Uncertainties* (Washington, DC: Electric Power Research Institute and U.S. Environmental Protection Agency, 1992).

[56] J. C. Bernabo, *Joint Climate to Project to Address Decision Makers' Uncertainties* (Washington, DC: Electric Power Research Institute and U.S. Environmental Protection Agency, 1992), 86.

[57] This is not the place to flesh out this argument, but see, e.g., T. C. Schelling, "What makes greenhouse sense?" *Foreign Affairs* 81 (May/June 2002): 2-9; R. A. Pielke Jr. and D. Sarewitz, "Wanted: scientific leadership on climate," *Issues in Science and Technology* (Winter 2003): 27-30; S. Rayner, "The International Challenge of Climate Change: Thinking Beyond Kyoto," Consortium for Science, Policy & Outcomes Perspectives (Jan. 2004); and D. G. Victor, J. C. House, and S. Joy, "A Madisonian approach to climate policy," *Science* 309 (2005): 1820-1821. While some would regard the coming-into force of the Kyoto Protocol as evidence of progress in this realm, no responsible scientific voices are claiming that Kyoto will have any discernible effect on negative climate impacts.

[58] B. Callahan, E. Miles, D. Fluharty, "Policy implications of climate forecasts for water resources management in the Pacific Northwest," *Policy Science* 32, no. 3 (1999): 269-293.

[59] M. C. Lemos, T. Finan, R. Fox, D. Nelson, and J. Tucker, "The use of seasonal climate forecasting in policymaking: lessons from northeast Brazil," *Climatic Change* 55 (2002): 479-507.

[60] S. Rayner, D. Lach, H. Ingram, and M. Houck, "Weather Forecasts are for Wimps: Why Water Resource Managers Don't Use Climate Forecasts," Final Report to NOAA Office of Global Programs (2002).

[61] E.g., R. O. Keohane, P. M. Haas, and M. A. Levy, "The effectiveness of international environmental institutions," in *Institutions for the Earth: Sources of Effective International Environmental Protection*, P. M. Haas, R. O. Keohane, and M. A. Levy, eds. (Cambridge, MA: MIT Press, 1993); J. Kingdon, *Agendas, Alternatives and Public Policies* (New York, NY: HarperCollins, 1984); F.

Laird, *Solar Energy, Technology Policy and Institutional Values* (Cambridge, UK: Cambridge University Press, 2001); D. A. Schön and M. Rein, *Frame Reflection: Toward the Resolution of Intractable Policy Controversies* (New York, NY: Basic Books, 1994); A. Wildavsky, "Choosing preferences by constructing institutions: a cultural theory of preference formation," *American Political Science Review* 81, no. 1 (1987): 3-21.

[62] E. C. McNie, "Reconciling the supply of scientific information with user demands: an analysis of the problem and review of the literature," *Environmental Science & Policy* 10, no. 1 (2007): 17-38.

[63] E.g., R. A. Pielke Jr., "Policy history of the U.S. Global Change Research Program. Part I. Administrative development," *Global Environmental Change* 10 (2000): 9-25; R. A. Pielke Jr., "Policy history of the U.S. Global Change Research Program. Part II. Legislative process," *Global Environmental Change* 10 (2000): 133-144; R. A. Pielke Jr. and D. Sarewitz, "Wanted: scientific leadership on climate," *Issues in Science and Technology* (Winter 2003): 27-30.

[64] L. Dilling, "Towards science in support of decision making: characterizing the supply of carbon cycle science," *Environmental Science & Policy* 10, no. 1 (2007): 48-61.

[65] L. Dilling, S. C. Doney, J. Edmonds, K. R. Gurney, R. C. Harriss, D. Schimel, B. Stephens, and G. Stokes, "The role of carbon cycle observations and knowledge in carbon management," *Annual Review of Environment and Resources* 28 (2003): 521-558.

[66] E.g., B. Bozeman, "Public Value Mapping of Science Outcomes: Theory and Method," Center for Science, Policy & Outcomes, Washington, DC (2003); B. Bozeman and D. Sarewitz, "Public value failures and science policy," *Science and Public Policy* 32, no. 2 (2005): 119-136; M. S. Garfinkel, D. Sarewitz, and A. Porter, "A societal outcomes map for health research and policy," *American Journal of Public Health* 96, no. 3 (2006): 441-446; D. H. Guston and D. Sarewitz, "Real-time technology assessment," *Technology and Culture* 24 (2002): 93-109; R. A. Pielke Jr., D. Sarewitz, and R. Byerly Jr., "Decision making and the future of nature: Understanding and using predictions," in *Prediction: Science, Decision Making, and the Future of Nature*, D. Sarewitz, R. A. Pielke Jr., and R. Byerly Jr., eds. (Washington, DC: Island Press,

2000), 361-387; D. Sarewitz, R. A. Pielke Jr., and R. Byerly Jr., eds., *Prediction: Science, Decision Making, and the Future of Nature* (Washington, DC: Island Press, 2000).

2

USABLE SCIENCE: A HANDBOOK FOR SCIENCE POLICY DECISION MAKERS*

The SPARC Project

1. Science for Decision Making

In 2010 the U.S. federal government will have spent more than $150 billion on research and development. What gets done with that enormous sum has important implications for the wide variety of problems facing our society today and in the years to come. Important decisions on challenges like national defense, environmental change, rapid urbanization, and public health rely on scientific knowledge to inform them. Given the complexity and the

---

* Originally published as SPARC, *Usable Science: A Handbook for Science Policy Decision Makers* (Boulder, CO: Science Policy Assessment and Research on Climate [SPARC], 2010). Available at: https://cspo.org/library/usable-science-a-handbook-for-science-policy-decision-makers/. The text was written by a team of SPARC researchers, including Marilyn Averill, Lisa Dilling, J. Britt Holbrook, Nat Logar, Genevieve Maricle, Elizabeth McNie, Ryan Meyer, and Mark Neff.

significance of such challenges, how can science funders effectively orient a vast research enterprise to make real progress toward desired social goals?

This guide is about the challenge of producing usable science, which we define as science that meets the changing needs of decision makers. Producing usable science requires smart choices about the support for and management of science. We refer to the people making these choices as "science-policy decision makers."

As anyone involved with federal research and development (R&D) knows, making choices about what science to do, and how to do it, is complicated. No single person or organization decides how to allocate resources to various research areas, and no single set of criteria can determine the best course of action. We cannot offer a simple explanation of how to navigate the complex politics of this process. However, the findings from our five-year, National Science Foundation-supported research program suggest some useful approaches to thinking about science management and science funding. We have condensed them in this short guide, along with some specific examples from across the federal government, in the hopes that science decision makers will find this an accessible and meaningful contribution to their work.

Our research has focused on the problem of reconciling the needs of potential science users ("demand") with the "supply" of scientific information (more on these terms in Section 3). Through interviews, workshops, and analyses, we have examined the interactions between these two sides of the equation, and the ways in which people seek to reconcile them with varying degrees of success. The results have implications for the practice of science and for the management of science programs by federal agencies and other actors.

The fundamental conclusion of our work: Science best meets the needs of decision makers when those needs are considered throughout the institutions, policies, and processes that comprise the scientific enterprise.

Our fundamental recommendation: criteria for verifying the *usability* of scientific results, and specific accounts of the *outcomes* which R&D programs aim to fulfill, are crucial to managing science for decision making.

Our research has focused largely on climate change and other environmental research programs, but our conclusions and recommendations apply to a much greater cross-section of federal R&D. Indeed, we feel that engagement across this landscape is crucial to improving the usefulness of science. Facilitating this will be an important part of our own work as we move forward.

2. Myths that Prevent Progress

In our research we encounter four common but misleading assumptions about science policy decision making. These assumptions have been and continue to be important drivers of the policies, practices, and institutions involved with science policy decision making. Not everyone holds these assumptions, but any individual in this arena must contend with them.

Myth #1: Usable Science = Applied Research

Many see the generation of usable science as synonymous with doing applied research. However, dealing with real world problems often requires advances in fundamental knowledge, or basic research. For example, much of the basic physical science research that the U.S. government funded after World War II was aimed at the military and political problems of the Cold War. A commitment to usable science for decision making does not imply the abandonment of basic research.

Myth #2: *The Benefits of Science are Completely Unpredictable*

Science is often described as an unpredictable process, in which the most important discoveries are serendipitous. Though new knowledge may lead down unexpected paths, it is also true that the history of science over the past sixty years is one of powerful linkages between research priorities and social goals, especially in the area of technological advance. Indeed, most federal science — including basic research — is justified in terms of particular desired benefits. We cannot pursue all possible research directions, so we need to be skillful in deciding which ones deserve attention and resources. This is both a matter of reality, in that choices will be made, and experience, which tells us that some choices have better results than others. There is no reason to avoid thoughtful planning in pursuit of explicit goals.

Myth #3: *More Knowledge Is Always Useful*

We often assume that solving a difficult problem requires more research, but not all knowledge is equally useful and technical information makes up just one part of a larger system in which problems occur. It is important to consider the role of evolving knowledge and the extent to which *more* of it is necessarily better. Sometimes we have adequate knowledge to address a problem and additional research may not be the best approach. And if we do want better information, we can ask "Better in what way?" before we decide what kind of research is most appropriate to the task.

Myth #4: Decision Makers Benefit from Science at the End of the Research Process

As part of controversial issues, one commonly hears debate over whether the science is "settled." But the scientific process almost never comes to final conclusions and often involves irreducible uncertainties. There is thus a tendency for scientists to want to wait until the end of a project or until all scientific uncertainties are resolved to engage decision makers. The problem is that without engagement early on, the research path taken may be irrelevant to decision maker needs. Moreover, there is valuable and useful knowledge to be imparted to decision makers despite uncertainties. For decision makers to benefit from science, they must be involved in the research process early and often.

Moving Beyond the Myths

When individuals and institutions embrace the myths outlined above, the scope of options that science-policy decision makers consider is reduced. By setting aside some of these common misconceptions, and adopting a set of guidelines and concepts that ensure a strong connection between research and improved societal outcomes, science policy decision makers can become more open, creative, and effective in pursuing usable science. This guide begins to outline principles that can help foster decisions about science that more reliably respond to societal goals, while making a case for further engagement to build on this effort.

We have divided the remainder of this guide into three sections. Section 3 presents a conceptual framework for thinking about science-policy decision making. Section 4 begins a discussion of how to use the framework in the real world. This section recognizes that many competing demands, and a variety of other obstacles, present challenges to science policy decision makers who wish to try a new way of doing things. Section 5 makes the case for continued engagement among science policy decision makers to share experiences and learn about best practices.

3. Supply of and Demand for Science

We suggest conceptualizing the problem of managing science for decision making in terms of the relationship between the "supply" of science information, and the "demand" for usable information. The notion of supply and demand and their relationship is borrowed from economics, where supply and demand are strongly interrelated, interdependent, and co-determined. In science policy, however, explicit demand for information by potential users outside of the scientific community is rarely a strong determinant of the supply of scientific information. Ensuring that the supply of scientific information is in line with the needs of decision makers requires attentive management. There is no "invisible hand."

Box 1. Responding to the Problem: Hazards Research

The costs of future disasters are projected to increase due to more frequent and intense extreme events such as storms and floods. But this is only explains part of expected growth in disaster losses. Damage from extreme events is largely determined by patterns of human development, e.g., the trillions of dollars' worth of beachfront housing and infrastructure. Development involves choices made every day in regions that experience extreme events, and these choices influence the nature of future disasters.

If policymakers wish to address the escalating costs of disasters then it is important to understand how alternative actions will influence future damages. Policy debates on

---

climate change tend to focus on energy policies, but increasingly acknowledge that adaptation must also be a part of the discussion, especially with regard to disasters.

In one application of this concept, we examined the sensitivity of future losses to changes in climate and changes in patterns of future development. Instead of predicting changes in climate, development, or future disaster losses, we assessed what factors are likely to be most responsible for any potential changes in those phenomena across a wide range of assumptions. We hoped to enable decision makers to identify beneficial policy actions despite uncertainties.

Our research found that, under any plausible scenario of climate change, the most important factors in the growing costs of disasters are patterns of development—what people build, and where. Studies indicate that for every dollar in damages in 2000, we should expect $4.60 in damages in 2050, or an increase of $3.60. Half of this increase is due to development, whereas only a sixth is directly due to the most serious projected changes in climate. The overwhelming importance of societal change in driving future losses is consistent across all scenarios of climate change, development, and damage projections. Thus any research program intended to address the problem of escalating disaster losses should address and inform the problems of social change and coastal development, and not just the physical impacts of a changing climate. This suggests that science policy decision makers should revise their definition of the problem, and the associated research priorities in order to address what most contributes to the problem.

Characterizing Supply

Awareness of the factors that steer science in one direction or another facilitates clearer thinking about research prioritization. How did some programs or particular issues come to win priority over others? Which inputs *should* inform one's choice of research pathways? How might those inputs change over time? How should one balance the many important priorities espoused by an agency or program in order to produce usable science?

When science policy decision makers are aware of the range of research currently under way to address a given problem, they may leverage areas of overlap, fill important gaps in existing knowledge, and generally direct agendas to where they are most needed. However, characterizing supply requires an assessment of information needs relative to a decision context, as opposed to a discipline or field.

Scientific research inevitably leads to more questions, expanding the possibilities for research. But the progress of knowledge within a particular scientific discipline (such as hydrology or ecology) is not necessarily linked to real-world problems (such as drought or species loss). For example, an incremental advance in the skill of a groundwater model may be of interest to hydrologists in the field; but that advance may not translate into any additional utility for water managers and others dealing with water scarcity issues. Producing science for decision making requires recognizing the differences between supporting research valued by the discipline itself, and supporting research for the purpose of solving a particular problem. Every research program will approach these trade-offs differently. When managers explicitly recognize this tension in their decisions about research funding, they are better positioned to make decisions that lead to useful knowledge.

Box 2. A Case for Organizational Change: NOAA and Hurricane Research

U.S. hurricane research largely focuses on prediction. Indeed, the FY2009 NOAA budget includes a four-fold increase for hurricane prediction research - to $17 million, of which only $350,000 funds research into human dimensions and implications. Accordingly, atmospheric scientists continue to develop ever better predictions of hurricane trajectories and intensity. Yet Hurricane Katrina remains a stark reminder that accurate prediction itself is not enough to prevent losses. While agencies like FEMA refocus to be more prepared for future extreme events, the research enterprise continues to give prediction research its highest priority rather than shift its focus, as the USGS did, to decision-maker needs as a means of reducing vulnerability. (See Box 3.)

Budgets for hurricane research are limited, and by emphasizing prediction as the primary means of reducing vulnerability, the need to understand the social and political network through which society responds to hurricanes is deemphasized. Prediction has proven valuable for hurricane response, but insufficient for vulnerability reduction. Societal factors and demographic patterns remain important causal factors for losses, as we have recently seen in the case of Hurricane Katrina. (See Box 1.)

Understanding Demand

A farmer making a decision about what crops to plant, and when, may benefit from a seasonal forecast. However, his ability to use and benefit from forecast information depends on his social and economic resources, his tolerance for risk, and his trust in those delivering the information, in addition to the climatological realities of the region. The forecast information needs of a subsistence farmer may differ widely from those of a large farming corporation.

The demand for information is rarely represented by a single perspective. The diversity of potential users may result in a cacophony of voices, each with a unique view of decision making problems and their solutions and unique information needs. For this reason, an all-inclusive approach to working with users could be as ineffectual as ignoring user needs altogether. There is no single process or set of criteria for determining the best way to incorporate user needs into a research program. However, based on our own studies of programs that have undertaken user engagement, we identify three considerations that play a prominent role in assessing demand:

- Carefully define (or identify) the broad societal problem a research program seeks to address;
- Define specific categories or groups of users that should be involved; and
- Identify the outcomes that would represent progress from the users' perspective.

Each of these considerations depends on the others. For example, one might want to identify users who can help to define the decision-making problem before describing desired outcomes. Alternatively, identifying a manageably narrow group of users might require careful definition of the problem in advance. In practice, this will almost certainly amount to a process of continual adjustment as knowledge advances, user needs change, and understandings of the problem evolve. In addition, some elements of the process may be beyond the control of a decision maker if, for example, they are specified as part of the legislative process. Decisions regarding the approach to creating usable science depend largely on the organizational context (e.g., mission, goals) of the research program, the resources available, and the context of the research to be undertaken.

Box 3. Organizational Change in the USGS

In the mid-1990s, the U.S. Geological Survey (USGS) faced intense scrutiny from Congress, accusations of irrelevance to societal problems, and threats of extinction. At the same time, the USGS's large-scale earthquake prediction program, the Parkfield Earthquake Experiment, was widely deemed a failure. This, combined with mounting discontent with the traditionally isolated, basic science approach of many of its scholars led the USGS to reconsider its approach. The mission of minimizing the loss of life and property during natural disasters remained the same, but instead of relying on better prediction to minimize losses, the USGS shifted its focus to the effects of, and responses to earthquakes. This required a reprioritization, and encouraged scholars to identify and actively work with users.

Consequently, USGS scientists have actively developed relationships with the users of their information — e.g., state departments of transportation, building engineers, utilities, and local governments — and have shaped their research agendas based in part on those lasting partnerships. In lieu of prediction, once a primary value driving their science portfolio, a large percentage of the agency budget now focuses on the decisions these users must make to reduce vulnerability. For example, in cooperation with lifeline operators (electricity, water, power) and the California Department of Transportation (Cal Trans), USGS scholars develop shake maps — assessments of the intensity of ground shaking around an earthquake site. They integrate these maps with Cal Trans's assessment of its infrastructure, and together with Cal Trans, send out automatic alerts when an earthquake hits. Owing to these developments and this new focus, earthquake research benefits from the buy-in, input, and understanding of its intended users. These USGS researchers actively work with users, and shape their research priorities to meet decision maker needs.

When Everyone's a Stakeholder ...

No program has the resources to involve every region and sector of society in the kinds of interactions necessary for setting responsive research priorities. In recent years, the U.S. Global Change Research Program (USGCRP) has been criticized for its failure to make scientific knowledge useful to decision makers (a major part of its mandate). Certainly, a major part of the problem is lack of resources.

But such efforts have also come up short because of a failure to identify, pursue, and build into the program relationships with stakeholders. For USGCRP, potential users have effectively been "anyone and everyone." With no clear idea of who they are targeting, and where they can make the most progress with their limited resources, the USGCRP's approach has been haphazard and passive, inviting participation without demanding the investment and mutual understanding needed to make meaningful progress.

Case Studies in Assessing Demand

1. Priority-Setting Workshops

The Agricultural Research Service's (ARS) Global Change research program convenes periodic workshops with scientists and users including those from federal agencies, agricultural nonprofits, and the agricultural producer community.

These workshops help the USDA set research priorities for the next planning cycle based in part on what customers want from research. Workshops of this kind not only directly inform priorities, but can also help to establish enduring lines of communication with potential end users, and move science closer to meeting demand. These workshops are typical of each of the ARS's National Research

Programs. Usually the Program Leaders, along with the rest of the program team consisting of three to four ARS scientists, are in charge of the workshops. The process runs on a five year cycle and features both backward-looking and forward-looking assessments of programmatic research. A common process will include a survey of the research that the program supplies and is proposing to supply, a needs assessment, during which the ARS invites users to discuss their informational requirements, and a discussion between users and suppliers on how researchers can work to meet those requirements.

2. Test Runs and Feedbacks

The Naval Research Laboratory's Meteorology Division works to enhance the value of meteorological tools that the Navy uses. These tools can range from short term regional weather forecasts to more specified applications, such as those that let officers in the Middle East track dust storms. When making a more advanced model, or when adding a new feature intended to aid decision makers, NRL staff will often test an early version of the new technology with users in the Naval fleet by simply e-mailing them a link to the new model and asking for feedback to help assess the added value of new developments.

Agricultural Research Service scientists also work directly with users to test and refine products such as new agricultural management strategies or decision tools for farmers. Through test runs coordinated with users, researchers thus learn about the value of their work in a real world environment from actual users.

A mandate from the Bush administration charged the ARS with developing mechanisms for accounting for agricultural carbon sequestration. In recent years, scientists in the ARS Global Change National Program have developed CQESTR, a computer model with the purpose of predicting carbon dioxide sequestration in agricultural land under different soil types, crops, and management regimes. In order for this model to actually help farmers in making decisions, however, they will need to see it as useful and understand how they will benefit from using it.

3. Review Protocols for Assessing the Impact of Research

As a director of the National Institute of Standards and Technology's (NIST) Material Science and Engineering Laboratory (MSEL), Richard Kayser worked at the helm of a research venture with the mission of meeting the materials science needs of industry. For the MSEL lab, and specifically, for the director, a significant challenge lies in creating an actual impact for those in the materials industry.

Kayser's protocol for assessing proposed research projects considers both the impact of the research and the risk of failure. Assessment of impact includes both the promised level of impact as well as how well that impact is articulated. Risk includes both risk of technical failure and risk of failed technology transfer. The highest ranked proposals have a low risk and high impact that is convincingly articulated. Assessing the risk of technology transfer reflects NIST's commitment to getting its products into the hands of industrial and academic users. Research is only usable to the extent that potential users are capable of adopting it.

Other decision makers have implemented or considered similar strategies. A consideration of impact during prioritization and evaluation could encourage projects that are more likely to address need. Thus, those proposals that are either better able to articulate eventual usability, or that might lead to a high impact (even if risks are moderate) become more likely to go forward. Scientific or technical excellence cannot stand alone as a criterion of usability or value.

4. Probing the Options: Heilmeier Questions

A series of appropriate questions can also be used as a general guide for making sure science policymakers are addressing the need to reconcile supply and demand. One example is the Heilmeier Questions, originated by George Heilmeier, a former director of DARPA and vice president at Texas Instruments:

1. What is the problem? Why is it hard?
2. How is it solved today? By whom?
3. What is the new technical idea? Why can we succeed now?
4. Why should your institution do this?
5. What is the impact if successful? Who would care?
6. How will you measure progress?
7. How much money? How long will it take?

The questions offer a way to address potential impacts of research. While the first three address the technical problem, and technical impact, the other four speak to issues of demand and fit to broader institutional goals. Finally, questions 6 and 7 address logistical research issues that affect implementation.

Box 4. Equity in Research Priorities

When public funds are expended in the service of a democratic society, the question of who benefits should come to the forefront. As individuals consider how to make their policies more effective at producing usable science, they also have an opportunity to ponder questions of equity, outcomes, and participation in the process. Science is used in a variety of ways, and new information is not always shared equitably, does not always lead to improved outcomes, and may even be detrimental to certain populations. These matters deserve careful consideration when assessing and responding to user needs.

Reconciling Supply and Demand

We have condensed the conceptual problem of reconciling the supply and demand of scientific information into a simple graphic called the "Missed Opportunity Matrix." All too often, the two simple questions proffered in the matrix do not play a role in the decision making of science managers. We believe that asking these questions in the normal course of writing requests for proposals, reviewing grant proposals, and evaluating results, involves a shift in attitude that can benefit users and researchers alike.

In working to reconcile supply and demand, science policy decision makers must:

- Relate the mission, goals, and results of research to specific, on-the-ground problems;
- Establish ongoing processes to engage with, and seek to understand, the needs of users;
- Incorporate the needs of users into the practice of science funding and science management; and
- Test and evaluate the results of research intended for use.

These are not incremental steps of a linear process; they are ongoing, complementary components of supporting research that helps people to make better decisions. Reconciling the supply and demand of scientific information requires more than a single workshop or focus group; it must be built into the institutions that make decisions about science priorities.

Box 5. Congress and Usable Science
Congress has supported science generously over the last half-century, but not without occasional calls for more accountability. Science is not an entitlement program, and has always needed justification as a national priority. Justifications have ranged over time, including issues such as

workforce preparedness, economic competitiveness, technological advantage, military superiority, and so on. But these debates tend to focus on broad national trends, and assume that science is useful regardless of the makeup of our nation's science portfolio. Whatever the merit of these arguments, they rarely propose that science funding programs reconcile supply and demand of information. For example, the Global Change Research Act of 1990, which required funded research to generate information useful to policymakers, did not specify the process for ensuring this outcome.

Nonetheless, calls for science to be more relevant to specific policy problems such as climate change, nanotechnology, and global health are becoming more prevalent. Congressional members and their staff can be quite influential in shaping this policy debate and ultimate national position toward usable science. Over the years, members of Congress have run hearings, introduced legislation, and initiated changes in science policy such as the broader impacts criterion for NSF proposals, an issue championed by Barbara Mikulski, and the integration of social, environmental, and ethical concerns into nanotechnology research priorities. (See Box 7.)

RISA Programs

NOAA's Regional Integrated Sciences and Assessments (RISA) programs use a variety of techniques to reconcile their scientific research efforts with their various users' information demands, ranging from the informal to the formal. All of the RISAs engage in frequent communication with their stakeholders, starting their conversations early. These events involve one-on-one meetings, group meetings, or conversations over the phone. Informal communication provides a forum for both sides to clearly identify and understand the nature of the problem they seek to resolve, and to understand the unique contexts of potential solutions. Through such informal, iterative meetings, RISA researchers were able to adjust their own research objectives, provide existing information to stakeholders, or could producing information for which the users had no useful purpose. Moreover, these meetings created opportunities for both sides to develop trusting, mutually respectful relationships that facilitate future efforts.

The RISAs also engaged in more formal efforts to reconcile supply with demand. For example, one RISA program created and administered formal surveys to thoroughly test the effectiveness of the RISA's data and information products. Other surveys investigated how well decision makers understood the particular ways in which the data presented. The RISAs used these engagement opportunities to assess, adjust, initiate or abate individual research streams.

As part of the RISA program researchers and program managers work closely to reconcile the supply and demand of scientific information. The program was designed with deliberate attention to the importance of understanding user needs and the usability of scientific results. Rather than relying on a traditional model of issuing a request for proposals — in which the request itself is the product of scientific advisory bodies — a new process was designed to require investigators to consult with stakeholders, and develop research agendas specific to the climate-related problems of a region. In addition to a high degree of interaction between the program managers and prospective research teams, managers worked hard to broaden participation in review and evaluation of individual RISAs, which has helped to widen the view of "excellence" espoused by the Program.

4. Making It Happen

Changing the processes of funding and managing science is not easy. In the course of our research we have identified a variety of challenges common to many organizations that support science for decision making. We present those below, followed by a preliminary list of opportunities for programmatic innovation, drawn from our interactions with program managers from across the federal government. As we argue in the final section, program managers could build on this list by coming together to share experiences and learn about new approaches.

Challenges

Supporting Researchers: Program managers wanting to encourage reconciliation of supply and demand need to be aware of the challenges this poses for grant recipients. In the case of university research, for example, these challenges require thinking creatively about how to reorient incentives in an academic system that traditionally emphasizes publications, citations, grant-writing, patenting, and other metrics of scholarly merit instead of relationship-building and decision support.

Funding Cycles: Research agendas are often geared to relatively short lifecycles of three to five years. This timeline does not always match the needs or expectations of users. The normal duration of a grant may be too short to establish trusting relationships among producers of information and potential users. As one individual involved with emergency planning and management in the Pacific said, "Don't even bother bringing your briefcase for the first two years… it takes that long before the stakeholders will trust you."

In many cases normal funding cycles may be too slow to respond to user needs. There are exceptions, however. In the anthrax attacks after September 11, decision makers urgently required new research on testing and monitoring for anthrax. While the National Institute of Standards and Technology's (NIST) normal research programs would not have addressed this need, they adapted to this timeline and successfully met the demand. It is important to understand the need for and create flexible structures that can be nimble in the face of changing problems.

Evaluation and Performance Measures: Evaluation of research often focuses on quantitative measures such as the number and citation impact of publications that emerge from a research grant. Such performance measures discourage and impede pursuit of outcomes that, while qualitative rather than quantitative, relate more strongly to the mission and goals of a program than traditional measures.

Justifications used to secure support should provide the basis for developing criteria for program evaluation and should extend to program metrics and accountability. Too often, considerations of use presented in the process of securing support for a program are forgotten once the funds arrive.

Organizations: The culture and inertia of an organization tend to favor the existing way of doing things. While not necessarily a bad thing, this constrains entrepreneurship. Disciplinary stovepipes do not lend themselves to addressing interdisciplinary, complex, societal issues. Individuals seeking to motivate more usable science must work to break down these divisions, or look for creative ways to organize in spite of existing structures. This means striving for a supportive environment where managers can take risks and be innovative in their development of programs.

Opportunities

There are many opportunities to enhance the creation of usable science and there have been many successes in the U.S. research enterprise, including within the climate science community. Many individuals make decisions that influence science programs, from congressional staff, to Office of Management and Budget (OMB) examiners, to agency program managers, to members of NRC panels proposing priorities for research. Science-policy decision makers, reflecting institutional, political, and other constraints, play an essential role in shaping programs and their outcomes. Leverage points in this shaping process include writing requests for proposals or announcements of opportunity, setting budget priorities or examining budgets during the agency pass-back process, conducting or testifying at hearings, writing legislation, contributing to expert reports, reviewing proposals, and making funding decisions on individual grants. Individuals involved in any of these at any level of the science policy process have an opportunity to make decisions that improve the usability of science.

Mandate and Mission: The mandate and mission driving an agency or program can be quite broad, leaving room for interpretation and opportunities for new approaches. In almost all cases, federally funded science *does have a mandate to address particular classes of problems*, whether in defense, energy, safety, health, or national competitiveness. Moreover, such problems are often articulated in terms of desired social outcomes.

Metrics: Science is changing. Interdisciplinary efforts are far more common, and "broader impacts" or evidence of use of science in society are becoming a more common goal. This sea change may accommodate new metrics commensurate with the task of creating usable science.

Review and Advisory Mechanisms: Through peer review and expert advice, the prioritization and decision-making process for science has remained largely within the scientific community. A science manager might consider expanding review and advisory processes to include a wider cross-section of experts, including potential users, who can assess usability and relevance along with scholarly merit. Both NOAA (RISA and Sectoral Applications Research Program [SARP]) and NASA Applied Sciences have experimented with this in some of their programs.

Science-policy decision makers, especially those involved with distributing resources, have a unique opportunity to foster dialogue among existing constituencies through workshops, town halls at science and professional conferences, hearings, and so on. Often these are high value activities taken on in addition to core responsibilities. Program managers can work to demonstrate the benefits of such endeavors, while looking for ways to make them a part of job descriptions, performance evaluations, and other metrics.

Box 6. Leadership in Agencies: Mike Hall

J. Michael (Mike) Hall demonstrates how one person can encourage the production of usable science throughout an agency and a research initiative. Hall was the Director of the Climate and Global Change Program at the National Oceanic and Atmospheric Administration, a Federal agency charged with understanding changes in the environment to support decision making. In the grand scheme of things, the program's budget was relatively small ($70M annually out of a $2B Federal investment), but the influence of the program was far-reaching because of the outlook and practices that Hall instilled in his employees. Hall himself was a systems thinker, looking at the big picture and encouraging others to do so. Many who worked for him were inspired by this larger vision, and an office atmosphere was created where civil service in the government was exciting, effective, and ground-breaking. Hall listened to everyone, and remained open and curious about new ideas his entire career, while remaining grounded in strategic thinking and a practical approach. He encouraged risk-taking, creating an environment where it was "ok to screw up," especially if that was done in the context of stretching and attempting something new and innovative.

Hall was fond of saying "sometimes you just have to break some pottery" in order to move forward with a different direction. He assembled a team that spanned across many different disciplines, and looked specifically for people who could think broadly and who came from different backgrounds, both within government and from academia. Most importantly, Hall empowered his employees to seize opportunity, do what needed to be done to address the important goals, and not shy away from larger challenges. For Hall, the bigger the challenge the better, and he did everything within his ability to support and protect his employees to reach for those challenges as well. For example, he created the space within a primarily physical sciences program to fund social sciences, and create new institutions and models to link science to society. Without his support, it is doubtful that employees would have felt comfortable challenging assumptions and moving in non-traditional directions.

Several innovative programs emerged from his leadership that still stand as model programs in the area of climate and service to society: the Tropical Ocean Global Atmosphere program, the International Research Institute for Climate and Society, the Regional Integrated Sciences and Assessment Program, the Human Dimensions Program (now the Sectoral Applications Research Program). These initiatives have all led to profound advances in science, along with valuable discoveries of how science is or is not used in decision making, while fostering entire communities of new scholars and science policy decision makers. Hall was awarded the Waldo E. Smith Medal in 2004 from the American Geophysical Union in recognition of "his vision, his innovations in program management, his nurturing of young talent, and his deeply held values that have so advanced science in the service of humanity." (See Box 7.)

Congress and NSF's "Broader Impacts" Criterion

In 1997, influenced by the demand for Federal agencies to produce "demonstrable results" expressed in the Government Performance and Results Act of 1993, the National Science Foundation (NSF) created what became known as the second or "broader impacts" criterion (BIC) for the assessment of grant proposals. Henceforth, in addition to assessing proposals in terms of their intellectual or scientific merit, proposers and reviewers of grant proposals were asked to answer the question: "What are the broader impacts of the proposed activity?"

Because of its emphasis on impacts beyond those of simply producing more knowledge, the introduction of BIC promoted reflection on whether a research program was responding effectively to a real social need. But over the last decade, BIC has increasingly been interpreted rather narrowly as encouraging the promotion of science for the sake of science. For instance, BIC is now most often satisfied by including public education and outreach activities, with little consideration for whether these are really demanded by the social context.

How, then, might BIC be addressed in ways that enhance the supply of scientific knowledge that responds to a real societal demand rather than simply trying to create a demand for a knowledge supply that scientists themselves want to create? In 2007 Congress proposed its own answer to this question in the form of the America COMPETES Act, which explicitly ties BIC to the promotion of Responsible

Conduct of Research (RCR) activities, such as mentoring post-doctoral researchers and instructing undergraduate and graduate students in the ethics of research. Such an answer, of course, interprets the question of the supply and demand of scientific knowledge as a question concerning the *quality* rather than the *quantity* of knowledge production. Instead of using BIC just to promote more science, Congress is expressing the demand for scientists to think in terms of producing *better* science.

This raises the question of what one means by "better science." Answers to this question will vary with the particular context, but the context of climate science presents a salient example. Although billions have been spent on increasing the quantity of our knowledge regarding climate change, not enough attention has been paid to the quality of that knowledge in terms of its usability by decision makers. Interpreted broadly, BIC might encourage climate scientists applying for NSF grants to conduct research that will respond to a specific need in addition to justifying the research on educational grounds alone.

Box 7. Leadership in Congress: George Brown

Congressman Brown was simultaneously a champion of science in the U.S. and a provocateur, challenging science to examine its role in serving society. Even before his election as Chair of the House Committee on Science, Space and Technology, Brown urged scientists to think hard about their role in society, and how their research might be useful, though it often put him at odds with Nobel-prize winning scientists. He did not accept that scientific research was automatically useful. Nor did Brown accept the premise that the application of science was uniformly beneficial to society—he recognized that negative consequences were also possible and that part of science's responsibility was in assessing the implications of science and technology and

---

their appropriate role in society. A man of impeccable integrity, Brown did not shy away from speaking the truth as
he saw it, no matter the constituency, and he consistently
opposed research he viewed as contributing to bad outcomes, such as breeder reactors and anti-satellite weapons.

Brown was instrumental in creating links between politics and science and technology, including the Office of
Technology Assessment and the Office of Science and
Technology Policy, which was formed to advise the President on matters of science and technology and their effects.
Among his many accomplishments, Brown led the establishment of the National Climate Program through passage
of the National Climate Program Act of 1978. Some of the
pioneering elements of that act have become an essential
part of climate science today: assessments of the effect of
climate on natural and social systems, conducting both
basic and applied research to understand natural processes
and the social and political implications of climate change,
and global monitoring and forecasting. These career
achievements reflect Brown's constant belief that scientists
had to accept accountability for the social outcomes they
helped to create. Through his tireless leadership, love of science, and passion for social justice, Brown enlarged the
boundaries on which science engaged societal values, pav-
ing the way for a new vision of usable science. (See Box 5.)

A New Take on Risk-Taking

Risk-taking is a widely embraced value in agencies
funding basic research. Program managers in agencies such
as the NSF, DOE, DOD, and NIST, often emphasize that
major scientific advance requires a willingness to fund
ideas that offer the combination of high risk and high potential payoff.

But the definition of risky research needs expansion.
Decision makers should not just fund high risk, high re-
ward scientific ideas, they should also apply this norm to

the incentive structures that govern research. This means exploring new kinds of collaboration, communication, and metrics. It could involve bringing in a completely foreign discipline to work on the problem, or requiring a different balance between formal research and "outreach" activities in the budget proposal. (See the RISA Programs section, above.)

5. Building Community

In addition to facilitating progress toward desired outcomes, reconciling supply and demand can greatly expand the community of individuals who recognize, trust, and become champions for both a program and the science it funds. Reconciling supply and demand can also lead in unexpected and exciting new directions for both science and social action. Some of NOAA's RISA programs, for example, have established a basis for extensive and lasting interdisciplinary and service-oriented research programs that have gained the attention and support of state and local governments.

In this guide we have tried to identify some issues, opportunities, and frameworks that may be shared among science managers and other individuals who wish to generate usable science, even if they work in vastly different organizations.

But there are likely many more.

Coming together to share experiences and best practices across a wide range of problem areas, from health and environment to homeland security and social justice, may prove mutually beneficial. Issues such as appropriate metrics, what works and what doesn't, how to involve stakeholders, and the role of champions may translate across cultures and contexts.

As we carry this research forward we will continue to engage with science managers, and attempt to build a critical mass of practitioners taking a creative approach to reconciling supply and demand. An effort to look for common ties also has benefits for creating a sense of community, fostering programmatic innovation, saving time, and helping to make science more useful.

3

DECISION MAKING AND THE FUTURE OF NATURE: UNDERSTANDING AND USING PREDICTIONS[*]

Roger A. Pielke Jr., Daniel Sarewitz, and Radford Byerly Jr.

A Prediction Enterprise

The story, by now, is familiar. A danger or opportunity is lurking out there, perhaps ill defined, imminent or in the more distant future, and decision makers must take action. While our ten cases are diverse, each is rooted in an effort to mobilize predictive science to pursue desired outcomes on behalf of society.

---

[*] Originally published as D. Sarewitz, R. A. Pielke Jr., and R. Byerly Jr., "Decision Making and the Future of Nature: Understanding and Using Prediction," in *Prediction: Science, Decision Making, and the Future of Nature*, D. Sarewitz, R. A. Pielke Jr., and R. Byerly Jr., eds. (Washington, DC: Island Press, 2000), 361-388. Copyright © 2000 Island Press. Reproduced by permission of Island Press, Washington, DC.

We know what undesired outcomes look like: more than ten thousand deaths from Hurricane Mitch in Central America in 1998; losses of $20 billion as a consequence of the 1993 Midwest floods; serpentine lines of cars waiting for gasoline during times of shortage; acidified lakes in temperate forests. Other outcomes are yet left to the imagination: toxic effluent leaching from pit mines and nuclear waste repositories into groundwater supplies; huge conflagrations ignited by giant asteroid impacts; fragile ecosystems collapsing under the pressure of rapid climate change. Of course, the future of human interaction with nature does not offer only disaster. Changing weather patterns might allow for more efficient agricultural harvests; the discovery of new hydrocarbon reserves (or new energy technologies) might enhance economic well-being and lessen the incentive to drill for oil in ecologically sensitive areas. But underlying every such scenario, whether pessimistic or hopeful, is the assumption by those demanding action that knowledge of the future is necessary to prevent negative outcomes and to capitalize on opportunities for gain.

It is not surprising, then, that each year policymakers invest tens of billions of dollars of public funds into technologies ranging from satellite-based observational platforms in the sky, to stream gauges on the ground, to seismometers in the deep ocean in an effort to monitor the environment and provide an ever-expanding database for scientific prediction of the future of nature. Prediction has been central to such organized efforts as the U.S. Global Change Research Program, the U.S. Weather Research Program, the National Earthquake Hazards Reduction Program, the Advanced Hydrological Prediction System, the National Acid Precipitation Assessment Program, the Yucca Mountain nuclear waste repository site assessment process, and the Near-Earth Asteroid Tracking Program. Each of these science programs has been justified in terms of the need to support decisions in the present through better scientific understanding of the future.

The quest for prediction of earth systems exists in a dynamic social and political milieu that we call the "prediction enterprise." The public demands action or useful information that can facilitate action. But because the public comprises a great diversity of interests and values, it rarely, if ever, speaks with one voice about what that action or information ought to be. Other participants in the prediction enterprise include policymakers looking to satisfy (or at least address) conflicting demands made by their constituents and a scientific community looking to help define and resolve problems while at the same time satisfying its own desire to expand the frontiers of knowledge.

The prediction enterprise also involves institutions. At the international level, the United Nations coordinates activities to address climate change and natural disasters. Within the United States, the Federal Emergency Management Agency and its state and local counterparts together help citizens prepare for and respond to disasters; the National Weather Service disseminates the latest meteorological information; the Bureau of Land Management seeks to manage public lands according to its legal mandate. Universities and federally funded laboratories are integral parts of the prediction infrastructure. Private-sector institutions are also involved: the insurance industry seeks profit from investments based on a balancing of risks; airlines depend on weather forecasts to maintain safety and schedules; and the construction industry implements building standards aimed at preventing damage from a variety of natural hazards.

How effectively does this prediction enterprise serve the common interest? Its sheer complexity — diverse participants, conflicting perspectives and values, numerous institutions representing different sectors of society, and significant resources at stake — makes evaluation a daunting task. In fact, the existence of a prediction enterprise has not been recognized as such, in part, perhaps, because prediction seems like such a "natural" part of science, society, and policy. Yet the prediction enterprise is as real and pervasive as "the economy" or "the medical system." As with the medical system, for example, one can look in many directions for accountability: to scientists, the media, government regulators, politicians, special interests, the nonexpert public. But unlike the economy or the medical system, little attention has been focused on the prediction enterprise. We therefore lack insight that can be applied to decision making at the intersection of predictive science and environmental policy. The cases in this volume begin the task of developing such insight.

Predictions are commonly viewed simply as pieces of information, as quantitative products of scientific research. From that perspective a prediction is understood as a "set of probabilities associated with a set of future events."[1] To understand a prediction, one must understand the specific definition of the predicted event (or events), as well as the expected likelihood of the event's (or events') occurrence. When predictions are seen in this light, then the goal of the prediction enterprise is simply to develop *good predictions*, as evaluated by objective criteria such as accuracy and skill.

Yet once we have recognized the existence of a prediction enterprise, it becomes clear that prediction is more than just a *product* of science. Rather, it is a complex *process*. This process includes all of the interactions and feedbacks among participants, perspectives, institutions, values, interests, resources, decisions, and other factors that constitute the prediction enterprise. From this perspective, the goal of the prediction enterprise is *good decisions*, as evaluated by criteria of common interests.[2] The common interest is often invoked in areas such as social security and health care policy, but it should also be a rationale for the prediction enterprise.

Prediction as a Product

A central irony of our book, *Prediction: Science, Decision Making, and the Future of Nature* (2000), from which this chapter is adapted, is that the quest for prediction products can in some cases undermine the societal goals that originally motivate the quest. In the cases of earthquakes, global climate change, beach nourishment, nuclear waste, and mine impacts, for example, decision making might be improved through less reliance on predictions. Effective decisions are not necessarily promoted by "good" prediction products and not necessarily prevented by "bad" ones. Even so, there will be cases in which reliance on prediction is unavoidable. Knowing when to depend on predictions is itself a challenge of the prediction process and one taken up in greater detail below. (See Box 1.)

Box 1. Design of Critical Facilities without Time-Specific Predictions

Thomas L. Anderson, Construction Engineer

The engineering community is moving away from traditional prescriptive building codes toward performance-based design criteria. Experience shows that prescriptive codes do not ensure that a critical facility will continue to function in case of a natural hazard event, while performance-based codes are designed to ensure a specified level of performance in the face of specified hazards. Natural hazards of traditional concern include earthquakes and high winds.

Performance codes do not depend on prediction of specific events at specific times or places; rather, they use information based on past events and general understanding of hazard phenomena to determine the maximum expected level of stress placed on a building by a potential event.

Two examples illustrate the effective use of earthquake-related information in the design and construction of critical facilities. The examples involve the Fire Command and Control Facility (FCCF) in Los Angeles County, California, and the proposed Alaska Natural Gas Pipeline (ANGP). The FCCF receives all fire and medical 911 calls for Los Angeles County and is responsible to over three million county residents. The proposed ANGP was to carry natural gas from the Prudhoe Bay fields to a terminal in southern Alaska along a route that generally paralleled the trans-Alaska oil pipeline.

The information needed for the FCCF design was the ground motions for the largest earthquake that could be expected from the several nearby faults in the region. The design requirement was for the FCCF to remain functional during and following such an event. Design alternatives were subjected to detailed calculations of their response to expected earthquake motions. All uncertainty factors were provided to the design team so that they could compare building designs based on equal values of assumed parameters and other forms of uncertainty. There was a very close and collaborative relationship between the seismologists and the design engineers at every step in the process. The final decision was based on lowest life-cycle cost and lower first cost to achieve the performance level demanded by the county.

The information needed for the ANGP was the expected ground movement where the pipeline crossed active faults. The performance requirement was to lower the risk of pipeline rupture to less than 1/2,500 a year. The project geotechnical team provided the required fault motion descriptions in great detail based on extensive research and fieldwork, and uncertainties were fully disclosed and expressed in terms understandable to the design engineers. Design engineers have a "tool kit" of strategies that allow a buried pipeline to withstand a wide range of abrupt fault movements, i.e., without having to resort to placing the pipeline above ground on sliding supports, where it is exposed to many other hazards. But use of those tools requires the predicted fault motions to be fully defined, including the nature of uncertainties in those motions. Armed with those data, lowest life-cycle cost designs were readily developed for each of the fault crossings to keep the risk of rupture below the acceptable level.

These examples show how in many situations experiential information coupled with understanding can be more useful than uncertain predictions. The construction engineer wants to build safely, i.e., to an acceptable level of risk, no matter when an earthquake occurs.

Accuracy

Given that one has decided to rely on predictions for decision making, how does one know whether a particular prediction product is a good one? A critical assessment criterion is accuracy — a measure of how closely a specific prediction product conforms to the actual event.[3] The value of accuracy may seem too obvious to merit discussion, but sometimes accuracy is impossible to evaluate; and other times, when evaluation is possible, decision makers fail to do it. The case studies of beach erosion and mining showed that once a forecast is produced and used in decision making, there may even be disincentives to looking back and assessing predictive accuracy.

Attempts to "retrodict" or "hindcast" past events can give a measure of the accuracy of predictive methods and has been central to assessment of global climate models.[4] Comparing different prediction methodologies can also give some indication of accuracy because if the results of independent predictions diverge, they cannot all be right (although they could all be wrong). However, the case of nuclear waste disposal showed that convergence of different predictions on a similar result is not necessarily a sign of accuracy, either. Shared scientific assumptions and political incentives may cause "independent" predictions to converge on a result that is palatable, even if incorrect.[5] Predictions of beach erosion and oil and gas reserves show similar evidence of such "convergence of convenience."

The ultimate test of a prediction, of course, is to evaluate its accuracy against actual events as they unfold, which is not as straightforward as it might seem. Consider the case of early tornado forecasts.[6] In the 1880s a weather forecaster began issuing daily tornado forecasts in which he would predict "tornado" or "no tornado." After a period of issuing forecasts, the forecaster found his predictions to be 96.6 percent correct—a performance that would merit a solid A in school. But others discovered that simply issuing a standing forecast of no tornadoes would result in an accuracy of 98.2 percent. This finding suggested that in spite of the high accuracy, action based on the forecaster's predictions could result in costs rather than benefits. In other words, *simply comparing a prediction with actual events does not provide sufficient information to evaluate its performance.* A more sophisticated approach is needed.

Scientists use a range of techniques to assess the skill of a prediction—skill being defined as the improvement of a prediction over some standard.[7] One way to evaluate skill is to compare the accuracy of a prediction with the accuracy of some naïve baseline. For example, historical weather information provides such a baseline because it yields the best estimate of the future occurrence of weather events, absent any other information. Thus, a forecast is considered skillful if it improves upon a prediction based on such climatological data. For instance, the average high temperature over the past one hundred years in London on September 6 (the climatological mean for that date) might be, say, 10 degrees Celsius. Absent any other information, the best prediction of the temperature on the next September 6 is thus 10 degrees. Any forecast for that particular day would be considered skillful if it were closer than the climatological mean to the actual temperature recorded on that date.

Such considerations suggest that our capacity to evaluate prediction as a technical product depends strongly on what is predicted. The accuracy of some types of predictions is clearly amenable to evaluation. Weather is the best example, because of the huge number of forecasts, their wide use by decision makers, and the ease of comparing forecasts with actual events, which reflects what science policy expert Radford Byerly Jr. has termed the short "characteristic time" of weather events.[8] In contrast, if an event has a long characteristic time, predictive accuracy often cannot be evaluated. This situation applies to cases such as global climate change, long-term mining impacts, and nuclear waste disposal. Decisions on such issues will have to be made long before the skill of the prediction can be assessed. The case of floods represents an intermediate case, amenable to some evaluation of skill, yet considerably less than weather.[9]

Uncertainty

The science fiction writer Isaac Asimov introduced, in his Foundation series, the notion of "psychohistorians," who could predict the future with scientific certainty based on complex mathematical models. We know that Asimov's characters lie squarely in the realm of science fiction — there can be no psychohistory. Yet the quest for a scientifically legitimated view of the future is no recent phenomenon; it dates back at least to the efforts of ancient Egyptian hydroengineers and astronomers to predict the stages of the Nile. Fifty centuries later, the future, as a weather predictor might say, still looks partly cloudy. Given today's circumstances, there are many possible ways that tomorrow might unfold (and even more possibilities for tomorrow's tomorrow). Prediction promises to narrow the range of possible futures so that decision making can be more successful. Occasional clearing can occur — we *can* predict some events with skill — but uncertainty can never be eliminated.

Cognitive psychologist Thomas Stewart distinguished between "aleatory" and "epistemic" uncertainty.[10] Aleatory uncertainty is irreducible, because it is introduced by random processes in a closed system — for example, a deck of cards or a pair of dice. Epistemic uncertainty, on the other hand, derives from incomplete knowledge of a system — perhaps the dealer is a cheat, or the dice are loaded. Epistemic uncertainty can sometimes be reduced through more and better knowledge.

Even though epistemic uncertainty can be reduced, if one is dealing with open systems (as is generally the case for environmental predictions), the level of uncertainty itself can never be known with absolute certainty. Seismologists assigned a probability of 95 percent to their prediction of the Parkfield earthquake, but the earthquake never occurred.[11] Were the scientists confounded by the unlikely but statistically explicable one-out-of-twenty chance of no earthquake? Or was their probability calculation simply wrong — i.e., was the uncertainty associated with the prediction in fact larger than initially thought? We would need many more Parkfield-like predictions to begin to answer such questions. Similarly, regardless of the sophistication of global climate models, many types of unpredictable events (changes in solar output, volcanic eruptions that cool the atmosphere, new energy technologies that reduce carbon emissions) can render climate predictions invalid and associated uncertainties meaningless.[12] One way scientists deal with such "unknowable unknowns" is by introducing fudge factors into their predictions, as we saw with beach models, asteroid impact predictions, and global climate models.

Moreover, many of our cases show that efforts to reduce uncertainty reveal vast, previously unrecognized complexities. In such cases, decision-relevant uncertainties can actually *increase* with more knowledge. This dynamic of spiraling uncertainty can have the perverse effect of increasing political controversy rather than reducing it, leading to calls for even more research to reduce uncertainties, while the problem that motivated the research goes unaddressed. As energy policy analyst John Bridger Robinson observes, "By basing present decisions on the apparent uncovering of future events, an appearance of inevitability is created that de-emphasizes the importance of present choice and further lessens the probability of developing creative policy in response to present problems."[13] The counterintuitive lesson for decision makers is that *uncertainties about the future can often be reduced more successfully through decision making than through prediction.* (See Box 2.)

Box 2. Ranching and Prediction

Rob Ravenscroft, Rancher

As a rancher, I deal with physical and biological systems, as well as economic and social systems. Since these are dynamic and interconnected, attempts to predict their behavior are probably wrong more often than right. If honestly done, there are no "bad" predictions. It's my responsibility as a manager to use them properly.

"Proper" use can be measured only by progress toward a goal. Technology (including predictions), financial and biological capital, labor, and (most important) creativity pretty well sum up the tools a manager can use to devise and implement a plan of operation.

The dynamic nature of the systems involved, and the inherent possibility of errors in predictions and assumptions made, means that a plan must have two essential

---

characteristics to be effective in achieving personal, family, and business goals. It must be monitored, and it must be flexible.

In ranching, as in most other businesses, the obvious monitoring areas are financially oriented. But cattle and beef production are just part of the entire biological system. Healthy plants, animals, and soils are critical to long-term sustainability of families, ranches, and communities. Biological alarms we watch for on our ranch are decreases in plant and animal diversity, which usually indicate some flaw in our plan that could hinder our ability to deal with future adversity.

Any plan that aims to achieve quality-of-life goals (which is the real need of the individuals and families implementing the plan) must be monitored for social impacts, too. If our ranching and business practices endanger our neighbors and community, our long-term goals can't be achieved. This is more difficult to measure but must be kept in mind.

Early warning is the most effective first step in reversing a planning mistake or reacting to a change in conditions. Flexibility built into the plan and the business is the next. For us, weather and prices are the major risk factors. Those are also factors that are regularly predicted. Experience shows that neither can be forecast with great reliability. This means that we can't afford to direct all our assets and efforts to best capitalize on any one set of predicted conditions. Here again, diversity enhances flexibility. Diverse plant communities support animals through a wider range of weather conditions. Diversity in the cattle enterprise can supply staying power as prices cycle from low to high. Monitoring lets us know when we're not achieving our goals; flexibility gives us the chance to replan and get back on track.

Science-based predictions can be enormously helpful. People are responsible for using such predictions appropriately. In most cases, that means recognizing that prediction is just one of the tools that can be used to help achieve goals. Quality-of-life-based, goal-driven plans that are economically, ecologically, and socially sound should be applied with flexibility and with a monitoring system that provides early warning when straying from the goal occurs. There are no bad predictions, only inappropriate uses of predictions.

Predictability

Asteroid orbits can be calculated from observations of the asteroid's positions combined with well-understood physical laws. But in the realm of earth science prediction, asteroid impacts are atypical. In most other cases, predictability is limited because knowledge of the future depends on knowing the present, which itself can never be completely or accurately characterized. For example, weather forecasts depend on knowing the present state of the atmosphere and then projecting the future behavior of the atmosphere, based on computer models. Because the future is dependent on initial conditions, small changes in these conditions can add up to large differences in outcomes. That is why maximum weather predictability is about two weeks: even though the system is well understood, measurement of initial conditions is invariably subject to error and omission.

The complexity of earth sciences phenomena of interest to policymakers increases when human and earth processes interact. Consider nuclear waste disposal. Predicting the performance of a waste facility ten thousand or more years into the future depends on knowing, among a multitude of other potentially relevant factors, how much precipitation might be expected at the site. Precipitation is a function of global climate patterns. And global climate patterns might be sensitive to human processes such as energy and land use. Energy and land use are functions of politics, policy, social changes, and so on. What at first seems a narrow scientific question rapidly spirals into unbounded complexity.

Finally, decision makers sometimes are led to believe that the sophistication of a prediction methodology contributes to greater predictive skill, i.e., that in a complex world, a complex methodology will enhance predictability. In reality, the situation is not so clear-cut. An evaluation of the performance of complex models in energy, economics, population, and other areas has shown that "methodological sophistication contributes very little to the accuracy of [predictions]."[14] Yet energy, economics, and population are integral to any long-term, policy-relevant predictive capability in the areas of global climate change, nuclear waste disposal, and oil and gas reserve assessment. Overall, more sophistication can introduce more uncertainty and more sources of error into a prediction. Our case studies suggest that better prediction products arise more from the feedback between predictions and experience than from the introduction of more sophisticated predictive methodologies. The lesson for decision makers is that they should not be overly impressed by claims of sophistication, unless those claims are backed up by demonstrable increases in accuracy. (See Box 3.)

Box 3. Perspective on Prediction Use in Funding Science

Jack Fellows, Government Executive

As someone who worked in the White House's Office of Management and Budget for many years and dealt with national public policy issues related to science, space, and the environment, the factors I would consider important for using or avoiding misuse of predictions include:

Problem dynamics. Is using or improving a model's prediction even germane to the problem? In the situations I most faced, I was being asked whether (1) it was worth the cost of improving a predictive model, or (2) the output from a model would be relevant to a public policy decision. With respect to the first point, it was difficult to tell many times whether a model improvement would contribute to policy-making or was only a challenging scientific topic. What could be a significant scientific advance might have little impact on those who might use the prediction in the real world. Depending on the nature of the situation, either outcome could have value, but if a model improvement was being proposed to address policy issues, then the value-added of the improvement to society needed to be demonstrated. Indeed, some problems are so oriented toward mitigation or adaptation that improvement in prediction is of little consequence. For example, better warning and storm shelter improvements probably would yield significantly more return to society than small improvements in tornado model predictions.

Uncertainty and risk. Can scientists adequately characterize the level of uncertainty associated with a prediction and how best to quantify the benefits or risks associated with those uncertainties?

Range of predictions. This might be viewed as another form of uncertainty, but there are uncertainties associated with a specific model, and then there is uncertainty associated with a range of models addressing the same issue. If most models tend to have similar results (assuming the physics, etc., are believable), then I would be more likely to accept the results than if the models significantly differed.

Fidelity of the model. How well does the model replicate the historical record? If not well, then I would discount the prediction or not use it at all. Also, does it fit the scale of the problem? Is the output global in nature when my problem is local or regional—can I scale down or up to my situation?

> *Affordability.* Can I afford the model, and do have the tools and data to run it for my application?

The Interface of Product and Process: Understanding Predictions

Given the many factors that influence the generation of a scientific prediction, one can see why accurate, useful predictions are so hard to make. Those same factors also ensure that the predictions are hard to understand. How should the numerical or statistical output of a given predictive effort be interpreted? That is a problem that plagues scientists (with their "unknowable unknowns") as well as the decision makers who try to use predictions.

The challenge of understanding predictions was aptly illustrated in the case of the 1997 flooding of the Red River of the North.[15] In February 1997, forecasters predicted that the river would see flooding larger than at any time in modern history. At Grand Forks, North Dakota, forecasters expected the spring flood to exceed the 1979 flood crest of 48.8 feet sometime in April. Forecasters issued a prediction that the flood would crest at a record 49 feet, hoping to convey the message that the flood would be the worst ever experienced. But the message sent by the forecasters was not the message received by decision makers in the community.

Decision makers in the community *interpreted the event* being predicted and the probabilities associated with the prediction within the context of their own experience. First, the prediction of 49 feet, rather than conveying serious concern to the public as the forecasters hoped, instead resulted in reduced concern. Local residents and officials interpreted the forecast in the context of the record 1979 flood, which caused damages but was not catastrophic. With the 1997 crest expected to be only a few inches higher than the record set in 1979, many expressed relief rather than concern, perhaps thinking: "We survived that one. How much worse can a few inches be?" Second, decision makers did not understand the uncertainty associated with the prediction. All flood forecasts are uncertain, but predictions of record floods, i.e., floods for which there is no experience, are especially uncertain. Yet forecasters issued a quantitative prediction with a simple qualitative warning about uncertainty. Hence, many decision makers could interpret the forecast uncertainty in their own terms: Some viewed the forecast as a ceiling: "The flood will not exceed 49 feet." Others viewed the prediction as uncertain, with different individuals estimating uncertainty in the crest prediction to range from 1 to 6 feet. The historical record showed that average error for flood crest forecasts was about 10 percent.

On April 22, 1997, the Red River crested at 54 feet, inundating the communities of Grand Forks, North Dakota, and East Grand Forks, Minnesota, and causing $2 billion in damages. In the aftermath of the flood, local, state, and national officials pointed to inaccurate flood predictions as a cause of the disaster. In fact, the accuracy of the predictions was not out of line with historical performance by any objective measure. Instead, forecasters failed to express, and decision makers failed to understand, the meaning of the prediction, in terms of what was being forecast and the uncertainty associated with it. The failure was one of process, not of product. (See Box 4.)

Box 4. Accuracy of Flood Predictions

Dennis Walaker, Public Works

My area of emergency decision making relates to weather-related events regarding straight-line winds, tornadoes, blizzards, heavy rains, and river flooding. Accuracy is what I most expect of predictions. Timeliness, of course, is also an important element. More lead time provides the ability to react efficiently to reduce damage, save lives, and make our communities more disaster resistant.

A flood forecast is a guide, not an absolute. If you expect absolute accuracy, you will be disappointed because weather-related events have numerous variables that are all subject to change. The best flood forecast model can be wrong if conditions (e.g., rainfall, temperature, etc.) change dramatically.

In spring of 1997, when the flood of the Red River of the North occurred, all flood forecasts were within acceptable ranges except in Grand Forks. We now focus on this one failure rather than the several other successes. In Fargo, we had severe weather, river gauge failures, and crest reversions, but we had time to adjust to those weather-related changes. Grand Forks had little time to react to a situation that overwhelmed them, as this was an unprecedented event.

We must rely on the National Weather Service and the Flood Forecast Center for reliable information. However, we must understand or at least better understand the variables, assumptions, and real value of their predictions. Society increasingly expects science to solve all problems. But not all problems are easily solved, and answers are not always absolute. Today when serious events are not accurately predicted, society seeks someone to blame.

Could the city of Grand Forks have been saved from the disaster if the forecasts had been absolutely correct? In my opinion, contingency dikes, earlier evacuation, and loss control were options, but they required difficult, unpopular decisions. Previous victories over floods gave a false sense of security. It would have been difficult to construct emergency measures against a 56-foot crest when dikes that were supposed to handle 52 feet failed at 51 feet.

Responsibility for protecting against disaster is a local one. Predictions are but one tool, albeit one of the most important, used by local officials along with political influence, historical reflection, acceptable loss, and other considerations.

In summary, we must support the scientists in gathering the information to achieve the best predictions. We then must question the predictions when life and property in our communities are at risk. We can't simply assume that the prediction is completely accurate without our own review. Predictions are based in part on historical data. If an event significantly exceeds all previous levels, accurate predictions may be difficult. Blaming others when failure occurs isn't enough. If we have done everything possible, we must accept the consequences — some events are beyond our control. An elderly woman victimized by a flood summarized this by saying, "Even if we lose the flood fight, you must feel that we have done everything possible to be successful."

Other cases presented in our book further illustrate that decision makers' understanding of predictive products has a profound influence on how — and how well — the products are used. Consider the following three examples:

1. Debate has raged for decades about the policy implications of possible future human-caused changes in climate. This debate has been about "global warming" expressed in terms of a single global average temperature. But no person and no ecosystem experiences global average temperature. Each policy advocate is thus free to interpret that prediction product in support of his or her particular interests, ranging from pending global catastrophe to benign (and perhaps beneficial) change. Uncertainty and the inability to compare predictions to experience allow even more interpretive freedom. Predictive science is thus used (and misused) to justify and advance the existing interests of contesting participants in the political process.

2. In recent years scientists have increased their ability to observe asteroids and comets that potentially threaten the earth. In this case, the "event" is clear enough—possible extinction of life on earth if a large asteroid slams into the planet. But public reaction to the discovery of asteroid 1997 XF11, and the associated prediction that it could strike the earth on October 26, 2028, illustrates that scientists, as well as the public, can fall prey to misunderstanding. Blame for the misunderstanding can be apportioned among scientists who hastily issued an erroneous prediction; the media, which jumped on the prediction because it was spectacular; and the public, which responded to the magnitude of the potential event, rather than its uncertainties or probabilities.

3. Weather forecasts afford decision makers the best opportunity to understand prediction products. It is well worth repeating that in the United States the National Weather Service issues more than 10 million predictions every year to hundreds of millions of users. (In contrast, we have seen less than a dozen scientifically legitimate earthquake predictions.) This activity provides a basis of experience from which users can learn, through trial and error, to understand the meaning of the prediction products they receive. Of course, in the case of weather prediction there is still room for confusion. People may fail to understand predictions even for routine events. The meteorologist Allan H. Murphy documents that when forecasters call for a 70 percent chance of rain, decision makers understand the probabilistic element of the forecast but do not know whether the rain has a 70 percent chance of occurring at each point in the forecast area, or whether 70 percent of the area is expected to receive rain with a 100 percent probability, and so on.[16] Even so, one of the important lessons of weather prediction is that decision makers, including the public, are in general able to use probabilistic information, and such products can have significant value.

These examples illustrate how viewing prediction solely as a product is inherently problematic, because doing so conceals the context that gives the product meaning. Thus, if one wants to improve the use of prediction, one must do more than simply develop "better" prediction products, whether more precise (e.g., a forecast of a 49.1652-foot flood crest at East Grand Forks), more accurate (e.g., a forecast of a 51-foot crest), or more robust (e.g., a probabilistic distribution of various forecast crest levels). While better prediction products are in many cases more desirable, *better decisions* in the common interest require attention to the broader prediction process. From this standpoint, better prediction products may be neither necessary nor sufficient for improved decision making, and hence desired outcomes. To effect better decisions, it is necessary to understand prediction as a process.

Prediction as a Process

The prediction process can be thought of as three parallel decision activities:

- *Research.* Including science, observations, modeling, etc., as well as forecasters' judgments and the organizational structure—all of which go into the production of predictions for decision makers.
- *Communication.* Both the sending and receiving of information—e.g., who says what to whom, how is it said, and with what effect.
- *Use.* The incorporation of predictive information into decision making. Of course, decisions are typically contingent on many factors other than predictions.

These activities are not sequential. They are more accurately thought of as integrated components of a broader *prediction process*, with each activity proceeding in parallel, and with significant feedbacks and interrelations between them.

A robust conclusion of this book is that good decisions are more likely to occur when all three activities of the prediction process are functioning well—and research activity is often the least critical of the three. Open communication and consideration of alternative policy approaches can lead to successful decisions in the face of unsuccessful prediction products, but the opposite is unlikely to occur.[17] Consider the following examples:

- The case of the Red River flood illustrates how a technically skillful forecast that is miscommunicated or misused can result in costs rather than benefits. The overall prediction process broke down in several places. No one in the prediction process fully understood the uncertainty associated with the prediction, hence little attention was paid to communicating the uncertainty to decision makers, and poor assumptions were made about how decision makers would interpret and use the predictions. As a result poor decisions were made. Given that that region will to some degree always depend on flood forecasts, the situation can be improved in the future by including local decision makers in the research activity in order to develop more useful products.[18]

- In the case of earthquake prediction, a focus on developing skillful predictions of earthquakes in the Parkfield region of California brought together seismologists, local officials, and emergency managers with the original goal of preparing for a predicted earthquake. A result was better communication among those groups and overall improved preparation for future earthquakes. In this case, even though the prediction product was a failure, the overall process adapted to that failure and made decisions that enhanced awareness, refocused attention on alternatives, and arguably reduced vulnerability to future earthquakes. (See Box 5.)

- Global climate change seems to display attributes similar to the early stages of earthquake prediction. Policy-making focused on prediction has run up against numerous political and technical obstacles, while alternatives to prediction are becoming increasingly visible. The prediction process will be said to work if it addresses the goals of climate policy — i.e., if it reduces the impacts of future climate changes on environment and society.[19] More and better predictions are not a prerequisite for this desirable outcome.

- Nuclear waste disposal has also evolved from a situation in which the development of skillful predictions played a central role into one in which decision making focuses on actions that can achieve desirable societal outcomes under various possible futures. Initially, the success of the repository seemed to be entirely dependent on predicting the hydrologic system at the disposal site over the next ten thousand years. Unanticipated complexities associated with this natural system led to decreased emphasis on prediction and increased emphasis on designing an engineered containment system. However, while the behavior of this engineered system is likely to be much more predictable than that of the hydrologic system, it will have its own problems, and uncertainty cannot be entirely eliminated. Additional options, such as monitored, retrievable storage, may be necessary to accommodate the remaining uncertainties.

Box 5. A User's Perspective on Earthquake Prediction and Public Policy

Shirley Mattingly, Emergency Management

As calamities go, earthquakes pose a special threat because the really disastrous events occur infrequently. Earthquakes challenge those who would predict them and

---

those who would respond to predictions because uncertainty surrounds the science and the response and provides an excuse for no action.

Predictions, per se, can disrupt life in a city at risk, and they don't have to be valid or even scientifically based. The self-proclaimed clairvoyant Nostradamus predicted a devastating event in May 1988 in the "new city," assumed to be Los Angeles. Widespread publicity fed rumors, which led to near panic in one community. Hundreds of families took their children out of school and permanently left their homes, relocating to the relative seismic safety of Fresno or Oregon. I was disheartened that earthquake drills at school were regarded as proof that the coming catastrophe was inevitable.

Panic is not a good thing. But emergency managers took advantage of the public's heightened awareness of earthquakes to explain the science and promote simple safety measures. Nevertheless, the Nostradamus "prediction" and similar incidents negatively impact public policymakers' regard for the predictive science.

Even apparently legitimate scientific disagreements justify inaction as the preferred policy option. A so-called seismic deficit postulated in 1994 by an official science working group was believed to mean that destructive quakes were more likely to strike the region in coming decades. Subsequently, earthquake insurance rates quadrupled (Kerr 1988). Eventually, the deficit was debunked and suddenly disappeared. But for four years Los Angelenos thought that they faced either twice as many large earthquakes as normal or one huge quake many times more powerful than the last Big One. This incident didn't improve policymakers' regard for the predictive science, either.

Science is often foreign territory for politicians, and politics is often foreign territory for scientists. Scientists and public policy setters often don't even begin to speak the same language. They generally have very different backgrounds, motivations, and aims, and they work in different milieus. So communication does not come naturally.

There's art and science in both predictions and politics. In my experience, decision makers rely on input from people they trust, people with whom they have a history. They like their advisors to do their homework, define the problem, identify alternative approaches, evaluate potential solutions, and find solid answers. And they want advice that is clear and easy to understand. Then they act based on what they've heard and on other factors we don't know about. While they are pragmatic, they can be swayed by people with passionate beliefs.

Scientists and policymakers can help each other to understand the environment that will receive—perhaps eagerly, perhaps kicking and screaming—a prediction. They should collaboratively decide how to communicate information, how to frame it, and when to release it. Both should pursue good relationships with the local media, even when there is little news, because if the media are well informed, they'll do a better job of reporting accurately when there *is* a story.

For local decision makers to take predictions seriously, they must have faith in the prediction and the predictor. Scientists must have credibility with peers and with the people they hope to influence into action. That requires sustained dialogue and mutual trust. The responsibility lies with both.

I remember one highly respected seismologist coming downtown to Los Angeles' city hall, more than once, to discuss his research findings with any public official who would listen. He came on his own initiative. He moved us, not immediately, but over time. He changed public officials' perceptions and influenced public policy. I saw it happen, and ever since, I've been trying to make it happen again, anytime and anywhere that anyone will listen.

A User's Guide to Prediction and Decision Making

When to Rely on Prediction Products

The case studies in this volume provide insight into when decision makers should look to prediction products and when they should look to alternative sources of information to help make decisions.[20] The conditions under which predictions should be relied on are easy to lay out in principle but may be difficult to apply in practice. In principle, predictions should be relied on when:

1. Predictive skill is known.
2. Decision makers have experience with understanding and using predictions.
3. The characteristic time of the predicted event is short.
4. There are limited alternatives.
5. The outcomes of various courses of action are understood in terms of well-constrained uncertainties (e.g., the likelihood and effects of false positives and false negatives).

Conversely, alternatives to prediction should be sought when:

1. Skill is low or unknown.
2. Little experience exists with using the predictions or with the phenomena in question.
3. The characteristic time is long.
4. Alternatives are available.
5. The outcomes of alternative decisions are highly uncertain.

Incorporating these principles into real-world decision processes may be difficult. Organizations often choose to gather more information (even if it is useless) rather than take action.[21] Political incentives favor "the basing of policy on supposedly neutral forecasts [that allow] decision making institutions to assume a cloak of objectivity."[22] Rejecting that cloak in favor of the hair shirt of realism requires decision makers to:

1. Be flexible.
2. Learn from experience.
3. Search for alternatives.
4. Hedge their bets.
5. Evaluate progress with respect to goals.
6. Evaluate predictive skill with respect to decisions.
7. Focus on good decisions, not just good predictions.

Each of these guidelines might seem obvious or commonsensical — but as the cases here dramatically show, they are often neglected. Overcoming this neglect requires decision makers to change their focus — from predictions as a product to predictions as a process.

Creating a Successful Prediction Process

If society is to benefit from the predictive information products of the earth sciences, scientists and decision makers should together pay attention to the broad process in which predictions are made. In particular, participants in the prediction process must take action in six areas.

Above all, users of predictions, along with other stakeholders in the prediction process, must *question predictions.* For this questioning to be effective, predictions should be as transparent as possible to the user. In particular, assumptions, model limitations, and weaknesses in input data should be forthrightly discussed. Institutional motives must be questioned and revealed. Especially in cases where personal experience may be limited (such as asteroid impacts and global warming), both scientific rigor and public confidence in the validity of the prediction will benefit from this open questioning process. "Black boxes," i.e., closed processes, generate public distrust, especially when a prediction can stimulate decisions that create winners and losers. They can also foster complacency among those doing the predicting. Even so, because of limited experience, many types of predictions will never be understood by decision makers in the way that weather predictions are understood. Table 3.1 lists seven general questions that can be asked about predictions and gives accompanying guidelines for seeking answers.

If users are to question predictions, then *the prediction process must be open to external scrutiny*. This means that policymakers must give procedural aspects of democratic openness, evaluation, and accountability the same priority as issues that may seem more directly connected to policy goals (e.g., funding predictive research or establishing environmental standards). Openness is important for many reasons, but perhaps the most interesting and least obvious is that the technical products of prediction are likely to be "better"—both more robust scientifically and more effectively integrated into the decision process—when predictive research is subjected to the tough love of democratic discourse. Scientists may reasonably fear that such attention could lead to politicization of research agendas, but many of our case histories show the opposite—that, in the absence of public openness, predictive science tends to converge on results that support the tacit assumptions of the administering organizations or policy regimes.[23] External scrutiny helps to reinvigorate the healthy skepticism that is supposed to be a part of the scientific process. Consider scientists working on the Yucca Mountain nuclear waste repository who converged on a predictive product that was consistent with their institutional interests. The presence of two oversight bodies provided the additional, outside scrutiny necessary to expose the technical flaws in those predictions. Similarly, Robert Moran, a geochemical and hydrogeologic consultant, shows that, in the effort to predict the environmental effects of mines, informed public scrutiny of environmental impact statements is necessary to ensure that significant uncertainties are brought to light.[24] Coastal geologist Orrin Pilkey describes a failed process for making decisions about beach nourishment that is, perhaps predictably, neither open nor subject to evaluation.[25] And as geologist Donald Gautier explains, when the U.S. Geological Survey opened up its oil and gas assessment program to a range of interested customers, it improved both its own technical capability, and the utility of its prediction products.[26]

In this same context of openness, *predictions must be generated primarily with the needs of the user in mind.* Television weather predictions focus primarily on temperature, precipitation, and wind, rather than temperature gradients, behavior of aerosols, and barometric pressure. Scientists must understand the broader goals of the process, not the narrow goals of science; they must listen to stakeholders. Stakeholders must work closely and persistently with the scientists to communicate their needs and problems. To ensure useful prediction products, prediction research programs should be designed from their inception to include mechanisms of formal and informal, regular and frequent dialogue between prediction researchers and prediction users. More communication between producers and users of predictions always benefits the prediction process and the quest for good decisions, even if it introduces inefficiencies in the generation of prediction products.

Uncertainties must be clearly understood and articulated by the scientists, so that users understand their implications. If scientists do not understand the uncertainties — which is often the case — they must say so. Failure to understand and articulate uncertainties contributes to poor decisions that undermine relations among scientists and decision makers. But merely understanding and articulating the uncertainties does not mean that the predictions will be useful decision tools. For example, if policymakers truly understood the uncertainties associated with predictions of global climate change, they might decide that strategies for action should not depend only on predictions.[27]

Decision makers must realize that predictions themselves can be significant events. Predictions can stimulate considerable action that can confer benefits or impose costs. False earthquake predictions have stimulated better earthquake preparedness, while false asteroid impact predictions have fueled needless alarm. More significantly, predictions can commit society to one course of action while foreclosing other options. The prediction of global warming, for example, has mobilized an international effort to reduce anthropogenic CO_2 emissions. Some would argue that such action is necessary to forestall disaster; others, that it is a fruitless and potentially dangerous distraction from more effective approaches to global environmental protection. In either case, the prediction itself has been a much greater catalyst for decision making than any unambiguous impact of global warming. A healthy prediction process depends on the recognition that predictions are themselves events.

Finally, *the quest for alternatives to prediction must be institutionalized in the prediction process,* especially when characteristic times are long, policy regimes are strong, and decision makers have limited (or no) experience with the predicted phenomenon. Alternatives to prediction should be debated and evaluated (and perhaps tried on a pilot basis) at the earliest stages of the prediction process. As our case studies show, alternatives are in fact often available. Rather than trying to predict the impacts of hard-rock pit mines on water quality as a basis for environmental regulation, spreading risk through bonding or other types of insurance might be preferable. Rather than depending on predictions of acid rain mitigation to design a regulatory command-and-control system,[28] the U.S. Congress actually implemented a system of tradable emissions permits that did not depend on predictive earth science.

Table 3.1: Questioning Predictions

Questions to Ask	Guidelines to Follow in Seeking Answers
What are the policy goals (i.e., outcomes) that prediction is intended to achieve?	Specify the purposes of the prediction
How does the process of developing predictions influence the policy process (and vice versa)?	Consider alternatives to prediction for achieving the purpose. Maintain flexibility of the system as work on predictions proceeds. Recognize that a choice to focus on prediction (as well as the choice of the specific predictive technique) will constrain future policy alternatives.
What are the direct societal impacts of the prediction?	Consider alternative societal impacts that might result from the prediction (including the different roles played by prediction). Evaluate past predictions in terms of impacts on society. Recognize that the prediction itself can be a significant event. If possible, assess the impacts of inadequate predictions relative to the impacts of successful ones.
What are the scientific limitations and uncertainties of prediction?	Evaluate past predictions in terms of scientific validity. Recognize that different approaches can yield equally valid predictions. Recognize that prediction is not a substitute for data collection, analysis, experience, or reality. Recognize that predictions are always uncertain; assess the level of uncertainty acceptable in the particular context. Beware of precision without accuracy.

	Recognize that quantification and prediction are not (a) accuracy, (b) certainty, (c) relevancy, or (d) reality.
	Recognize that computers hide assumptions; computers don't kill predictions, assumptions do.
	Recognize that the science base may be inadequate for a given type of prediction.
What factors can influence how a prediction is used by society?	Recognize that prediction may be more effective at bringing problems to attention than forcing them to effective solution.
	Recognize that perceptions of predictions may differ from what predictors intend and may lead to unexpected responses.
	Recognize that the societal benefits of a prediction are not necessarily a function of its accuracy.
	Recognize that there are many types of prediction, and their potential uses in society are diverse.
What political and ethical considerations are raised by the generation and dissemination of a prediction?	Pay attention to conflicts of interest among those soliciting and making predictions.
	Understand who becomes empowered when the prediction is made. Who are the winners and losers?
	Pay attention to the ethical issues raised by the release of predictions.
How should predictions be communicated in society?	Make the prediction methodology as transparent as possible.
	Predictions should be communicated (a) in terms of their implications for societal response, and (b) in terms of their uncertainties.

In Conclusion: Question Predictions!

The emergence of an environmental challenge appears to stimulate an almost automatic call for scientific prediction as the first step toward meeting the challenge. The possible sources of this reaction range from the desire to find an objective source of information that can dictate action while protecting against political backlash, to an unquestioning modern confidence in our technological ability to control the future.[29] Whatever the cause, the scientific establishment of the United States focuses a not inconsiderable proportion of its intellectual energy and technological wherewithal on predicting the future of nature in order to promote a variety of desired societal outcomes.

Considered as a whole, the cases in this book portray a pervasive and energetic societal activity — a prediction enterprise supported by substantial federal and private funds — that is unified by shared assumptions about the necessity and value of scientific foresight in environmental decision making, and rooted in a strong belief in predictability itself. The recognition that such an enterprise exists is a crucial first step toward fulfilling the goal set out at the beginning of this book: to improve environmental decision making. Only when the prediction enterprise is recognized can critical scrutiny begin.

Predictions — information products — lie at the heart of this enterprise. They are its rationale, its currency, its legitimacy. For this reason, any effort to assess the prediction enterprise must openly and persistently *question predictions*. This questioning has to occur on two levels simultaneously. Of course it is important to question accuracy, uncertainty, and predictability. But we have seen that prediction products mean little by themselves. Predictions must also be questioned in the context — political, cultural, economic, or environmental — of the larger enterprise. Given a particular environmental problem, we need to ask: How does the enterprise operate in this case? Who are the players, and how is power, legitimacy, and participation apportioned among them? What conflicting values are hidden by debate over technical matters? What criteria should be used for judging the output of the enterprise and the outcomes of that output?

Technically "good" predictions used in a healthy decision environment can of course facilitate better decisions, as illustrated by the case of weather predictions — our only candidate for the prediction hall of fame. But the "goodness" of weather predictions arises not just from their accuracy and skill, but also from the capacity of society to make effective use of them. A pretty good flood prediction did not forestall disaster in Grand Forks, North Dakota, and a pretty bad earthquake prediction did not prevent better earthquake preparedness in central and Southern California. These types of outcomes are paradoxical or confusing only if one persists in viewing predictions as simple information products. When the whole enterprise is seen, sense and order begin to emerge.

The central issue is an uncertain future. The cause of this uncertainty is a dynamic planet, an evolving society, and the interaction between the two. Scientific prediction is one tool for coping with this uncertainty — a tool with some promise, some problems, and much unacknowledged complexity, but only one tool among many. Given the uneven performance and our lack of understanding of the prediction enterprise, a good argument can be made for the following: First, our dependence on scientific prediction has become uncritical, and at times excessive and counterproductive. Second, we need to be more careful about how and when to make prediction a central activity in addressing environmental problems. Third, as soon as new environmental problems begin to command public attention, we need to resist the urge to immediately prescribe a predictive approach and should consider instead a range of possible actions. And finally, we should worry less about making good predictions and more about making good decisions.

Notes

[1] B. Fischoff, "What Forecasts (Seem to) Mean," *International Journal of Forecasting* 10 (1994): 387-403.

[2] As contrasted with narrow or parochial interests, which may conflict with common interests.

[3] W. Ascher, "The Forecasting Potential of Complex Models," *Policy Sciences* 13 (1981): 247-267.

[4] See S. Rayner, "Prediction and Other Approaches to Climate Change Policy," Ch. 13 in *Prediction: Science, Decision Making, and the Future of Nature*, D. Sarewitz, R. A. Pielke Jr., and R. Byerly Jr., eds. (Washington, DC: Island Press, 2000), 269-298.

[5] See D. Metlay, "From Tin Roof to Torn Wet Blanket: Predicting and Observing Groundwater Movement at a Proposed Nuclear Waste Site," Ch. 10 in *Prediction: Science, Decision Making, and the Future of Nature*, D. Sarewitz, R. A. Pielke Jr., and R. Byerly Jr., eds. (Washington, DC: Island Press, 2000), 199-230.

[6] A. H. Murphy, "The Finley Affair: A Signal Event in the History of Forecast Verification," *Weather and Forecasting* 8 (1996): 281-293.

[7] A. H. Murphy, "Forecast verification," in *Economic Value of Weather and Climate Forecasts*, R. W. Katz and A. H. Murphy, eds. (Cambridge, UK: Cambridge University Press, 1997), 19-74.

[8] R. Byerly Jr., "Prediction and Characteristic Times," Ch. 16, in *Prediction: Science, Decision Making, and the Future of Nature*, D. Sarewitz, R. A. Pielke Jr., and R. Byerly Jr., eds. (Washington, DC: Island Press, 2000), 327-340.

[9] S. A. Changnon, "Flood Prediction: Immersed in the Quagmire of National Flood Mitigation Strategy," Ch. 5 in *Prediction: Science, Decision Making, and the Future of Nature*, D. Sarewitz, R. A. Pielke Jr., and R. Byerly Jr., eds. (Washington, DC: Island Press, 2000), 85-106.

[10] T. R. Stewart, "Uncertainty, Judgment, and Error in Prediction," Ch. 3 in *Prediction: Science, Decision Making, and the Future of Nature*, D. Sarewitz, R. A. Pielke Jr., and R. Byerly Jr., eds. (Washington, DC: Island Press, 2000), 41-60.

[11] J. M. Nigg, "Predicting Earthquakes: Science, Pseudoscience, and Public Policy Paradox," Ch. 7 in *Prediction: Science, Decision Making, and the Future of Nature*, D. Sarewitz, R. A. Pielke Jr., and R. Byerly Jr., eds. (Washington, DC: Island Press, 2000), 135-158.

[12] E.g., B. Keepin, "Review of Global Energy and Carbon Dioxide Projections," *Annual Review of Energy* 11 (1986): 357-392.

[13] J. B. Robinson, "Backing into the Future: On the Methodological and Institutional Biases Embedded in Energy Supply and Demand Forecasting," *Technological Forecasting & Social Change* 21 (1982): 249.

[14] W. Ascher, "The Forecasting Potential of Complex Models," Policy Sciences 13 (1981): 258; see also B. Keepin, "Review of Global Energy and Carbon Dioxide Projections," *Annual Review of Energy* 11 (1986): 357-392.

[15] See W. H. Hooke and R. A. Pielke Jr., "Short-Term Weather Prediction: An Orchestra in Need of a Conductor," Ch. 4 in in *Prediction: Science, Decision Making, and the Future of Nature*, D. Sarewitz, R. A. Pielke Jr., and R. Byerly Jr., eds. (Washington, DC: Island Press, 2000), 61-84. See also R. A. Pielke Jr., "Who Decides? Forecasts and Responsibilities in the 1997 Red River Flood," *American Behavioral Science Review* (1999): 83-101.

[16] A. H. Murphy, S. Lichtenstein, B. Fischhoff, and R. L. Winkler, "Misinterpretations of Precipitation Probability Forecast," *Bulletin of the American Meteorological Society* 61 (1980): 695-701.

[17] See R. D. Brunner, "Alternatives to Prediction," Ch. 14 in in *Prediction: Science, Decision Making, and the Future of Nature*, D. Sarewitz, R. A. Pielke Jr., and R. Byerly Jr., eds. (Washington, DC: Island Press, 2000), 299-314.

[18] R. A. Pielke Jr., "Who Decides? Forecasts and Responsibilities in the 1997 Red River Flood," *American Behavioral Science Review* (1999): 83-101.

[19] R. A. Pielke Jr., "Rethinking the Role of Adaptation in Climate Policy, *Global Environmental Change* 8, no. 2 (1998): 159-170.

[20] There are other such "user's guides" for understanding predictions. One notable example, which focuses on economic and technological forecasts, is J. S. Armstrong, "Introduction," in

Principles of Forecasting: A Handbook for Researchers and Practitioners, J. S. Armstrong, ed. (Norwell, MA: Kluwer Academic Publishers, 1999. See also N. Nicholls, "Cognitive Illusions, Heuristics, and Climate Prediction," *Bulletin of the American Meteorological Society* 80, no. 7 (1999): 1385-1397.

[21] E.g., M. S. Feldman and J. G. March, "Information in Organizations as Signal and Sign," *Administrative Science Quarterly* 26 (1981): 171-186.

[22] J. B. Robinson, "Backing into the Future: On the Methodological and Institutional Biases Embedded in Energy Supply and Demand Forecasting," *Technological Forecasting & Social Change* 21 (1982): 240.

[23] See C. Herrick and J. M. Pendleton, "A Decision Framework for Prediction in Environmental Policy," Ch. 17 in *Prediction: Science, Decision Making, and the Future of Nature*, D. Sarewitz, R. A. Pielke Jr., and R. Byerly Jr., eds. (Washington, DC: Island Press, 2000), 341-360.

[24] R. E. Moran, "Is this Number to Your Liking? Water Quality Predictions in Mining Impact Studies," Ch. 9 in *Prediction: Science, Decision Making, and the Future of Nature*, D. Sarewitz, R. A. Pielke Jr., and R. Byerly Jr., eds. (Washington, DC: Island Press, 2000), 185-198.

[25] O. H. Pilkey, "What You Know Can Hurt You: Predicting the Behavior of Nourished Beaches," Ch. 8 in *Prediction: Science, Decision Making, and the Future of Nature*, D. Sarewitz, R. A. Pielke Jr., and R. Byerly Jr., eds. (Washington, DC: Island Press, 2000), 159-184.

[26] D. L. Gautier, "Oil and Gas Resources Appraisal: Diminishing Reserves, Increasing Supplies," Ch. 11 in *Prediction: Science, Decision Making, and the Future of Nature*, D. Sarewitz, R. A. Pielke Jr., and R. Byerly Jr., eds. (Washington, DC: Island Press, 2000), 231-250.

[27] E.g., R. A. Pielke Jr., "Rethinking the Role of Adaptation in Climate Policy, *Global Environmental Change* 8, no. 2 (1998): 159-170.

[28] See C. Herrick, "Predictive Modeling of Acid Rain: Obstacles to Generating Useful Information," Ch. 12 in *Prediction: Science, Decision Making, and the Future of Nature*, D. Sarewitz, R. A. Pielke Jr., and R. Byerly Jr., eds. (Washington, DC: Island Press, 2000), 251-268.

[29] E.g., R. L. Heilbroner, *The Future as History: The Historic Currents of Our Time and the Direction in Which They are Taking America* (New York, NY: Harper and Brothers, 1959).

4

A TYPOLOGY FOR ASSESSING THE ROLE OF USERS IN SCIENTIFIC RESEARCH[*]

Elizabeth C. McNie, Adam Parris, and Daniel Sarewitz

Overview

Decision makers call upon and fund science to help clarify and resolve many types of problems.[1] They expect research to create useful information to help inform solutions to intractable problems, catalyze innovation, and provide information that not only educates stakeholders, but also expands alternatives, clarifies choices, and aids in formulating and implementing policy decisions.[2]

But linking science with decision making to help solve problems is challenging. Often when responding to such

---

[*] This is a preliminary report. A revised, peer-reviewed version was published as E. McNie, A. Parris, and D. Sarewitz, "Improving the Public Value of Science: A Typology to Inform Discussion, Design, and Implementation of Research," *Research Policy* 45, no. 4 (2016): 884-895.

problems we simply produce more science, and not necessarily "the right science."[3] Intended users of the scientific information may be unaware that it exists, or be unable to use what is available. The difficulty of actively linking the supply of scientific information with users' demands leads to missed opportunities for science to better inform policy (see Figure 4.1).[4] Such "missed opportunities" occur for many reasons. Here we are concerned with the tendency to view and assess research in isolation from the context of its use, and simply in terms of whether it is "basic" or "applied." Such science-centric approaches have great value in producing new knowledge, but are inadequate to address the growing complexity of problems typically facing decision makers, and may in fact simply reinforce a structural gap between the "production and use of scientific information."[5]

Figure 4.1: The Missed Opportunity Matrix

DEMAND: Do users have specific information needs?

		YES	NO
SUPPLY: Is scientific information produced?	**YES**	*SUPPLY & DEMAND RECONCILED:* Users' information needs reconciled with the production of scientific information.	*MISSED OPPORTUNITY:* Research priorities misaligned or users are unaware of possible utility of information produced.
	NO	*MISSED OPPORTUNITY:* Research priorities need modification in order to respond to users' information needs.	*SUPPLY & DEMAND RECONCILED:* Information not produced nor needed by users.

Over two dozen different terms describing scientific research have been described or adopted by the National Science Foundation, National Science Board, Office of Management and Budget, Organisation for Economic Cooperation and Development (OECD), and science-policy researchers and others during this century and the last (see

Table 4.1). Research types have been defined by many variables, although the differences between many types are often minor or semantic.[6] Nonetheless the research categories of "basic" and "applied" remain the epistemic norms in the science community, and as a result, most research types are classified as one or the other, and distinguished primarily by two overarching criteria: the motivation for research (fundamental discovery vs. application of knowledge) and temporal delay to application of research results (from a few years to decades).[7] Despite many efforts to refine research typologies, *none of the types considered and adopted by national or international science policy bodies identifies the role of users in the shaping of research*, and none of the types adequately address the need to reconcile the production of scientific information with the context in which such information is used. In fact the OECD even goes as far as disqualifying from consideration as basic or applied research any activities or personnel that are actively engaged with potential users.[8]

Table 4.1: Common Research Types

Ad hoc	Development	Normal Science
Applied	Directed	Oriented-Basic
Background	Experimental	Pure
Baconian	Free-Basic	Pure-Basic
Basic	Fundamental	Purposive-Basic
Clinical	Jeffersonian	Strategic
Committed	Mode 1	Tactical
Curiosity-Driven	Mission-Oriented	Uncommitted
Curiosity-Oriented	Newtonian	Use-Inspired

Many practitioners and scholars of science policy have come to recognize that the basic/applied typology may conceal as much as it reveals. For example, in political scientist Donald Stokes's well-known conception of use-inspired research, he added to the standard dichotomy a new dimension (Pasteur's Quadrant) that accommodated the recognition that research, whether basic or applied, is commonly influenced by considerations of use.[9] Little to no progress has been made in translating such insights into criteria for research design,[10] and even Stokes failed to consider the role of users themselves. Our perspective here is that the character of scientific knowledge, the intended use of science, and the role of users in the research process will often be directly pertinent to appropriate research design.

Some have suggested that directing research toward specific outcomes is unproductive, may limit scientists' exploration of possible alternative solutions,[11] may lead to concerns over scientific accountability,[12] and may even be harmful to science.[13] Such concerns in total question whether science can be shaped, let alone shaped by users. But extensive research has shown that science is a social process influenced by societal and individual values and norms[14] and is therefore amenable to being shaped and informed by scientists and users alike (as well by as other factors such as institutional culture and professional incentives). Directing research toward practical ends has always been a part of our scientific enterprise, and doing so need not drive out fundamental and novel discoveries.[15] Increasingly, the scientific community itself is coming to recognize the need for new science institutions that better support, incentivize, and train scientists to perform research to meet societal needs.[16] To do that, we need better approaches to view, deliberate on, shape, implement and evaluate research. The typology presented here has been developed as a tool for supporting such approaches. It is intended for use especially by science program managers and designers, although we anticipate that it will be modified, adapted, and improved both through use by practitioners and through further scholarly analysis.

An Expanded Typology

This paper introduces a new, multidimensional research typology that can describe different research types in order to improve our understanding of research in general, help inform research design, and assess the organizational and institutional resources needed to manage different types of research. Application of this typology may help improve science-policy decisions by revealing the ways in which science programs may or may not be appropriately reconciled with the problem context they are supposed to address.

One consideration that cuts across the typology is the role of the knowledge user. "Users" constitute a broad category that includes people or organizations that bring the results of research into decision making contexts and activities. But users also engage with researchers at various times and venues in the research process, and this engagement itself influences research and its value for users. As well, users may need or benefit from different kinds of information at different points in any decision process. For example, in the early phases of decision making, users may need to simply improve their understanding of the problem, whereas in later phases of decision making users may need highly context-specific information. Given the continuum of decision making, users themselves may change as the problem or context for action evolves. Users may be program managers, the media or other science communicators, educators, policymakers, elected officials, interested citizens, and more. Other researchers or technologists may also be users. Given such variety, it is important to understand and articulate who the intended users of the research outputs are, as this will help inform and characterize the research activity.

Underlying this discussion of users are questions of influence: Who gets to influence the design, implementation, and use of research? What is the extent of that influence? The distribution of influence among unique users is not uniform and varies by social, political, economic, intellectual, and cultural dimensions.

The typology divides research by three general activities, each of which is subdivided into more specific attributes. *Knowledge Production* describes attributes such as the nature of expertise, goals of research, and treatment of uncertainty. *Learning and Engagement* describes attributes such as what is learned, how knowledge is exchanged with users, who participates in the exchange network, and the role of social capital in transferring knowledge. *Organizational and Institutional Processes* describes attributes such as research outputs, human capital, institutional accessibility, organizational flexibility, boundary work, and approaches for evaluation, which together help inform how resources can be identified and deployed to support research. The attributes are situated on an idealized spectrum bound by value-laden criteria ranging from strongly science-centric to strongly user-oriented (see Figure 4.2). The left side of each spectrum represents research criteria focused on achieving ends internal to science — what we term "science values."[17] This research tends to be more disconnected from explicit consideration of the context of use and involvement of users, that is, science is treated as a closed system. The right side represents research criteria focused on achieving ends external to the research itself — what we term "user values." Such research is open to engagement with actors other than the core researchers themselves and is justified by the expectation of providing information and knowledge for various users and uses. A research activity is characterized in full by assessing where it lies on the spectrum of value criteria for the entire suite of attributes.

Figure 4.2: Typology of Research

Activity	Attribute	Spectra of Research Criteria	
		Science Values	User Values
Knowledge Production	Expertise	Epistemic	Experiential
	Relevance	General	Contextual
	Disciplinary Focus	Singular, Narrow	Transdisciplinary, Diverse
	Uncertainty	Reduce Uncertainty	Manage Uncertainty
	Goals for Research	Exploratory	Outcome Oriented
Learning & Engagement	Learning	Theoretical	Social, Practical
	Knowledge Exchange	Restricted, Linear	Iterative, Influential
	Network Participation	Homogeneous	Heterogeneous
	Social Capital	Negligible	Significant
Organizational & Institutional Processes	Accessibility	Constrained	High
	Outputs	Narrow	Diverse
	Evaluation & Effectiveness	Science-Centric	Public-Value Oriented
	Flexibility	Constrained	Responsive
	Human Capital	Narrow	Broad
	Boundary Management	Limited	Broad

Research Activities

In this section we briefly describe and define each element of the typology. The typology is divided into three organizing categories (columns in Figure 4.2): Activity, Attribute, and Spectra of Research Criteria. The Activity column separates the research endeavor into major subcomponents; the Attribute column identifies the key subcategories of each Activity; and the Spectra of Research Criteria column shows, for each Attribute, a pair of evaluative criteria that define a spectrum along which any given research program can be qualitatively located. For example, in considering Knowledge Production, approaches to addressing the attribute of Uncertainty may range along a spectrum from those aimed at reducing uncertainty to those aimed at managing it. Of course, most research activities lie between the extremes. They typology allows this intermediate domain to be explored and characterized with attention to any or all of the fifteen research attributes. We intend it to be a heuristic device that can help inform and improve science-policy decisions.

Activity 1: Knowledge Production

Knowledge Production addresses what is credible, who is credible, and what ways of creating knowledge are credible.[18] Knowledge Production consists not just of facts but includes tacit skills and the wisdom of lived experiences, while acknowledging that freedom from bias and social influence is never entirely possible.[19]

Attributes and Spectra of Research Criteria

A. Expertise: Who has the credibility to produce knowledge?

<u>Epistemic</u>: Experts have specific norms and behaviors consistent with their epistemic communities. Expertise tends to be oriented by discipline and is established by attainment of a Ph.D.

<u>Experiential</u>: Expertise expands from disciplines to include policy, economic, bureaucratic, community, and lay expertise, each of which comes with its own norms and criteria for quality. Expertise also includes lived experiences and proximity to the problem.

B. Relevance: What is the source of relevance to solving the specific problem?

<u>General</u>: Research is oriented toward developing and testing hypotheses with the aim of informing theories. Consequently, outputs from research tend toward global instead of local scales and are broadly relevant. Significant time delay between research and application also reduces relevance.

<u>Contextual</u>: Research is oriented toward producing knowledge that focuses on spatial and temporal scales specific to various dimensions of a pre-identified decision.

Solving discrete problems requires that information be context-sensitive and needs to consider the appropriate physical, social, and natural scales.

C. Disciplinary Focus: How discipline-driven are the knowledge production activities?

<u>Singular, Narrow</u>: Research is largely guided by single or sub-disciplines. Knowledge is often characterized by a reductionist worldview in which systems are divided into smaller parts and analyzed in isolation, and is guided by problem formulation rooted in disciplines. Interdisciplinary research may also occur, but research questions are still largely informed by a reductionist worldview and organized around problems that are defined scientifically.

<u>Transdisciplinary, Diverse:</u> Research is transdisciplinary, that is, is organized around problems that are defined by the context of use, and will often incorporate social, physical, and natural sciences. Such research is necessary, for example, when knowledge is sought to inform decisions related to coupled human-environmental systems.[20]

D. Uncertainty: How do researchers understand and address the problem of uncertainty in knowledge production?

<u>Reduce</u>: Uncertainty and statistical errors are to be reduced as much as possible, while simultaneously ensuring the highest degree of accuracy and precision.

<u>Manage:</u> In some problems uncertainty is irreducible and must be managed as an accepted condition of more complex and interconnected realities.[21] More information does not necessarily reduce uncertainty and can in fact increase it.[22] Reducing uncertainties, often considered essential for policy, is not necessarily a pre-condition for making robust decisions that reduce vulnerabilities.[23]

E. Goals for Research: Is the knowledge produced to provide insights into science itself, or into questions and problems outside of science?

<u>Exploratory</u>: Research is driven by curiosity and not constrained by specific goals. If diffuse goals are informing research questions, application of knowledge may be years or decades away.

<u>Outcomes-oriented</u>: Research is shaped by those people who will use the knowledge. Use may involve expanding understanding of a discrete problem or may feed into specific decisions, policies, plans, etc.

Activity 2: Learning and Engagement

Learning requires information and a process of transformation in which behavior, knowledge, skills, etc. are developed or changed.[24] Social learning is contextual and iterative[25] and requires systems thinking, communication, and negotiation.[26] Learning becomes more difficult as problems become less structured and more complex.[27]

Attributes and Spectra of Research Criteria

A. Learning: In what ways do the research outputs change the knowledge or decision-making system?

<u>Theoretical</u>: Learning is focused on understanding theories and focuses on the absorption of explicit knowledge that can be easily transferred between people through documents, patents, and procedures.

<u>Social, Practical</u>: Learning is about understanding new things, but is also focused on new techniques, better approaches, and developing new policies, plans, and behavior by exchanging tacit knowledge that is difficult to codify, takes time to explain and learn, and is embedded in relationships.[28]

B. Knowledge Exchange:[29] To what extent, and how, is knowledge exchanged?

<u>Restricted, Linear:</u> Exchange is limited primarily to within the researchers' own epistemic community and occasionally to the general public through the form of press releases or news articles. If it occurs, communication is one-way from science to society.

<u>Iterative, Influential:</u> Methods can include knowledge brokering, informing, consulting, collaborating, mediating, and negotiating, among others,[30] and leads to more "novel forms of the contextualization of knowledge."[31] Two-way, iterative or "multi-way" communication is needed for the production of useful information to inform decisions.[32] Knowledge may need to be "brokered" by individuals or organizations that are trained or designed to do this work.[33] Brokering is fundamentally about building relationships between the different actors (hence the need for social capital) and leveraging knowledge networks.

C. Network Participation: Who participates in the knowledge network?

<u>Homogeneous:</u> Participation in research is limited to other researchers or sometimes to a single researcher. Users or the public are not included in the shaping of research agendas.

<u>Heterogeneous:</u> Users play a moderate to major role in the shaping of research agendas. Participants may include researchers from multiple disciplines, as well as policy, economic, bureaucratic and lay experts. The researcher network is larger, spanning multiple scales (e.g., local to global).

D. Social Capital:[34] How important is the development and deployment of social capital?

Negligible: The need for creating or deploying social capital may be non-existent or exist only within the researchers' epistemic community.

Significant: Social capital, trust, and relationships are necessary to create and share knowledge.[35] People are more willing to share useful information, listen, and absorb knowledge when the relationship is grounded in trust.[36]

Activity 3: Organizational and Institutional Processes

The organization of work, research, incentives, and both formal and informal rules, all shape the process of work, knowledge production, and interactions between groups.[37] Research processes and organizations are also subject to the same socio-technical considerations as other forms of work, albeit with different characteristics, norms, identities, and processes.[38]

Attributes and Spectra of Research Criteria

A. Accessibility: How accessible to users are the researchers and their organizations or institutions?

Constrained: Research organizations and researchers are often difficult to access due to physical constraints (location of researchers or their organization) or institutional constraints (placement of the research organization within other organizations or institutions), making it difficult for users to gain access.

High: Researchers and their organizations are located proximate to the user and problem. Organizations are often designed to facilitate easy access to researchers and knowledge resources. Access by users is prioritized in organizational activities.

B. Outputs: How various are the research outputs?

Narrow: Outputs are directed toward a limited audience. The most common output is the peer-reviewed publication, followed by reports, patents, conference attendance, new methods and processes, workshops, etc.

Diverse: These approaches yield similar outputs to research disconnected from users' needs, but also include trainings, public outreach activities, educational materials, press releases, meetings, plans, expanded social networks, decision frameworks and decision support tools, etc.

C. Evaluation and Effectiveness: What factors shape the evaluation of research?

Science-centric: Quantitative and statistical approaches are used to evaluate outputs and are consistent with a linear, "knowledge transfer" framework.[39] Evaluation is most commonly performed through bibliometric analysis by quantifying the number of peer-reviewed publications, the impact factor of the journals where the papers are published, and the number of times the papers are cited. Newer methods include the "h-index" and network analysis of research collaborations, however these are not widely used by funding agencies to evaluate research productivity. Outcomes are not typically evaluated.

Public-value oriented: Evaluation includes the aforementioned approaches but also includes an "extended peer community" beyond the world of researchers.[40] Using traditional bibliometric analyses alone limits our evaluation of these approaches and may even deter interdisciplinary research.[41] Evaluating research productivity needs to include qualitative approaches using network and systems approaches to describe how knowledge is used in policy and the impacts it has on social values and preferences.[42] Producing, exchanging and integrating knowledge to support decisions is a complex process, thus the widest array of outcomes should be evaluated, including outcomes oriented to process and interactions between researchers and users.[43]

Evaluating outcomes related to social capital, knowledge exchange, and influence is best served by the use of qualitative methods. Evaluating outcomes remains challenging due to long temporal delays between knowledge production, integration, and application, and because the effects of some decisions may not be able to be assessed for years afterward (e.g., flood mitigation planning or earthquake retrofitting).

D. Flexibility: How easy is it to alter research to better respond to users' needs, and changes in those needs?

Constrained: Research organizations are relatively inflexible with formal rules of operations. The inflexibility is not a problem given the rather predictable forms of research conduct and applications.

Responsive: Responding to users' needs, emerging problems, and expanding research windows of opportunities requires higher degrees of organizational flexibility.[44]

E. Human Capital: What kinds of skills and training are needed to do the research?

Narrow: Researchers are trained almost exclusively as Ph.D.s and have gone through rigorous training as doctoral and post-doctoral researchers.

Broad: Researchers have a broader array of skills, training, and experiences and may include people with master's degrees or even individuals with expertise gained from lived experiences.

F. Boundary Management:[45] To what extent must efforts be made to actively manage the boundary?

Limited: The risk of politicization of science is low, although it varies by discipline, but increases somewhat with more applied research. Society, especially politically marginalized populations, has little or no voice in research.

Thus, little attention to boundary management is necessary.

Broad: Active involvement of users in shaping research brings science and users closer together, inevitably increasing the risks of its credibility being impugned or of science becoming politicized. Such conditions will require greater efforts in boundary work by individuals and organizations.

Using the Typology

The typology provides a richer depiction of the character and conduct of science than permitted by terms like "basic" and "applied." Such terms are often used with vague and varied definitions, often for political purposes in the competition for resources. Moreover, individual science projects, programs, and institutions change over time in response to many of the contextual factors mentioned in the attributes. For example, leaders of science institutions can have a dramatic effect, shifting the focus of an institution to or from particular goals or societal needs. Also, federally funded, national scale programs are being designed with the goal of building capacity to connect science with societal needs. But science managers lack methods to empirically assess whether this capacity is actually being achieved, a wholly different process than that of evaluation of impact, outcomes, or public value of an individual effort.

The typology provides a framework to visualize the range of activities of a science project or several projects across a program or institution at both fixed points in time and over a succession of years. To operationalize the use of the typology, one might allow the spectra to vary on a scale of one (science-centric values are dominant) to five (user-oriented values are dominant), and expert judgments can be applied to classify the full menu of attributes for a given project or set of projects (e.g., program).

Example 1: Southwest Monsoon Fire Decision Support

Wildfire suppression in the United States is built on a three-tiered system of geographic support: a local area, one of the 11 regional areas, and finally, the national level. When a fire is reported, the local agency and its firefighting partners respond. If the fire continues to grow, the agency can ask for help from its geographic area. When a geographic area has exhausted all its resources, it can turn to the National Interagency Coordination Center (NICC) at the National Interagency Fire Center (NIFC) for help in locating what is needed, from air tankers to radios to firefighting crews to incident management teams. Predictive Services was developed to provide decision-support information needed to be more proactive in anticipating significant fire activity and determining resource allocation needs. Predictive Services consists of three primary functions: fire weather, fire danger/fuels, and intelligence/resource status information. Predictive Services involves participation from representatives of the Bureau of Land Management, Bureau of Indian Affairs, National Park Service, Forest Service, U.S. Fish and Wildlife Service, Federal Emergency Management Administration, and the National Association of State Foresters. In this project, researchers from the Desert Research Institute (Reno, NV) and the University of Arizona identified needs within the Southwest Area, Rocky Mountain, and Great Basin Predictive Services information in relation to the Southwest Monsoon to better understand the physical relationships between monsoon atmospheric processes and fire activity. The results of the project will provide operational fire staff and managers with information and products to improve prediction of monsoon impacts on fire, and climatological information on monsoon-fire relationships for assessments and planning. Figure 4.3 represents the program manager's classification of this research for each attribute, based on elements of the project description above and extensive interaction with the researchers on the project.

While the activities may be idealized, the example in Figure 4.3 illustrates how research projects are not idealized. If the Spectra of Research Criteria vary on a generic scale of 1 to 5, then a science manager could assign a score of 3 to Relevance, given that the monsoon information may not fit the decisions of both the Southwest and Great Basin. Similarly, a science manager could assign a score of 5 to Expertise, since the experience of fire managers and agency personnel help shape the decision support information. Moreover, this example illustrates how research directed toward satisfying the needs of decision makers need not have every attribute scored as a 5, which adequately reflects the complexity of research design and implementation.

Figure 4.3: Southwest Fire Monsoon Decision Support

Activity	Attribute	Spectra of Research Criteria				
		Science Values				User Values
		1	2	3	4	5
Knowledge Production	Expertise	Epistemic				Experient
	Relevance	General		Contextual		
	Disciplinary Focus	Singular, Narrow			Transdisciplinary, Diver	
	Uncertainty	Reduce Uncertainty			nage Uncertainty	
	Goals for Research	Exploratory		Outcome Oriented		
Learning & Engagement	Learning	Theoretical		Social, Practical		
	Knowledge Exchange	Restricted, Linear			Iterative, Influen	
	Network Participation	Homogeneous			Heterogened	
	Social Capital	Negligible			Significa	
Organizational & Institutional Processes	Accessibility	Constrained			Hig	
	Outputs	Narrow			Diverse	
	Evaluation & Effectiveness	Science-Centric			ic-Value Oriented	
	Flexibility	Constrained			Responsive	
	Human Capital	Narrow			Broad	
	Boundary Management	Limited		Broad		

Example 2: Indonesian Agroforestry

On the island of Sumatra, "protection forests" provide several economic and ecosystem services including erosion control, water filtration, and timber production. Agroforestry practices, such as coffee cultivation, were not allowed in protection forests limiting the opportunity for people to improve their livelihoods. The Ministry of Forestry believed that coffee trees were not "trees" in that they could not provide the same ecosystem services as timber species. In the interest of improving livelihoods for impoverished farmers living in the protection forests, the World Agroforestry Centre sought to determine if coffee trees were in fact trees in terms of providing similar ecosystem services as timber species. From a disciplinary perspective the research was fairly narrow, scoring a 2 on the spectra (see Figure 4.4). Research determined that coffee trees did in fact provide similar ecosystem services as timber varietals. This research was complex for many reasons. One is that findings from the research had implications in how protection forests were managed that could result in transferring some power for land management from the government to local tenant farmers. The World Agroforestry Centre was largely seen as a trusted broker of information, but significant mistrust existed between the government and farmers, consequently increasing the need for the research to be both credible and legitimate, and for managing the boundary between science and society thus scoring a 5 on the spectra.

In both examples, producing scientific information to inform decision making and improve societal outcomes was the goal. Yet each project had different characteristics including users, role of expertise and disciplinary foci, knowledge exchange, and others. Differences between approaches does not indicate that one is better than the other, but rather, that shaping research to meet the needs of users requires different approaches.

Figure 4.4: Indonesian Agroforestry

Activity	Attribute	Spectra of Research Criteria Science Values			User Values	
		1	2	3	4	5
Knowledge Production	Expertise	Epistemic				Experiential
	Relevance	General				Context
	Disciplinary Focus	Singular, Narrow			Transdisciplinary, Diverse	
	Uncertainty	Reduce Uncertain			Manage Uncertainty	
	Goals for Research	Exploratory			Outcome Oriented	
Learning & Engagement	Learning	Theoretical			Social, Practical	
	Knowledge Exchange	Restricted, Linear			Iterative, Influential	
	Network Participation	Homogeneous			Heterogeneo	
	Social Capital	Negligible			Significa	
Organizational & Institutional Processes	Accessibility	Constrained			High	
	Outputs	Narrow			Diverse	
	Evaluation & Effectiveness	Science-Centric			P-Value Oriented	
	Flexibility	Constrained			Responsive	
	Human Capital	Narrow			Broad	
	Boundary Management	Limited			Broad	

For the science manager, the most important element of putting the typology into practice through such graphical tools is in bringing to the fore aspects of the research process that are often unexamined, assumed, or excluded. Using the typology will create a process of developing and visualizing empirical evidence and expert judgments about the internal coherence of science projects, programs, and institutions. It will also allow deeper understanding of how they are evolving over time. For a program or institution, this exercise could be done for any number of projects to yield an aggregated sense of the type of research being performed. This process would allow science managers to: (a) form mental models about mechanisms that might support different attributes and activities over time, (b) dispel bias about whether or not the research is complementing mission and goals that support user-driven science, and (c) link observed changes in the character and conduct of science to observations of contextual factors (e.g., a decrease in knowledge exchange resulting from a different project or program leader). The typology can aid in the development of proposal solicitations, in allocation decisions about resources to support research, and in the development of more valuable grant-reporting processes. The tool still requires intimate familiarity with the research in question, which should be developed through extensive interaction with knowledge producers and users as partners in a collective endeavor. This task often requires the soft skills and expertise referenced in the Knowledge Exchange attribute.

For the science policy community as a whole, putting the typology to use over time can help bring the expert judgment of science managers to bear on understanding the relations among (a) the complex attributes of research activities, (b) the expectations for and promises about the goals of science, and (c) the extent to which research activities actually are appropriately structured to advance desired societal outcomes. Applying the typology, or other rigorous methods of science policy assessment, across broad portfolios of science can support responsible decision making about science that is justified by, and aimed at, the achievement of public values in addition to simple knowledge creation.

Notes

[1] Organisation for Economic Co-operation and Development, *Frascati Manual: Proposed Standard Practice for Surveys on Research and Experimental Development* (2002); America Competes Act, H.R. 2272, 100th Congress, 2007-2009, signed Aug. 9, 2007.

[2] L. Dilling and M.C. Lemos, "Creating Usable Science: Opportunities and Constraints for Climate Knowledge Use and Their Implications for Science Policy," *Global Environmental Change* 21 (2011): 680-689; D. Sarewitz, and R. A. Pielke Jr. "The Neglected Heart of Science Policy: Reconciling Supply of and Demand for Science," *Environmental Science & Policy* 10, no. 1 (2007): 5-16.

[3] National Research Council, *Decision Making for the Environment: Social and Behavioral Science Research Priorities* (Washington, DC: National Academies Press, 2005); National Research Council, *Informing Decisions in a Changing Climate – Panel on Strategies and Methods for Climate-Related Decision Support* (Washington, DC: National Academies Press, 2009).

[4] D. Sarewitz, and R. A. Pielke Jr. "The Neglected Heart of Science Policy: Reconciling Supply of and Demand for Science," *Environmental Science & Policy* 10, no. 1 (2007): 5-16.

[5] C. J. Kirchhoff, M. C. Lemos, and S. Dessai, "Actionable Knowledge for Environmental Decision Making: Broadening the Usability of Climate Science," *Annual Review of Environment and Resources* 38, no. 1 (2013): 407.

[6] D. E. Stokes, *Pasteur's Quadrant: Basic Science and Technological Innovation* (Washington, DC: Brookings Institution Press, 1997); J. Calvert, "What's Special about Basic Research?" *Science, Technology & Human Values* 31, no. 2 (2006): 199-220.

[7] National Science Board, *Key Science and Engineering Indicators: 2010 Digest*, C. Roesel, ed., NSB 10-02, National Science Foundation (2010); Organisation for Economic Co-operation and Development, *Frascati Manual: Proposed Standard Practice for Surveys on Research and Experimental Development* (2002).

[8] Organisation for Economic Co-operation and Development, *Frascati Manual: Proposed Standard Practice for Surveys on Research and Experimental Development* (2002).

[9] D. E. Stokes, *Pasteur's Quadrant: Basic Science and Technological Innovation* (Washington, DC: Brookings Institution Press, 1997).

[10] Here we assume "design" to be an ongoing and iterative process such that our use of the word implies not only the design of particular science study, project, or program, but its ongoing management and evaluation.

[11] R. K. Merton, "Role of the intellectual in public bureaucracy," *Social Forces* 23, no. 4 (1945): 405-415.

[12] E. Lövbrand, "Co-Producing European Climate Science and Policy: A Cautionary Note on the Making of Useful Knowledge," *Science and Public Policy* 38, no. 2 (2011): 225-236.

[13] M. Polanyi, "The Republic of Science," *Minerva* 1 (1962): 54-73.

[14] B. Latour, *Science in Action: How to Follow Scientists and Engineers through Society* (Cambridge, MA: Harvard University Press, 1987); S. Jasanoff, "The idiom of co-production," in *States of Knowledge: The Co-production of Science and Social Order*, S. Jasanoff, ed. (London, UK: Routledge, 2004), 1-12; S. Van den Hove, "A Rationale for Science-Policy Interfaces," *Futures* 39, no. 7 (2007): 807-826.

[15] D. E. Stokes, *Pasteur's Quadrant: Basic Science and Technological Innovation* (Washington, DC: Brookings Institution Press, 1997); N. Logar, "Towards a Culture of Application: Science and Decision Making at the National Institute of Standards & Technology," *Minerva* 47, no. 4 (2009): 345-66; E. C. McNie, "Co-Producing Useful Climate Science for Policy: Lessons from the RISA Program," monograph, University of Colorado, Boulder (2008).

[16] K. Averyt, K. 2010. "Are we successfully adapting science to climate change?" *Bulletin of the American Meteorological Society* 91 (2007): 723-726; C. N. Knapp and S. F. Trainor, "Adapting science to a warming world," *Global Environmental Change* 23 (2013): 1296-1306; National Research Council, *Decision Making for the Environment: Social and Behavioral Science Research Priorities* (Washington, DC: National Academies Press, 2005); National Research Council, *Informing an Effective Response to Climate Change* (Washington, DC: National Academies Press, 2010).

[17] R. Meyer, "The Public Values Failures of Climate Science in the U.S.," *Minerva* 49, no. 1 (2011): 47-70.

[18] S. Epstein, "The Construction of Lay Expertise: AIDS Activism and the Forging of Credibility in the Reform of Clinical Trials. Science," *Technology and Human Values* 20, no. 4 (1995): 408-437.

[19] S. Jasanoff, "The idiom of co-production," in *States of Knowledge: The Co-production of Science and Social Order*, S. Jasanoff, ed. (London, UK: Routledge, 2004), 1-12; B. Latour, *Science in Action: How to Follow Scientists and Engineers through Society* (Cambridge, MA: Harvard University Press, 1987); B. Latour and S. Woolgar, *Laboratory Life: The Construction of Science* (Princeton, NJ: Princeton University Press, 1979).

[20] W. C. Clark and N. M. Dickson, "Sustainability Science: The Emerging Research Program," *Proceedings of the National Academy of Sciences* 100, no. 14 (2003): 8059-8061; F. Berkes, "Evolution of Co-Management: Role of Knowledge Generation, Bridging Organizations and Social Learning," *Journal of Environmental Management* 90, no. 5 (2009): 1692-1702; R. Ziegler and K. Ott, "The Quality of Sustainability Science: A Philosophical Perspective," *Sustainability: Science, Practice, & Policy* 7, no. 1 (2011): 31-44.

[21] S. Van den Hove, "A Rationale for Science-Policy Interfaces," *Futures* 39, no. 7 (2007): 807-826; S. O. Funtowicz and J. R. Ravetz, "Science for the Post-Normal Age," *Futures* 25, no. 7 (1993): 739-55.

[22] D. Sarewitz, "How Science Makes Environmental Controversies Worse," *Environmental Science & Policy* 7, no. 5 (2004): 385-403.

[23] R. Lempert, N. Nakicenovic, D. Sarewitz, and M. Schlesinger, "Characterizing Climate-Change Uncertainties for Decision-Makers," *Climatic Change* 65, no. 1 (2004): 1-9.

[24] M .S. Knowles, E. F. Holton III, and R. A. Swanson, *The Adult Learner* (New York, NY: Routledge: 1998); J. Mezirow, *Transformative Learning: Theory and Practice*, New Directions for Adult and Continuing Education, no. 74 (San Francisco, CA: Jossey-Bass, 1997).

[25] C. Pahl-Wostl, "A Conceptual Framework for Analysing Adaptive Capacity and Multi-Level Learning Processes in Resource Governance Regimes," *Global Environmental Change* 19, no. 3 (2009): 354-365.

[26] M. Keen and S. Mahanty, "Learning in Sustainable Natural Resource Management: Challenges and Opportunities in the Pacific," *Society and Natural Resources* 19, no. 6 (2006): 497-513.

[27] C. Argyris, "Single-Loop and Double-Loop Models in Research on Decision Making," *Administrative Science Quarterly* 21, no. 3 (1976): 363.

[28] I. Nonaka, "A Dynamic Theory of Organizational Knowledge Creation," *Organization Science* 5, no. 1 (1994): 14-37.

[29] A process of "generating, sharing, and/or using knowledge through various methods appropriate to the context, purpose, and participants involved." I. Fazey, L. Bunse, J. Msika, M. Pinke, K. Preedy, A. C. Evely, E. Lambert, E. Hastings, S. Morris, and M. S. Reed, "Evaluating Knowledge Exchange in Interdisciplinary and Multi-Stakeholder Research," *Global Environmental Change* 25 (Mar. 2014): 204-220.

[30] S. Michaels, "Matching Knowledge Brokering Strategies to Environmental Policy Problems and Settings," *Environmental Science & Policy* 12, no. 7 (2009): 994-1011; M. C. Lemos and B.J. Morehouse, "The co-production of science and policy in integrated climate assessments," *Global Environmental Change* 15 (2005): 57-68.

[31] H. Nowotny, P. Scott, and M. Gibbons, *Re-Thinking Science: Knowledge and the Public in an Age of Uncertainty* (London, UK: Polity Press, 2002), 206.

[32] M. C. Lemos and B.J. Morehouse, "The co-production of science and policy in integrated climate assessments," *Global Environmental Change* 15 (2005): 57-68.; C. J. Kirchhoff, M. C. Lemos, and S. Dessai, "Actionable Knowledge for Environmental Decision Making: Broadening the Usability of Climate Science," *Annual Review of Environment and Resources* 38, no. 1 (2013): 393-414.

[33] D. H. Guston, "Boundary organizations in environmental policy and science: An introduction," *Science, Technology & Human Values* 26, no. 4 (2001): 399-408; W. C. Clark, T. P. Tomich, M. van Noordwijk, D. Guston, D. Catacutan, N. M. Dickson, and E. McNie, "Boundary Work for Sustainable Development: Natural Resource Management at the Consultative Group on International Agricultural Research (CGIAR)," *Proceedings of the National Academy of Sciences* (August 2011).

[34] Relationships and "goodwill that others have toward us," the effects of which flow from the "information, influence, and solidarity such goodwill makes available." P. S. Adler and S. W. Kwon, "Social Capital: Prospects for a New Concept," *The Academy of Management Review* 27, no. 1 (2002): 17-40.

[35] D. Z. Levin and R. Cross, "The Strength of Weak Ties You Can Trust: The Mediating Role of Trust in Effective Knowledge Transfer," *Management Science* 50, no. 11 (2004): 1477-1490.

36 D. Z. Levin and R. Cross, "The Strength of Weak Ties You Can Trust: The Mediating Role of Trust in Effective Knowledge Transfer," *Management Science* 50, no. 11 (2004): 1477-1490; M. C. Lemos, C. J. Kirchhoff, and V. Ramprasad, "Narrowing the Climate Information Usability Gap," *Nature Climate Change* 2 (2012): 789-794.

37 E. Trist, "The Evolution of Socio-Technical Systems: A Conceptual Framework and an Action Research Program," Occasional Paper No. 2, York University, Toronto, Canada (June 1981); F. W. Geels, "From Sectoral Systems of Innovation to Socio-Technical Systems" *Research Policy* 33, nos. 6-7 (2004): 897-920.

38 S. Jasanoff, "The idiom of co-production," in *States of Knowledge: The Co-production of Science and Social Order*, S. Jasanoff, ed. (London UK, Routledge, 2004), 1-12.

39 B. Godin, "The Linear Model of Innovation: The Historical Construction of an Analytical Framework. Project on the History and Sociology of S&T Statistics," Working Paper No. 30 (2005); A. Best and B. Holmes, "Systems Thinking, Knowledge and Action: Towards Better Models and Methods," *Evidence & Policy: A Journal of Research, Debate and Practice* 6, no. 2 (2010): 145-159.

40 S. O. Funtowicz and J. R. Ravetz, "Science for the Post-Normal Age," *Futures* 25, no. 7 (1993): 739-755.

41 T. Penfield, M. J. Baker, R. Scoble, and M. C. Wykes, "Assessment, Evaluations, and Definitions of Research Impact: A Review," *Research Evaluation* 23, no. 1 (2014): 21-32; I. Rafols, L. Leydesdorff, A. O'Hare, P. Nightingale and A. Stirling, "How journal rankings can suppress interdisciplinarity. The case of innovation studies and business and management," *Research Policy* 41, no. 7 (2012): 1262-1282.

42 S. Cozzens and M. Snoek, "Knowledge to Policy: Contributing to the Measurement of Social, Health, and Environmental Benefits," white paper prepared for the "Workshop on the Science of Science Measurement," Washington, DC (Dec. 2-3, 2010); B. Bozeman and D. Sarewitz, "Public Value Mapping and Science Policy Evaluation," *Minerva* 49, no. 1 (2011): 1-23; R. Meyer, "The Public Values Failures of Climate Science in the U.S.," *Minerva* 49, no. 1 (2011): 47-70; A. Best and B. Holmes, "Systems

Thinking, Knowledge and Action: Towards Better Models and Methods," *Evidence & Policy: A Journal of Research, Debate and Practice* 6, no. 2 (2010): 145-159; C. Donovan, "State of the Art in Assessing Research Impact," *Research Evaluation* 20, no. 3 (2011): 175-179.

[43] I. Fazey, L. Bunse, J. Msika, M. Pinke, K. Preedy, A. C. Evely, E. Lambert, E. Hastings, S. Morris, and M. S. Reed, "Evaluating Knowledge Exchange in Interdisciplinary and Multi-Stakeholder Research," *Global Environmental Change* 25 (Mar. 2014): 204-220; J. Molas-Gallart, P. D'Este, Ó. Llopis, and I. Rafols, "Towards an Alternative Framework for the Evaluation of Translational Research Initiatives," INGENIO (CSIC-UPV) (2014); S. Moser, "Making a Difference on the Ground: The Challenge of Demonstrating the Effectiveness of Decision Support," *Climatic Change* 95, nos. 1-2 (2009): 11-21.

[44] E. C. McNie, "Delivering Climate Services: Organizational Strategies and Approaches for Producing Useful Climate Science Information," *Weather, Climate, and Society* 5 (2013): 14-26.

[45] The boundary between science and society needs to be managed to accomplish two mutual goals: ensuring that research responds to the needs of users and assuring the credibility of science; boundary work involves communicating between science and society, translating information, and mediating and negotiating across the boundary.

II. IMPROVING THE PUBLIC VALUE OF SCIENCE

How can science agendas and programs be assessed in terms of their capacity to achieve desired public values?

Public investments in science are typically promoted on the basis of promised contributions to solving real-world problems and improving human welfare. Yet assessments of science's value are usually conducted in terms of either knowledge outputs (like publications or patents), or economic activity (like social rate of return on investment). Science policy decision makers lack the tools to evaluate, either retrospectively or prospectively, the capacity of research investments to achieve the social benefits upon which the investments are justified. These three chapters present a conceptual framework, a practical method, and a detailed case study for mapping the linkages between science investments and public values.

5

PUBLIC VALUES AND PUBLIC FAILURE IN U.S. SCIENCE POLICY*

Barry Bozeman and Daniel Sarewitz

The processes of economic valuation do not easily accommodate public values.[1] However, in part because of their concreteness, a focus on economic values sometimes displaces consideration of public values in political discourse. In science policy, market-based arguments and outcomes dominate political thinking and action, despite the fact that science and technology hugely influence public values in ways that are independent of the marketplace.

In this paper, we apply a new analytical and rhetorical framework — public-failure theory[2] — to science policy. Our goal is to make available an intellectual approach that can compete with market logic in thinking about, and making, science policy decisions.

We start out by briefly discussing the ways in which marketplace logic has become dominant in science policy.

---

* Originally published as B. Bozeman and D. Sarewitz, "Public Values and Public Failure in U.S. Science Policy," *Science and Public Policy* 32, no. 2 (2005): 119-136. Reprinted with permission from Oxford University Press.

We then discuss the concept of public values and introduce the theory of public failure as a complement to the idea of failure. Using brief case discussions, we illustrate six criteria of public failure in science policy. We then present a simple graphical tool for conceptualizing the relationship between market failure and public failure, before concluding with a brief discussion of why public failure might succeed in breaking the hegemony of economic rationality in science policy.

Background

Domestic science policy in the United States is linked inextricably to economic thinking, making it no different from many other policy domains. When Americans consider institutional arrangements for delivery of public goods and services, they either begin with systematic economic reasoning or, more often, with less systematic assumptions filtered through the laissez-faire nostrums embedded deeply in U.S. political culture.[3] When Americans seek to determine the value of resources, goods, and services, they reflexively look for price indices, eschewing more complex and indeterminate approaches.

The focus of our paper is on developing a practical analytical and rhetorical framework that confronts the manifest problems of economic valuing for science and technology activities. We argue that pervasive use of market valuation, market-failure assumptions and economic metaphors shapes the structure of science policy in undesirable ways. In particular, reliance on economic reasoning tends to shift the discourse about science policy away from political questions of "Why?" and "To what end?" to economic questions of "How much?"

If we assume that everyone is made better off by investments in science, then the only sensible policy question is "How much science can we afford?" Yet, if we assume that science's benefits and costs affect citizens in very different ways and to different degrees, and that those benefits and costs are in turn affected by the composition of society's science portfolio, then public value questions emerge as at least as important as economic ones.

Critiques of post-World War II U.S. science policy have recognized in its operation the subservience of a broadly construed but difficult to measure public interest to more easily recognizable economic interests.[4] Indeed, a central dilemma of postwar science policy has been this: the value of science is commonly promoted in terms of concrete social outcomes (say, curing a disease), but the process by which the products of science permeate society are largely through the marketplace and the tools for measuring value are largely economic.

Yet the tension between the public value embodied in promise of science and the market value realized through its commercialization is real and pervasive. For example, the doubling of the budget for the National Institutes of Health between 1998 and 2002 was justified by the promise of health benefits for Americans,[5] even as health care becomes increasingly unaffordable to increasing numbers of citizens, health disparities persist across socioeconomic and ethnic divides, and the public health returns on research investments remain difficult to document.[6]

The most resilient justification for publicly funded science has been job creation and increased standards of living.[7] Yet GDP (gross domestic product) per capita is the coarsest possible proxy for quality of life; indeed the affluent-world experience of the past thirty years shows that science- and technology-based economic growth is accompanied by increasing inequality in distribution of economic benefits, including increasing unemployment or underemployment, decreasing real wages, increasing wage inequality, and increasing wealth concentration within nations and between nations.[8]

We might imagine that such tensions between public values and economic values in science policy would strengthen political motives to ensure that publicly funded science effectively served public values. Yet scholars in disciplines ranging from economics of technology to history of science have been documenting a fifty-year increase in the influence of the marketplace on the agendas of public science.

To some extent this rising influence can be seen as an explicit transition in national priorities from Cold War competition with the USSR to economic competition with emerging economies such as Japan. Yet even during the Cold War, science policies justified in terms of national defense were tightly coupled to private-sector innovation processes.[9]

More subtly still, the dynamics of science's role in economic growth seems to promote very strong coupling between public agendas and private motives. For example, technological frontiers (generally pursued in the private sector) have a strong influence on academic research by revealing new phenomena and problems for scientists to confront.[10]

Also, a progressive increase in the ratio of private to public funding in the United States, combined with changing intellectual property regimes, is continually strengthening the linkages between private-sector priorities and publicly funded science.[11] In some sense this is not surprising. If several decades of scholarship in science and technology studies (STS) have demonstrated the co-evolution of science and society,[12] then in modern liberal democracies the place where we would most to see this co-evolution expressed is in the economic realm.

There is nothing inherently wrong with the idea of science as catalyst for economic activity — a healthy economy is essential to the functioning of the modern state. Rather our concern is with science's insufficiency in meeting public values. As the political theorist Yaron Ezrahi has provocatively argued, the gradual delegitimation of science as a source of authority leaves the economic role as the only one that no longer demands a defense. [13] All that matters is economic growth.

It is therefore sufficient to know that, as the philosopher David L. Hull[14] observed, science "works," and works quite well enough to contribute robustly to economic growth.[15] When it comes to economic value, the cultural or political construction of science is neither here nor there. Thus, the last bastion of "exceptionalism" for science may well be its role in economic growth.[16]

What Is "Science Policy"?

Throughout the paper we use the term "science policy" in its broadest and most encompassing sense. Indeed, most "science policies" are actually subsidiary to other policies, such as higher-education policy, defense policy, agricultural policy, energy policy, and space policy. For many purposes, distinguishing among these is vital, but not for our purposes. When we use "science policy" we refer to all these efforts to bring technical knowledge to fruition and application.

We do not distinguish among basic research, applied research, and development, nor among discovery, invention, and innovation. As important as these distinctions may be for some types of policy decision, our analysis is at the highest level of aggregation. We also note that these distinctions are far from clear in many situations.

We are concerned about the values of this enterprise, writ large. Since all acts of knowledge creation, use, and distribution have the potential to have impact on people, all such acts are united in their normative implications if in no other way. Each element of the technical enterprise has implication for public value.

We also note that when we refer to "science policy" we are *not* concerned with the hundreds of thousands of decisions and the hundreds (at least) of decision processes pertaining to specific research grants for individual scientists. We *are* concerned with the broad policies and policy processes that guide those micro-level behaviors, policies governing allocation of research funding, and institutional arrangements for the conduct and delivery of research. We are also concerned with the mental models and rhetorical constructs that help guide decision making throughout the research and development (R&D) enterprise.

Public Values and Failure

Social theory offers few alternative ways of thinking systematically about science policy. There is no social theory of scientific outcomes; there is no social choice for science. There *is* a market-failure model that tells us conditions under which government should "intervene." What is missing in most contemporary rationales for science policy, at least as manifested in actual public policy deliberations, is a sense of the specific ways science does and does not serve public values.

One of the difficulties of previous work in public values and the public interest[17] is that these key concepts, important as they are, do not easily match with extant institutions and processes. The elegance of market solutions is that to achieve their result we, allegedly, need to do nothing other than restrain barriers to competition. The argument spills over easily into science: in a seminal paper, Michael Polanyi portrayed science as a self-regulating marketplace whose efficiency could not be improved, but could only be compromised, by outside intervention.[18]

Such economic metaphors have had a powerful impact on public discourse about science policy.[19]

To enact public values, something more than philosophy and reticence is required. Thus, we examine not only the possible role of public values in science policy but also identify a set of criteria that can assist policymakers in identifying public values issues in much the same way as they now use market-failure models to identify economic aspects of science policy. We provide an alternative schema, which we call the public-failure model.[20] This model gives rise to criteria that can allow policymakers to make rigorous judgments about the public value and distributional implications of science policy, in addition to questions of economic efficiency and economic growth.

The public-failure model depends on the notion that there are such things as "public values," just as the market-failure model derives from an idealized notion of a market, generally defined in terms of efficiency. The term public value has many meanings.[21] What we mean by "public values" are those that embody the prerogatives, normative standards, social supports, rights, and procedural guarantees that a given society aspires to provide to all citizens.

This is not the same as a public good because public values are not goods, either tangible (dishwashers) or less tangible (for instance scientific information). Public values are not Platonic ideals, rather they vary across cultures and time, depending on the common values prized in the culture. Public values can be identified in empirical inquiry into the particular public values of particular cultures, but, even absent an empirical anchor, public value is a useful enabling concept, not unlike that of the perfectly competitive market.

A key assumption of our paper, and the public-failure model, is that market efficiency and public value are not closely correlated. Public failure can occur with market success, public failure and market failure can occur simultaneously, and in some happy circumstances, public success and market success can coincide.

To illustrate the disjunction between market efficiency and public value, we need only return to the case of AIDS drugs, an excellent illustration that market failure and public failure are not the end points of a dimension. AIDS drugs represent a remarkable market success, where initial public investment in research under conditions of market failure led to private-sector development of effective pharmaceutical interventions that also generate considerable profit. However, the vast majority of HIV and AIDS sufferers worldwide do not have access to these expensive drugs.

It is possible, that is, to have governments intervene effectively through R&D to correct a market failure, and to have markets operate with great efficiency once the market failure has been addressed, and yet still have unconscionable failure of public values. The case of AIDS medicines is an illustration of the constricting moral and operational knots we tie ourselves in when we have no frameworks or criteria to compete with market efficiency as a guide to science policy and its concomitant social outcomes.

An Introduction to Public-Failure Theory

Policymakers of every ideological stripe have long been comfortable with the idea that the private sector will never make sufficient investments in basic scientific research to generate the necessary knowledge to support robust innovation and economic growth. This market-failure argument has long been accepted as good sense,[22] but since World War II it also been vindicated by economic scholarship.[23]

In this paper, we present an analytical and rhetorical counterbalance to the economic rationality that has so successfully justified and vindicated science policies for the past fifty years. Our approach, following Barry Bozeman,[24] is to develop a framework that is conceptually symmetrical to the market-failure rationale used to justify government investment in science. We call this framework "public-failure theory."

"Public failure" occurs when neither the market nor public sector provides goods and services required to achieve core public values. A public-failure approach changes the discussion of public policy by making government (and public values) something other than a residual category or an issue of technical efficiency in pricing structures. With the public-failure model, the key policy question becomes: "Even if the market is efficient, is there nonetheless a failure to provide an essential public value?"

Using a market-failure model, government involvement is thus justified only when market processes fail and "prices lie — that is, when the prices of goods and services give false signals about their real value, confounding the communication between consumers and producers." The causes of such failure are oft-articulated and well-understood: externalities; steep transaction costs; distortion of information or inhibition of information flow about a good or service; and monopolistic behavior or other competitive failures.[25] A public-failure model eschews assumptions about the correspondence of efficient markets and desirable social outcomes and focuses instead on social values criteria.

With respect to science policy, economics is about the private value of public things. Despite the relative rigors of market-failure theory, no economic analysis can encompass the full range of policy choices facing society. Efficient pricing cannot solve all problems of public values, and indeed there is a strong societal sense that, in some domains, economically optimal solutions are entirely inappropriate, for example, in creating a market for blood or organ donors. Some political actions explicitly eschew economic efficiency in favor of social equity, for example, the Americans with Disabilities Act. Yet economic approaches have been applied, often controversially, in domains that encompass public values, such as in the valuation of natural resources, the creation of markets for pollution-permit trading, and the design of science and technology programs.

Even if we accept the market-failure rationale on its own terms, it is unavoidably incomplete, for two rather obvious reasons. First, just because markets fail, it does not mean that government action can eliminate or avoid the causes of failure. For example, environmental externalities may signal market failure, but a government decision to respond to these externalities is not an *a priori* demonstration that doing so will lead to more social benefit. While the U.S. government invested billions in collaboration with the big three automakers in the Partners for a New Generation of Vehicles program, Japanese automakers on their own produced a first generation of hybrid-electric automobiles that outstripped anything the Americans had to offer.

Second, the absence of market failure does not *a priori* imply public success, and therefore is not a sufficient reason to eschew government investment. That is, market value does not equal public value. The situation with AIDS drugs in the developing world is archetypal: the market has succeeded and millions wait to die.

As obvious as these arguments may be, they are insufficiently available for purposes of public policymaking. The aim of public-failure theory is to provide an analytical framework that can be set alongside market failure as an alternative set of policymaking criteria. The notion of public failure derives from the reality that sometimes neither the market nor the public sector is providing goods and services necessary to achieve certain core public values.

A public-failure approach to policymaking changes the terms of debate by making government (and public values) something other than a subsidiary issue of efficiency in market performance. The key question in market-failure rhetoric is: "Are prices distorted due to a failure of communication between consumers and producers?" The key question in public failure goes an essential step further: "Regardless of market efficiency, is there nonetheless a failure to provide an essential public value?"

We recognize, of course, that "prices" are more tangible, or at least quantifiable, than "public values" as a unit of analysis. However, there is very little, if any, fundamental disagreement in the United States about the existence of a fairly comprehensive set of core public values, especially those embodied in the nation's founding documents, such as the right to subsistence, the rule by consent of the governed, freedom of speech and religious practice, and *habeas corpus*. This basis is more than sufficient for us to proceed, because public-failure theory is not a decision-making tool (*à la* cost-benefit analysis), but rather a framework (*à la* market failure) to promote rigorous deliberation about the relation between economic value and public value.

Public-Failure Criteria

Public failure occurs when core public values are not reflected in social relations. Bozeman elucidates criteria for identifying public-values failure, criteria that to some extent mirror market-failure criteria, but that focus on public values rather than efficiency of market transactions.[26] In applying this framework to science policy, we identify six public-failure criteria:

- Inadequate values articulation
- Imperfect monopolies
- Scarcity of providers
- Short time horizons

- Non-substitutability of resources
- Benefit hoarding

While we do not claim this set of public value criteria to be canonical, it provides a starting point to enhance discourse and decisions for the allocation of responsibilities between public and private sectors, and for shaping allocations within the public sector. Table 5.1 provides diagnostic criteria of the public-failure model, illustrated by examples specific to science policy.[27] In the next section, we discuss in greater detail specific illustrations of each criteria, to show the applicability of public-failure theory to real-world science-policy dilemmas.

Table 5.1: Public Failure and Public Policy: A General Diagnostic Model

Public Failure Criterion	Failure Definition	Science Policy Example
Mechanisms for values articulation and aggregation	Political processes and social cohesion insufficient to ensure effective communication and processing of public values.	Peer review, the favored means of making decisions of individual-level projects, is appropriated for decisions about huge scientific programs, resulting in the displacement of social goals for more easily resolved technical goals.
Imperfect monopolies	Private provision of goods and services permitted even though government monopoly deemed in the public interest.	When public authorities abrogate their responsibility for overseeing public safety in clinical trials for medical research, there is potential for violation of public trust and public value.

Scarcity of providers	Despite the recognition of a public value and agreement on the public provision of goods and services, they are not provided because of the unavailability of providers.	The premature privatization of the Landsat program shows that a scarcity of providers can create a public failure potentially remediable by government action.
Short time horizon	A short-term time horizon is employed when a longer term view shows that a set of actions is counter to public value.	Policy for energy R&D, by considering the short term, fails to fully capture the costs of global climate change on future generations.
Substitutability vs. conservation of resources	Policies focus on either substitutability or indemnification even in cases when there is no satisfactory substitute.	"No-net-loss" policies fail to take into account the non-substitutability of many natural organisms ranging from wetlands protection to prohibiting the sale of human organs on the open market.
Benefit hoarding	Public commodities and services have been captured by individuals or groups, limiting distribution to the population.	A prime technical success of genetic engineering, the "terminator gene," proves an excellent means of enhancing the efficiency of agricultural markets, potentially to the detriment of millions of subsistence farmers throughout the world.

Cases in Public Failure and Science Policy

Case 1. Public Failure in Values Articulation and Aggregation: Priority Setting in Science

Public failure can occur when expression of public values is stifled or distorted. For example, if campaign financing procedures lead to conspicuous conflict between public values (as elicited, say, through polling) and the values of elected officials, then there is a potential for public failure. This type of conflict may provide an incentive for private investment in lobbying that is rational by economic standards yet counter to the larger public interest—as when efforts by the insurance industry and its allies to prevent healthcare reform have overcome a broader public desire for a more affordable and equitable healthcare delivery system.

In science policy, a pervasive cause of values articulation public failures is an absence of mechanisms that allow non-scientists to have a significant say about public investments and priorities in most areas of science. The reasons for this failure are clear. How can a non-scientist be expected to make a sensible choice between, say, funding two distinct areas of health research, for instance, research aimed at understanding the contribution of polycystic ovarian syndrome versus research on understanding the impact of bovine hormone in milk or breast cancer?

It would take a great deal of effort even for most scientists to have an informed opinion about the largely unknowable trade-off between two important lines of applied medical research. Moreover, politicians (and the general public) are as likely as scientists to understand their own preferences for, say, favorable outcomes in breast cancer research versus favorable outcomes in astronomy or in polar sciences or in mental health. This is not an overestimation of the ability of the "median voter" to understand science trade-offs but, rather, a perhaps more realistic (and pessimistic) estimate of the relative ability of experts to make high-level values choices.[28]

Science policymakers have evinced some concern about the balance between scientific values (for instance, what constitutes "good" science?) and social values (for instance, how is the public good being advanced?). In response to congressional prodding, the National Science Foundation

(NSF) has sought to use the peer-review process to enhance the societal value of its research portfolio. In addition to standard criteria of scientific merit, NSF added in 1997 the criterion of social benefit to its peer review process.

NSF then commissioned the National Academy of Public Administration (NAPA) to evaluate how well this effort to incorporate public values into peer review was working. NAPA[29] reported back the changes, as implemented, were unlikely to have much positive effect. Problems with NSF's approach ranged from lack of "quantitative measures and performance indicators to track the objectives of the new merit review criteria,"[30] to skepticism or even outright opposition on the part of reviewers to the inclusion of social impact criteria to begin with. NAPA went on to recommend a variety of actions that NSF could take to correct these problems, such as improving "the conceptual clarity of the objectives of the new criteria,"[31] and ensuring "genuine attention to the goals of the new criteria throughout the entire review cycle."[32]

Yet neither the NSF social impacts criteria nor the NAPA report addressed the underlying source of public failure. Nobody denies that the scientific community has great skill in assessing technical quality of research, but who has vested it with special training, skill, or legitimacy in assessing the social value of research? Moreover, there is no particular reason to believe that the social priorities of scientists are representative of society. Indeed, surveys of scientists' political opinions and values suggest there are often large differences between scientists and the general public,[33] though scientists are closer to other elite groups such as journalists.

Just as with other professions and demographic groups, scientists' values probably resemble those of persons who have socioeconomic attributes and life experiences similar to their own. Also, citizens have not voted for scientists or in any way designated them as the "official" articulators or judges of public value. Finally, the public value of science is rarely ascertainable at the individual project level, where peer review most often operates.

Public values operate at a level where science policy receives very little attention: cross-science comparisons and the opportunity costs associated with resource allocation decisions. It is also at this level of broad preferences where the general public, or at least the attentive public, may plausibly contribute (for instance, Carnegie Commission), but the structure of U.S. science policy provides little opportunity to do so. Congress, because of its jurisdictional structure, is generally unwilling to make either cross-science choices or systematic choices among the public values that science serves. Likewise, the science bureaucracy works within scientific fields, disciplines, or objectives, rarely among them.

Scientists themselves have even less incentive for the internecine warfare that would arise with a more systematic assessment of the values associated with a diverse set of desired scientific outcomes, thus militating against even expert-driven processes of choosing among disciplines.[34] This is a built-in public failure affording limited opportunity for values articulation.[35]

When the putatively "value neutral" science policy funding machine is temporarily thrown off kilter, it is generally because an issue emerges that grips the public imagination, or a highly motivated special interest group, to such a degree that public value issues simply cannot be ignored. The most recent case in point is the stem cell controversy, which provides an excellent proof that it is not the complexity of scientific issues that forestalls public participation and public values articulation. The scientific issues the various stem cell debates are technical and esoteric, but the values issues are so fundamental and compelling that research cannot proceed apace.[36]

When the conduct of research requires one to consider such issues as "What constitutes a human being?" the momentum of the science policy funding machine slows down and the role of public values is brought to the fore. The results of the stem cell controversy highly the dearth of institutions and analytical frameworks available for values articulation and analysis.

Case 2. Public Failure and "Imperfect Monopolies": Clinical Trials

Whereas private-sector monopoly is an indication of market failure, in some cases the inability of a government activity to protect its monopoly may lead to erosion of a public value. For example, foreign policy is a legitimate government monopoly, and any competition from unauthorized envoys could damage the broader public interest.

Regulation of private-sector activities to protect public welfare is a widely accepted role of government, although the appropriate degree of regulation is often highly contentious. In the area of clinical trials to determine the efficacy of pharmaceuticals and other medical interventions, the government has granted research institutions and scientists considerable autonomy. This autonomy is justified by faith in the self-policing capacity of the scientific community, especially as embodied in its claim to objectivity — or at least disinterest — through the scientific method, and to quality control through peer review.

The protection of humans in scientific experiments is a well-established public value, enshrined in international law through the Nuremburg Code and Helsinki Declaration,[37] and nationally through such codified principles as informed prior consent. All experiments involving humans that are funded, in whole or part, with federal dollars, are overseen by Institutional Review Boards — decentralized, self-policing oversight bodies aimed at "protecting the rights and welfare of human subjects of research"[38] and ensuring that "risks to the subjects are reasonable in relation to anticipated benefits."[39] Such experiments include tests and trials to demonstrate the efficacy of new drugs, therapies, and procedures, both as part of the process of gaining government approval for general use and as a means of informing physicians about the relative value of available options.

In September 1999, 18-year-old Jesse Gelsinger died while undergoing gene therapy for a rare liver disease. Gene therapy had long been touted as potentially miraculous emerging line of treatment for a wide variety of serious genetic disorders, but its promise had remained unfulfilled and Gelsinger's death made national news. Early reporting on his death suggested only that something had gone terribly wrong in the experiment, but that all appropriate processes and procedures had been followed to ensure that risk was minimized and his participation was fully consensual.[40]

Deeper investigations revealed irregularities. The consent forms that Gelsinger signed misrepresented the dosages that were to be administered and did not include information about animal deaths from similar treatments. Evidence of high toxicity and adverse side effects in earlier experiments was ignored. The doctor in charge of the experiments, and the university he worked for, had a financial stake in the company that would have produced the new gene therapy.[41]

Before Gelsinger's death grabbed the headlines, academic studies of clinical trials had been painting a more dispassionate, less publicized picture of public failure. A number of studies revealed that clinical trials directly or indirectly supported by pharmaceutical companies often yielded more favorable assessments of new therapies than trials that were not tied to the private sector in any way. In one analysis, only 5% of company-sponsored studies on anti-cancer drugs yielded unfavorable assessments, while for studies sponsored by nonprofits, the unfavorable rate was 38%.[42]

An investigation of calcium-channel antagonists, a class of drug used to treat cardiovascular disease, demonstrated "a strong association between authors' published positions on the safety of calcium-channel antagonists and their financial relationships with pharmaceutical manufacturers."[43] An analysis of published symposia proceedings showed that "articles with drug company support are more likely than articles without drug company support to have outcomes favoring the drug of interest."[44]

Few have argued that such results demonstrate scientific fraud. More likely, "close and remunerative collaboration with a company naturally creates goodwill [that] can subtly influence scientific judgment in ways that may be difficult to discern."[45] Some scientists have publicly claimed that they are not subject to such influences. James Wilson, the researcher in charge of the Gelsinger trial, said, "To suggest that I acted or was influenced by money is really offensive to me.... You've got to be on the cutting edge and take risks if you're going to stay on top [scientifically]."[46]

While such claims to immunity from human weakness may or may not ring true, researchers' ties to industry by definition create a conflict of interest, which, if not revealed to patients in trials, undermines the principle of informed consent, and, if not apparent to peer reviewers and publishers of research articles, can obscure the implications of research results. Thomas Bodenheimer[47] catalogued a variety of ways in which a drug test can be carried out to favor one result or another without rendering the data itself invalid. For example, "if a drug is tested in a healthier population ... than the population that will actually receive the drug, a trial may find that the drug relieves symptoms and creates fewer adverse effects than will actually be the case."[48]

In terms of public-failure theory, a particularly trouble-some attribute of this problem lies in the difficulty of actually documenting the threat to public values. The Gelsinger story was atypical in that the connection between the conflict of interest and the public consequence—Gelsinger's death—was obvious (even if not demonstrably causal). However, when published studies comparing one drug to another influence a physician to prescribe one drug rather than another, the very existence of the public failure may be difficult to ascertain, and the public-failure consequences highly diffused. It is, indeed, a testimony to the transparency of the biomedical and medical-legal research enterprises that this problem did emerge.

Federal regulations for oversight of human subjects research do not explicitly require Institutional Review Boards to consider conflict of interest in the approval process,[49] although the Food and Drug Administration, for example, requires that applications for drug approval must be accompanied by disclosure of investigator conflicts in all research supporting the application. The final report of the now-defunct National Bioethics Advisory Commission[50] recommended that the government develop specific guidelines for defining and regulating conflict of interest in human-subjects research, and that conflict of interest should be disclosed to research participants as part of the prior consent process. Enforcement of these recommendations would help to reestablish the government monopoly over protecting human subjects of medical research and thus help to reverse a case of public failure in science.[51]

Case 3. Public Failure Due to Scarcity of Providers: Geographic Information

Protection of a core public value may depend on the presence of a sufficient number of providers of that value. If market signals are insufficient to attract the necessary number of providers, and if the government fails to step in, then public failure may occur. Few would disagree that the number of high quality public school teachers is less than optimal, due to many factors, including relatively low salaries and other disincentives. This may be counted a public failure. When certain government activities are deregulated, provider scarcity may follow. For example, when airline deregulation leads to decreased services for rural areas, significant portions of the population may be adversely affected. The market may be operating efficiently, but public failure has occurred.

The federal government has long been recognized as the appropriate source of support for developing and disseminating data on the geographic and physiographic characteristics of the nation. The Lewis and Clark expedition was a famous early example of a government research project aimed at garnering geographic information, and surveying and mapping activities were early mainstays of federal support for science prior to World War I.[52]

In recent decades, the importance of geographically referenced, or geospatial, data has increased rapidly. This growth has been fueled by new technologies, from remote sensing and global positioning satellites to sophisticated computer graphics software, and also by societal demand for new capabilities to monitor and address complex challenges, ranging from environmental protection to emergency management.

At the same time, private-sector involvement in both the collection and use of geospatial data has increased, leading to a number of dilemmas regarding the appropriate allocation of public and private activities. Considerable attention has been focused on the need to ensure that this increasing private-sector role does not result in erosion of public access to information and products that are recognized as public goods.

The revolution in geographic information began with NASA's launching of the first civilian remote sensing satellite—Landsat 1—in 1972. Efforts to gradually privatize the Landsat program were initiated in 1979 by the Carter administration. Two years later, the Reagan administration began advocating a more rapid shift to privatization, which in turn led to legislation in 1984 that privatized the sale of Landsat data, and encouraged private-sector development of future satellites.

These actions took place despite studies indicating that privatization was not economically sustainable. Indeed, for the next five years, the Landsat program was in a state of constant fiscal crisis. By the early 1990s, with the operational satellites (Landsats 4 and 5) beyond their design life, and no concrete plans for replacing them either with public or private satellites, the very existence of the Landsat program was in jeopardy.[53]

In 1992, Congress took action to ensure the continued provision of satellite-based geospatial data. In doing so, it explicitly noted that the privatization effort interfered with the provision of public goods: "The cost of Landsat data has impeded the use of such data for scientific purposes, such as for global environmental change research, as well as for public-sector applications."[54] A new law was enacted (P.L. 102-555) to ensure the continuity of the Landsat program, but also to ensure that publicly supported scientists and others who depend on satellite imagery for non-commercial uses would have access both to archived data and to newly acquired data—access that had been compromised by high prices during the privatization effort.

The near debacle created by the premature privatization of Landsat demonstrates how a scarcity of providers can deprive society of a public good upon which it depends, and how such public failure can be corrected by appropriate government action. In this case, the obvious failure of a putative market solution—privatizing Landsat—made it easy to recognize the public failure. That is, public failure and market failure existed hand-in-hand.

The more interesting and problematic case, however, occurs when the markets are functioning well, but the provision of the public good is not automatically preserved. Recent development of geospatial data policy exemplifies an awareness of this tension, and is in fact something of a success story: a case where policy intervention ensures that market success is combined with the support of public values.

As we have discussed, overcoming public failure depends on general agreement about the desirability of a particular public value, and indeed the idea of geospatial data as a public good is well accepted. For example, a study by the National Academy of Public Administration states that "many believe that [geospatial] data should be made widely available at no cost or at reasonable cost to the user, and that this will satisfy an almost infinite variety of governmental, commercial, and societal needs."[55]

One National Research Council (NRC) committee asserted that "it is in the public interest for government to play a leading and facilitating role in coordinating the development of spatial data and to make those data available for public use and exchange."[56] Another NRC committee made the even more specific claim "that it is in the public interest and a federal responsibility for the ... development of an interdisciplinary, multi-database architecture that will allow disparate databases to become nondestructively interoperable in a geospatial context."[57]

While such language cannot easily be derived from the U.S. Constitution, it can nonetheless be justified by "countless applications (for instance, facility management, real estate transactions, taxation, land-use planning, transportation, emergency services, environmental assessment and monitoring, and research),"[58] and the consequent public benefits that access to geospatial data can confer.

The major obstacle to ensuring such benefits has become the coordination of rapidly expanding private- and public-sector capabilities in acquiring, processing, and disseminating a wide variety of geographic information. The transition from analog ("paper") maps and photos to digital databases has enabled a thriving private-sector effort to apply spatial data to a diversity of public and private needs. In particular, the rise of "geographic information systems" (GIS) has created the capability of bringing together very different types of data to support decision making. The challenge of assuring that data, software, and hardware capabilities arising from a multitude of providers did not create a sort of geographic information tower of Babel even led to the formation, in 1994, of a nonprofit organization, the Open GIS Consortium, to "address the lack of interoperability among systems that process georeferenced data."[59]

The situation had rapidly changed from one of providers of a single type of data satellite imagery to a scarcity of providers of an integrated product. The point is worth emphasizing because it illustrates the subtlety and power of public-failure theory: in the first case, the public failure of provider scarcity correlated with market failure; in the second, the correlation was with market success. A new need rapidly arose: to ensure "a common spatial data foundation organized according to widely accepted layers and scales (or resolution) that is available for the entire area of geographic coverage ... to which other geospatial data can be easily referenced."[60]

For example, if a municipality needed to develop geospatial data to support ecosystem management, it might require spatially referenced data about the location of wetlands and other sensitive areas, about demographic and land-use trends, groundwater chemistry, surface water flow, sources of pollution, distribution of animal and plant species, power lines and pipelines, and of course traditional physiographic data. For these data to be useful, they must be combined as part of a single geospatial database, which means they must be available in compatible formats and coverage, and usable with one software package, on one computer. Such compatibility was not arising from private-sector providers acting individually to maximize profit and capture market share.

The need for government intervention has been broadly accepted and recognized in both the public and private sectors. In 1994, President Clinton issued Executive Order 12906, "Coordinating geographic data acquisition and access: the national spatial data infrastructures [NSDI]," to establish:

1. A Federal Geographic Data Committee to coordinate the development of the NSDI;
2. A national geospatial electronic data clearinghouse that would encompass all data collected by the public sector;
3. A process of developing standards to ensure compatibility among public, private, and nonprofit sector sources of geospatial data; and
4. A framework of basic geospatial data—"data you can trust"—for a variety of applications that would be available for all.

The framework represented a clear embodiment of public action to protect a public good: "basic geographic data in a common format and an accessible environment that anyone can use and to which anyone can contribute ... a nationwide community for data sharing."[61]

Case 4. Public Failures and Short Time Horizons: Energy R&D

Human beings pay attention to unborn generations, but they do not do so out of economic rationality. Pricing will not account for consequences that are expected to emerge in the distant future. Thus, there is clearly a public role in guaranteeing the long-term perspective even if there is no short-term market failure.

This type of problem has emerged most conspicuously in the area of environmental protection. For example, the price of gasoline in the past did not reflect the public health costs associated with high levels of lead in the air; currently gas prices do not account for the long-term global environmental costs associated with climate change. In the case of lead, government action created a public success — mandatory introduction of lead-free gasolines — in the absence of market signals. For climate change, the necessary regulatory and R&D investments have to be made, so here we see both public failure and market failure arising from short time horizons.

The market-failure paradigm has provided a politically robust rationale for long-term investment in research where no foreseeable application exists. Oddly enough, the paradigm has been less successful as a justification for public research investment where the long-term application is clear, but the short-term incentives for private-sector involvement are weak. This irony reflects the apparent repugnance in market-failure dogma to choose "winners and losers," or at least to significantly alter the balance between current winners and losers. The consequences are starkly illustrated in the case of energy R&D.

The energy crises of the 1970s demonstrated that the long-term U.S. dependence on foreign sources of oil could have far-reaching economic and political consequences. More recently, the growing awareness of the connections between fossil fuel use and global climate change have created an additional long-term rationale to switch to other types of less-polluting energy technologies. In the face of these two realities, trends in both public and private investment in energy R&D are quite amazing: they have declined by almost two-thirds, in real dollars, since the late 1970s.[62]

The reasons for this lack of investment are clear: over short time horizons, the market has been working quite well. In particular, and contrary to general extractions, oil prices have been fairly stable as a result of aggressive exploration, enhanced extraction technologies, open global markets, and the willingness of the United States to intervene militarily to protect access to oil supplies. In market-failure thinking, continued low energy prices justify neither aggressive public funding of energy R&D, nor government regulatory action to promote efficiency, which could stimulate private-sector R&D. Absent the price pressures of oil embargoes, there has been little motive to innovate. Annual energy technology patents, for example, have been declining since the 1980s.[63]

Reduced commitment to research seems to be reflected in both energy production and consumption trends. In 1970, fossil fuels accounted for 93% of all U.S. energy production. This proportion declined 5% over the next five years (during the first energy crisis) but only 8% more over the succeeding fifteen years.[64] On the consumption end, energy intensity (energy use per unit of economic output) declined 2.4% per year in the 1980s; in the 1990s, the average annual decline was only 1.5%.[65]

Given the ongoing volatility of politics in the Middle East and the increasing evidence that carbon emissions influence the behavior of the global climate, it is difficult not to see the declining public investment in research on alternative energy sources and more efficient energy technologies as deeply problematic. This declining investment documents a continued failure to overcome the short-term thinking in government energy R&D policy that is made possible by a well-functioning market that continues to deliver stable energy supplies and low prices.

Case 5. Over-Reliance on Substitutability of Resources: Organ Sales as a Medical Public Failure

Market mechanisms may indemnify against the loss of particular resources, or offer substitutes for lost resources. While such mechanisms may be efficient from a market perspective, they may also represent public failure. An obvious example is the calculation that automobile manufacturers might use when determining how safe to make a vehicle. Part of this calculation includes the price of adequate indemnification against lawsuits for wrongful death.

While such trade-offs are unavoidable (a totally safe car would be either unaffordable, or immobile), they may still represent public failure, for example, if the manufacturer determines that the costs of fixing a known problem exceed the expected legal costs, as occurred when Ford failed to correct the exploding gas tanks in its Pinto model.[66] The idea that life is explicitly substitutable offends sensibilities of most non-economists, and may often imply public failure.

A related example comes from environmental policy. "No-net-loss" policies allow for developers who fill in existing wetlands to construct artificial wetlands as a substitute. However, ecological research suggests that artificial wetlands tend not to have the same species diversity or ecological value as the natural ones that they replace.[67] Similarly, when old-growth forests are clear-cut and replaced by planting of monoculture forests, the ecological value of the original forest has not been retained, even if the economic value, as measured by board-feet of lumber, is maintained.

In market-failure-based policies, public-value failures are most often a result of the substitution of money for a tangible or natural resource. One especially interesting case implicating science policies and pertaining to medical practice is money-for-body-parts transactions. In the United

States, trafficking in human organs is illegal — a clear signal that public values should take precedence over market efficiency. Elsewhere in the world, evidence of a market in human organs to supply rapidly advancing capabilities in medical science continues to crop up. An active market in kidneys and corneas has been documented in India,[68] and an organ market is also thought to exist in the Philippines.[69]

Such transactions degrade humans, victimize the poor, and invariably occur under some type of economic or political duress; they exemplify public failure. Yet, from a market standpoint, money-for-body-parts transactions may be viewed as efficient, with money being an acceptable substitute for personal health. From a consumer standpoint this logic is unimpeachable. As one Harvard economist writes: "If a desperately ill individual who would die without a kidney is able to buy one from a healthy individual, both are made better off. Why … stand in the way of market transactions that will not only make those who engage in them happier but also save lives?"[70]

Perhaps whether or not one keeps one's corneas is really a matter of one's view about the substitutability of health for other assets. Nevertheless, in a world where millions live in abject poverty, the notion of consumer sovereignty and of rational choice of one good for another seems less about markets than about massive public-values failure.

Case 6. Public Failure and Benefit Hoarding: Terminator Technology

In the marketplace, externalities may distort prices and thus skew costs or benefits toward particular consumers. For example, the costs of cleaning up pollution are rarely included in the price of the polluting good. Thus, those who produce and consume that good may benefit preferentially. Analogously, if the benefits of a public policy meant to aid a large group are captured preferentially by a much smaller group, public failure may be occurring.

165

Recent attention to the "digital divide" may illustrate such a failure. Disparities in health care may be another example. Development of the internet and many medical technologies was made possible by public support of the necessary R&D. If only certain segments of the population are benefiting from this investment, then benefit hoarding may be taking place.

In the early 1980s, following a decade of disappointing economic performance, U.S. policymakers were anxious to find ways to stimulate economic growth. One area of action focused on creating incentives to transfer the results of government-funded research to the private sector as a stimulus to technological innovation, and resulted in such laws as the Stephenson-Wydler Act of 1980, the Bayh-Dole Act of 1980, and the Federal Technology Transfer Act of 1986.

The Technology Transfer Act legalized public-private research partnerships, called CRADAs (cooperative research and development agreements), meant to stimulate collaboration between government and corporate laboratories. The "Findings" that articulate the rationale for the act include brief mention of "social well-being," "increased public services" and "public purposes," but in fact focus almost entirely on economic arguments, for example: "Increased industrial and technological innovation would reduce trade deficits, stabilize the dollar, increase productivity gains, increase employment, and stabilize prices."[71] While these are all laudatory goals, they make no mention of possible social impacts that could undermine public values.

On March 3, 1998, the U.S. Patent Office granted a patent jointly to the U.S. Department of Agriculture's (USDA) Agricultural Research Service and the Delta and Pine Land Co., a breeder of cotton and soybeans, entitled "Control of Plant Gene Expression." This patent arose from joint work funded through a CRADA, and embodied the type of technology transfer envisioned by legislators more than a decade earlier.

The patent covered a process, called the Technology Protection System (TPS), that would allow seeds to be genetically engineered so that they did not give rise to fertile offspring. The intention was to protect the technological innovation embodied in new varieties of seeds (for example, resistance to drought or herbicides), by ensuring that farmers could not plant second-generation seeds produced by the first generation crop. Rather, they would have to buy new seeds for each planting. In the words of the USDA, the new technology "would protect investments made in breeding or genetically engineering these crops. It would do this by reducing potential sales losses from unauthorized reproduction and sale of seed."[72] This economic argument was causally linked to a social-benefits argument via standard market logic:

> *The knowledge that the seed companies could potentially recoup their investment through sales will provide a stronger incentive for the companies to develop new, more useful varieties that the market demands. Today's emerging scientific approaches to crop breeding – especially genetic engineering – could be crucial to meeting future world food needs, conserving soil and water, conserving genetic resources, reducing negative environmental effects of farming, and spurring farm and other economic growth. TPS technology will contribute to these outcomes by encouraging development of new crop varieties with increased nutrition to benefit consumers and with stronger resistance to drought, disease, and insects to benefit farmers, for example.[73]*

TPS technology does appear to hold considerable interest for plant-breeding companies, and TPS patents continue to be granted in the United States and abroad.[74] In essence, TPS makes protection of intellectual property a biological process, rather than a legal one. At present, seed

companies must count on the honest farmers to honor intellectual property by not "brown-bagging" second-generation seeds, or the companies must resort to policing of
farms to enforce their intellectual property. Indeed, in pursuing the latter course, Monsanto suffered a public relations disaster when they sued a Saskatchewan rape-seed
farmer for patent infringement.[75]

TPS is a testimony to amazing progress in genetic engineering. The process described in the original patent involves enormously complex, integrated manipulation of
transgenic components that are inserted into the DNA of
the plant to be protected. A plant gene "normally activated
late in seed development" must be fused with a "promoter
to the coding sequence for a protein that will kill an embryo
going through the last stages of development" and then
coupled to a mechanism to repress the promoter until it is
treated with a specific chemical.[76]

Less than two years after the TPS patent was granted,
M. S. Swaminathan, one of the founders of the Green Revolution and an advocate of biotechnology in the service of
global agriculture, declared that if TPS was widely
adopted, "small farmers will then experience genetic en-
slavement since their agricultural destiny will be in the
hands of a few companies."[77] The Consultative Group on
International Agricultural Research (CGIAR, the organization that provided much of the science for the Green Revolution) banned TPS from their research agenda[78] and Monsanto, which was attempting to acquire Delta and Pine
Land Company (co-holder of the original patent), pledged,
under pressure from public interest groups and philan-
thropic foundations, "not to commercialize sterile seed
technologies."[79]

The Rural Advancement Foundation (RAFI, later re-
named ETC Group), which mobilized opposition to TPS,
coined the phrase "terminator technology" and asserted
that the "seed-sterilizing technology threatens to eliminate

the age-old right of farmers to save seed from their harvest and it jeopardizes the food security of 1.4 billion people — resource-poor farmers in the [global] South — who depend on farm-saved seed."[80] RAFI also argued that TPS would further contribute to diminution of global agricultural genetic diversity, especially for plant varieties of importance to developing countries.

The argument against TPS is multifaceted.[81] At the heart of the issue is the practice by many farmers, especially (but not only) in the developing world, to continually seek better plant varieties for local growing conditions through careful selection of kept seed, as well as purchase of new varieties from both private and public seed distributors.

TPS was alleged to threaten this process in many interconnected ways. First, it would allow commercial breeders to capture markets for crops that are not amenable to hybridization, including wheat, rice, and cotton. (Commercial breeders do not focus on such crops precisely because they cannot control farmers' use of kept seed. Hybrid seed, on the other hand, tends not to express its engineered attributes homogeneously in the second generation, and thus offers some inherent protection of intellectual property.)

This commercialization of seed varieties in turn would inevitably reduce the available commercial sources of such seed because of advantages conferred to larger breeders and seed purchasers by economies of scale. Local plant breeders' access to new genetic materials would thus become increasingly restricted, and their ability to select for improved seed varieties would be impaired.

Secondly, because commercial plant breeders would be aiming their products at the most profitable markets — those of the rich countries — they would be unlikely to engineer plant varieties to meet the needs of poorer farmers, as has been the case generally with hybrid products. At the same time, publicly funded plant breeding organizations, such as CGIAR, might be blocked from using engineered traits developed by private breeders unless they also accepted TPS. Such trends would exacerbate agricultural technology gaps between rich and poor.

Thirdly, because poor farmers would find it increasingly difficult to acquire seed without terminator technology, their exposure to year-to-year food-supply disruption as a result of economic, political, climatic, or other factors would increase. Finally, genetic diversity of agricultural varieties would decline, because the largest source of such diversity is the seed-production activities of farmers themselves. Large breeding companies tend to reduce, not increase, genetic diversity.

In defense of TPS, USDA focuses on market arguments:

Loss of cost savings from brown-bagging [kept seed] also must be weighed against the productivity gains to the farmer from having superior new varieties that could increase crop values such as yield and quality, input cost reductions such as for fertilizers and pesticides, and reduced losses such as those due to pests or adverse soils and weather.[82]

Such arguments assume a level playing field, where the attributes of new, engineered seed varieties will be those needed by small farmers and poor farmers, where such farmers will be able to afford the new varieties, and where they will, therefore, no longer be dependent on their own seed selection skills to optimize crops for particular local growing conditions. Even should such an optimistic scenario transpire, it ignores the effects of reduced genetic diversity on the resilience of agricultural systems worldwide.

Terminator technologies thus create a possibility for corporations to gain control of a process — seed selection — and a product — plant varieties — that have been in the hands of farmers for millennia. The effect is a private hoarding of what had been a public good — the plant-genetic commons. This effect is less troubling in the context of affluent nations, where agriculture has become increasingly industrialized, than for poor ones, where small farmers continue to depend upon kept seed and selective breeding for crop improvement and adaptation, and for food security from year to year.

A particularly conspicuous element of this story is that the original research was partly funded by public money and conducted at a public research laboratory. As such, it is an exemplar of the way that market values displace public values in justifying public funding of science and technology.

Science Policy and the "Public Value Grid"

Among other implications of these examples and the criteria they illustrate is that public failure and market failure are *not* single poles on a dimension or even two orthogonal dimensions. Instead, it is best to view the two as axes of a grid, as in Figure 5.1, which provides a depiction of the ways in which science policies can have very different economic and public values outcomes.

Figure 5.1: Public Failure Grid and Examples

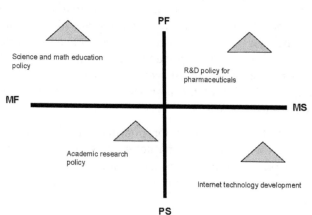

The notion of setting market values against other values not easily encompassed by market framework is not new. For example, environmental economist R. Talbot Page suggested contrasting dimensions of market efficiency and conservation of resources.[83] Bryan Norton and Michael Toman speak of "two tiers," one an efficiency criterion, the other a conservation criterion.[84] Figure 5.1 provides a highly simplified depiction of public failure and market failure, illustrating the possibility of a virtually infinite range of outcomes among the extremes of complete public failure, complete public success, complete market failure, complete market success. One obvious point is that market failure and public failure need not be correlated at all.

Figure 5.1 is broadly illustrative. We might easily quibble with the exact location of the policies depicted. Another obvious limitation is that such broad categories as "academic research policy" are little more than stand-in symbols for many diverse science (and other) policies. However, the lack of precision should not undercut the chief point.

Take the case of internet technology development. We might argue, for example, that the history of internet technology development provides a happy example of a public values success and, at the same time, a market success. While the internet, much as any ubiquitous social phenomenon, has not been a success in every possible respect (witness controversies about privacy, pornography, intellectual property, and spam), most would, on balance, assess the commercialization of the internet as both a market and public values success.

Similarly, R&D policy for pharmaceuticals could be viewed as a considerable market success but in many respects a public failure. In neither instance is it a "pure" success or failure and thus not at the extreme end of either pole.

One point worth noting is that over time policies move in "normative space," repositioning themselves in Figure 5.1. Thus, at the beginning of internet technology development, the best description would be "modest public values success combined with market failure." That is, in 1992, the internet (not yet called that) served some significant if limited public values in linking scientists and a few other users. However, at that time, the internet was a nearly perfect market failure in the sense that no commercial value had yet been harvested, nobody was in a position exclusively to appropriate its benefits, and no price mechanisms were in place.

The public-failure grid provides a simple analytical tool for thinking about the public values and economic values served by science policies. We need not be "right" in the positioning of policies to find such deliberation useful. Likewise, we need not entertain each public failure (and each market failure) diagnostic criterion to employ the grid and to obtain its value as a common sense check on deliberations about the values served by science policies.

For the past fifty years, questions of choice have been central to science policy discourse. In a world of finite resources, how shall we choose among various portfolios of scientific investments and research strategies, and who shall do the choosing? The famed Bush–Kilgore debates of the late 1940s, which sought in part to establish the degree to which publicly funded science should be linked to specific social goals,[85] set the stage for an initial phase of intellectual debate that took as its starting point the assumption that science needed to be insulated from the vulgarities of democracy, and proceeded to ask how, then, choices might be made to serve the best interests of society.[86]

Yet the texture and depth of thinking about choice in science policy has had remarkably little impact on the actual science policy process, which remains, above all, a competition for incremental budget increases. Each year, science policy, as so much of the rest of federal policy, becomes riveted on the federal budget and, specifically, the amount of money available for science. There is great deliberation about the actual amount, the rate of growth, the percentage of the budget, the amount for science as opposed to other outlay categories, and the amount (and percentage and rate of growth) for particular agencies and particular programs within agencies, as compiled annually by the American Association for the Advancement of Science,[87] and biennially by the National Science Board.[88]

Every year, even during periods of considerable growth in spending, there are at least a few "funding crises" identified and these become grist for op-eds, sound bites, lobbying, and anguish. (The latest example is the concerns voiced on behalf of the National Institutes of Health, whose budget doubled between 1998 and 2002, and must now suffer a reversion to rates of increase typical of its prior history of robust growth.)[89]

The fact is, few people (and more likely no people) have the breadth of understanding to even begin to provide a valid account of what will happen as a result of a 5% decrease or increase in, say, biochemistry funding. Yet, in the world where science policy decisions are actually made, science funding acts as a proxy for public value; more of the former is assumed to yield more of the latter. Policy documents[90] and scholarship[91] have made the case for greater diversity of voices in science policy priority setting, a recommendation that we would support, yet one that does little to address the more complex question of how successfully a given line of research may actually connect to advancing public values. It is telling that successful efforts to influence the internal conduct of science to achieve particular societal outcomes are relatively rare, and have mostly been driven by highly motivated and politically empowered groups focused on changing the norms of clinical health research.[92]

We suggest that, while democratizing choice is important, it is insufficient for enhancing the public value of science. Indeed, in one very real sense, choice in science policy has been highly democratized. In the words of the late Congressman George E. Brown Jr., perhaps the most thoughtful of all practitioners of the politics of science: "Congress does have a rational priority-setting system. Unfortunately it is largely zip-code based: Anything close to my district or state is better than something farther away. Individual colleges and universities and many federal labs know this system well and have used it to their advantage for decades."[93]

The problem is that what really counts when it comes to the public values flowing from science policy is not so much budgetary level of effort as the institutional, cultural, political, and economic contexts in which science is produced and applied. So why, in the face of decades of critical STS scholarship about these complex contextual relations, does the formula that equates more-money-for-science with more-public-value assert itself with undiminished vigor? We suggest this is a consequence of two factors: first, the bipartisan power of economic thinking, bolstered by evidence of the key role for science in economic growth, and rationalized by the market-failure model for government intervention; and, second, the absence of analytical and rhetorical tools that can match the simplicity and potency of economic argumentation.

Here we have presented simple criteria that can be used to test claims that more science equals more public value. If values are not well articulated or aggregated; if public monopolies are imperfect; if providers are scarce; if time horizons are short; if resources are viewed as substitutable; if benefits can be captured by small groups; then the translation of science investments into public values may well be compromised, regardless of how well the market is operating, or how much money the science receives.

Notes

[1] A. Sen, *The Standard of Living* (Cambridge, UK: Cambridge University Press, 1987).

[2] B. Bozeman, "Public value failure: When efficient markets may not do," *Public Administration Review* 62, no. 2 (2002): 134-151.

[3] In the United States, public schools are free, tax-supported schools controlled by a local government authority

[4] For instance, D. Dickson, *The New Politics of Science* (New York, NY: Pantheon, 1984); L. Winner, *The Whale and the Reactor: A Search for Limits in an Age of High Technology* (Chicago, IL: University of Chicago Press, 1986); D. L. Kleinman, *Politics on the Endless Frontier: Postward Research Policy in the United States* (Durham, NC: Duke University Press, 1993); S. Cozzens and E. Woodhouse, "Science, government, and the politics of knowledge," in *Handbook of Science and Technology Studies*, S. Jasanoff, G. Markle, J. Petersen, and T. Pinch, eds. (Thousand Oaks, CA: Sage Publications, 1995); D. Sarewitz, *Frontiers of Illusion: Science, Technology, and the Politics of Progress* (Philadelphia, PA: Temple University Press, 1996); D. Greenberg, *Science, Money, and Politics* (Chicago, IL: University of Chicago Press, 2001).

[5] For instance, Federation of American Societies for Experimental Biology (FASEB), "FASEB President says Bush's budget for the NIH is a 'Great Start,' but vows to push for more on Capitol Hill," *FASEBnews*, press release (Feb 21, 2001).

[6] For instance, R. G. Evans, M. L. Barer, and T. R. Marmor, eds., *Why Are Some People Healthy and Others Not? The Determinants of Health of Populations* (New York, NY: Aldine de Gruyter, 1994); R. G. Wilkinson, *Unhealthy Societies: The Afflictions of Inequality* (New York, NY: Routledge, 1996); D. Callahan, *False Hopes: Why America's Quest for Perfect Health is a Recipe for Failure* (New York, NY: Simon & Schuster, 1998); B. D. Smedley, A. Y. Stith, and A. R. Nelson, eds., *Unequal Treatment: Confronting Racial and Ethnic Disparities in Health Care* (Washington, DC: National Academies Press, 2002).

[7] For instance, V. Bush, *Science, the Endless Frontier* (Washington, DC: National Science Foundation, 1945); W. J. Clinton and

A. Gore Jr., *Science in the National Interest* (Washington, DC: Office of Science and Technology Policy, 1994), 1; L. Lindsay, Speech (untitled) to the American Association for the Advancement of Science, Science and Technology Policy Colloquium (May 3, 2001).

8 For instance, D. F. Noble, *Progress without People: New Technologies, Unemployment, and the Message of Resistance* (Toronto, Canada: Between the Lines, 1995); A. Sen, "Inequality, unemployment, and contemporary Europe," *International Labour Review* 136, no. 2 (1997): 155-171; United Nations Development Programme, *Human Development Report 1994* (New York, NY: Oxford University Press, 1999); M. Castells, *End of Millennium* (Malden, MA: Blackwell, 1998); J. K. Galbraith and M. Berner, eds., *Inequality and Industrial Change: A Global View* (Cambrige, UK: Cambridge University Press, 2001); R. Arocena and P. Senker, "Technology, inequality, and underdevelopment: The case of Latin America," *Science, Technology, & Human Values* 28, no. 1 (2003): 15-33.

9 For instance, E. Mansfield, "Basic research and productivity increases in manufacturing," *American Economic Review* 70 (1968): 863-873; D. F. Noble, *Forces of Production* (New York, NY: Alfred A. Knopf, 1984); S. W. Leslie, *The Cold War and American Science* (New York, NY: Columbia University Press, 1993); A. L. Norburg and J. E. O'Neill, *Transforming Computer Technology: Information Processing for the Pentagon, 1962-1986* (Baltimore, MD: Johns Hopkins University Press, 1996).

10 For instance, N. Rosenberg, *Inside the Black Box* (New York, NY: Cambridge University Press, 1982), chapter 7; F. Narin and D. Olivastro, "Status report: Linkage between technology and science," *Research Policy* 21 (1992): 237-249; N. Rosenberg and R. R. Nelson, "American research universities and technical advance in industry," *Research Policy* 23, no. 8 (1994): 323-348; K. Pavitt, "The social shaping of the National Science Base," *Research Policy* 27, no. 12 (1998): 793-805.

11 For instance, E. Press and J. Washburn, "The kept university," *Atlantic Monthly* 285 (2000): 39-54; R. R. Nelson, "The market economy, and the scientific commons," *Research Policy* 33, no. 3 (2004): 455-471.

[12] For instance, see S. Jasanoff, G. Markle, J. Petersen, and T. Pinch, eds., *Handbook of Science and Technology Studies* (Thousand Oaks, CA: Sage Publications, 1995).

[13] Y. Ezrahi, *The Descent of Icarus: Science and the Transformation of Contemporary Culture* (Cambridge, MA: Harvard University Press, 1990), chapter 11.

[14] D. L. Hull, *Science as a Process: An Evolutionary Account of the Social and Conceptual Development of Science* (Chicago, IL: University of Chicago Press, 1998), 31.

[15] For instance, R. R. Nelson, M. J. Peck, and E. D. Kalachek, *Technology, Economic Growth, and Public Policy: A Rand Corporation and Brookings Institution Study* (Washington, DC: Brookings Institution, 1967); R. Rosenbloom and W. Spencer, *Engines of Innovation: U.S. Industrial Research at the End of an Era* (Boston, MA: Harvard Business School Press, 1996); D. C. Mowery and N. Rosenburg, *Technology and the Pursuit of Economic Growth* (New York, NY: Cambridge University Press, 1989); Z. Griliches, "R&D productivity: Econometric results and measurement issues," in *The Handbook of the Economics of Innovation and Technological Change*, S. Paul, ed. (Oxford, UK: Blackwell, 1995); E. Denison, *The Sources of Economic Growth in the United States and the Alternatives before Us* (New York, NY: Committee for Economic Development, 1962).

[16] B. Bimber and D. Guston, "Politics by the same means: Government and science in the United States," in in *Handbook of Science and Technology Studies*, S. Jasanoff, G. Markle, J. Petersen, and T. Pinch, eds. (Thousand Oaks, CA: Sage Publications, 1995).

[17] For instance, R. Flathman, *The Public Interest* (New York, NY: Wiley, 1966); V. Held, *The Public Interest and Individual Interests* (New York, NY: Basic Books, 1972); C. E. Cochran, "Political science and 'the public interest,'" *Journal of Politics* 36 (1974): 327-355.

[18] M. Polanyi, "The republic of science: Its political and economic theory," *Minerva* 1 (1962): 54-73.

[19] See discussion in chapter 3 of D. Guston, *Between Politics and Science: Assuring the Integrity and Productivity of Research* (Oxford, UK: Oxford University Press, 2000).

[20] B. Bozeman, "Public value failure: When efficient markets may not do," *Public Administration Review* 62, no. 2 (2002): 134-151.

[21] For instance, G. Schubert, *The Public Interest* (Glencoe, IL: The Free Press, 1960); F. Sorauf, "The public interest reconsidered," *Journal of Politics* 19 (1957): 616-639; L. Fuller, *The Morality of Law* (New Haven, CT: Yale University Press, 1964).

[22] For instance, V. Bush, *Science, the Endless Frontier* (Washington, DC: National Science Foundation, 1945).

[23] For instance, R. R. Nelson, "The simple economics of basic scientific research," *Journal of Political Economy* 67 (1959); E. Mansfield, *The Economics of Technical Change* (New York, NY: W. W. Norton, 1980).

[24] B. Bozeman, "Public value failure: When efficient markets may not do," *Public Administration Review* 62, no. 2 (2002): 134-151.

[25] For a precise definition of market failure, see G. Bannock, R. Baxter, and E. Davis, *The Penguin Dictionary of Economics* (New York, NY: Penguin Books, 1998), 117.

[26] B. Bozeman, "Public value failure: When efficient markets may not do," *Public Administration Review* 62, no. 2 (2002): 134-151.

[27] Adapted from B. Bozeman, "Public value failure: When efficient markets may not do," *Public Administration Review* 62, no. 2 (2002): 134-151.

[28] For discussions of basic questions involved in scientific choice, see, for instance, S. Fuller, *The Governance of Science* (London, UK: Open University Press, 2000).

[29] National Academy of Public Administration, *A Study of the National Science Foundation's Criteria for Project Selection* (Washington, DC: NAPA, 2001).

[30] Ibid., 7.

[31] Ibid., 8.

[32] Ibid., 9.

[33] For instance, M. Bauer, K. Petkova, and B. Boyadjieva, "Public knowledge and attitudes to science: Alternative measures that may end the 'science war,'" *Science, Technology, & Human Values* 25, no. 1 (2000): 30-51; E. Plutzer, A. Maney, and R. O'Connor, "Ideology and elites' perceptions of the safety of new technologies," *American Journal of Political Science* 42, no. 1 (1998): 190-209; R. Barke and H. Jenkins-Smith, "Politics and scientific expertise: Scientists, risk perception, and nuclear waste policy," *Risk Analysis* 13, no. 4 (1993): 425-439.

[34] For instance, as originally suggested by A. M. Weinberg, "Criteria for scientific choice," *Minerva* 1, no. 2 (1963): 159-171, and revisited by S. Fuller, *The Governance of Science* (London, UK: Open University Press, 2000).

[35] See P. Kitcher, *Science, Truth, and Democracy* (New York, NY: Oxford University Press, 2001), for a formal argument about enhancing the public role in articulating public values for science.

[36] For instance, F. Fukuyama, *Our Post-Human Future: Consequences of the Biotechnology Revolution* (New York, NY: Allen and Unwin, 2002).

[37] B. Woodward, "Challenges to human subject protection in U.S. medical research," *Journal of the American Medical Association* 282, no. 20 (1999): 1947-1952.

[38] Code of Federal Regulations, "Title 45, Public Welfare, Department of Health and Human Services, National Institutes of Health, Office for Protection from Research Risks, part 46, Protection of Human Subjects" (Washington, DC: U.S. Government Printing Office, 1993), 112-113.

[39] Ibid.

[40] N. Wade, "Patient dies during a trial of therapy using genes," *New York Times* (Sept. 29, 1999).

[41] R. Nelson and R. Weiss, "Hasty decisions in the race to a cure? Gene therapy study proceeded despite safety, ethics concerns," *Washington Post* (Nov. 21, 1999): A1.

[42] M. Friedberg, B. Saffran, T. Stinson, W. Nelson, and C. L. Bennett, "Evaluation of conflict of interest in economic analyses

of new drugs used in oncology," *Journal of the American Medical Association* 282, no. 15 (1999): 1453-1457.

[43] H. T. Stelfox, G. Chua, K. O'Rourke, and A. S. Detsky, "Conflict of interest in the debate over calcium-channel antagonists," *New England Journal of Medicine* 338, no. 2 (1998): 101.

[44] M. Cho and L. Bero, "The quality of drug studies published in symposium proceedings," *Annals of Internal Medicine* 124, no. 5 (1996): 485.

[45] M. Angell, "Is academic medicine for sale?" *New England Journal of Medicine* 342, no. 20 (2000): 1517.

[46] R. Nelson and R. Weiss, "Hasty decisions in the race to a cure? Gene therapy study proceeded despite safety, ethics concerns," *Washington Post* (Nov. 21, 1999): Al.

[47] T. Bodenheimer, "Uneasy Alliance — Clinical Investigators and the Pharmaceutical Industry," *New England Journal of Medicine* 342, no. 20 (2000): 1539-1544.

[48] Ibid., 1541.

[49] Code of Federal Regulations, "Title 45, Public Welfare, Department of Health and Human Services, National Institutes of Health, Office for Protection from Research Risks, part 46, Protection of Human Subjects" (Washington, DC: U.S. Government Printing Office, 1993), 112-113.

[50] National Bioethics Advisory Commission, *Ethical and Policy Issues in Research Involving Human Participants* (Bethesda, MD: NBAC, 2000).

[51] See J. A. Goldner, "Dealing with conflicts of interest in biomedical research," *Journal of Law, Medicine, & Ethics* 28, no. 4 (2000): 379-404, for a comprehensive discussion of conflict of interest in biomedical research.

[52] For instance, A. H. Dupree, *Science in the Federal Government* (Baltimore, MD: Johns Hopkins University Press, 1986).

[53] NASA, "Landsat program chronology" (1998); National Research Council, *Assessment of Satellite Earth Observation Programs 1991* (Washington, DC: National Academy Press, 1991).

[54] Land Remote Sensing Policy Act of 1992, H.R. 6133, 102nd Congress (1992).

[55] National Academy of Public Administration, *Geographic Information for the 21st Century - Building a Strategy for the Nation* (Washington, DC: NAPA, 1998), 2.

[56] National Research Council, *A Data Foundation for the National Spatial Data Infrastructure* (Washington, DC: National Academy Press, 1995), 1.

[57] National Research Council, *Future Roles and Opportunities for the U.S. Geological Survey* (Washington, DC: National Academy Press, 2001), 77.

[58] National Research Council, *Toward a Coordinated Spatial Data Infrastructure for the Nation* (Washington, DC: National Academy Press, 1993), 2.

[59] Open GIS Consortium, "Spatial Connectivity for a Changing World," promotional brochure (1999), 2.

[60] National Academy of Public Administration, *Geographic Information for the 21st Century - Building a Strategy for the Nation* (Washington, DC: NAPA, 1998).

[61] Federal Geographic Data Committee, "Overview: What the framework approach involves" (2001).

[62] J. J. Dooley, *Energy Research and Development in the United States* (Washington, DC: Pacific Northwest National Lab, 1999), Figure 4.

[63] R. M. Margolis and D. M. Kammen, "Underinvestment: The energy technology and R&D challenge," *Science* 285 (1999): 690-692.

[64] Energy Information Administration, *Annual Energy Review*, Table 1.2 (2000).

[65] Energy Information Administration, *Annual Energy Outlook*, Table 7 (2001).

[66] G. F. Tietz, "Strict products liability, design defects, and corporate decision-making: Greater deterrence through stricter process," *Villanova Law Review* 38 (1993): 1361-1459.

[67] J. Kaiser, "Wetlands restoration: Recreated wetlands no match for original," *Science* 293, no. 5527 (2001): 25.

[68] S. Kumar, "Curbing the trade in human organs in India," *Lancet* 344 (1994): 750.

[69] *Medical Industry Today*, "Suspected murder for organ trade probed in Philippines" (Sept. 9, 1998): 127-128.

[70] S. Shavell, "Why not sell organs?" *New York Times* (May 11, 1999): 22.

[71] 15 USC Sec. 3701.

[72] USDA Agricultural Research Service, "Why USDA's Technology Protection System (a.k.a. 'Terminator') benefits agriculture," ARS News and Information website (2001).

[73] Ibid.

[74] ETC Group, "Sterile harvest: New crop of terminator patents threaten food sovereignty," news item (Jan. 31, 2002).

[75] For instance, D. Margoshes, "Saskatchewan farmer battles agrochemical giant," *Vancouver Sun* (Aug. 14, 1999): B1.

[76] M. Crouch, "How the terminator terminates: An explanation for the non-scientist of a remarkable patent for killing second generation seeds of crop plants," Occasional Paper Edmonds, Edmonds Institute, WA, revised edition (1998).

[77] M. S. Swaminathan, "Genetic engineering and food, ecological livelihood security in predominantly agricultural developing countries," speech to CGIAR/NAS Biotechnology Conference (Oct. 21, 1999).

[78] R. F. Service, "Seed-sterilizing 'terminator technology' sows discord," *Science* 282 (1998): 850-851.

[79] R. B. Shapiro, "Open letter from Monsanto CEO Robert B. Shapiro to Rockefeller Foundation President Gordon Conway" (Oct. 4, 1990).

[80] ETC Group, "Terminator technology targets farmers," communique (Mar. 30, 1998).

[81] Our summary is drawn from: B. Visser, I. van der Meer, N. Louwaars, J. Beekwilder, and D. Eato, "The impact of 'terminator' technology," *Biotechnology and Development Monitor* 48 (2001): 9-12; D. Eaton, F. van Tongeren, N. Louwaars, B. Visser, and I. van der Meer, "Economic and policy aspects of 'terminator' technology," *Biotechnology and Development Monitor* 49 (2002): 19-22; R. F. Service, "Seed-sterilizing 'terminator technology' sows discord," *Science* 282 (1998): 850-851; ETC Group, "Terminator technology targets farmers," communique (Mar. 30, 1998); 1999)

[82] USDA Agricultural Research Service, "Why USDA's Technology Protection System (a.k.a. 'Terminator') benefits agriculture," ARS News and Information website (2001).

[83] R. T. Page, *Conservation and Economic Efficiency* (Baltimore, MD: Johns Hopkins University Press for Resources for the Future, 1977).

[84] B. Norton and M. Toman, "Sustainability: Ecological and economic perspectives," *Land Economics* 73, no. 4 (1997): 553-568.

[85] D. J. Kevles, *The Physicists: The History of a Scientific Community in Modern America* (Cambridge, MA: Harvard University Press, 1987).

[86] For instance, M. Polanyi, "The republic of science: Its political and economic theory," *Minerva* 1 (1962): 54-73; A. M. Weinberg, "Criteria for scientific choice," *Minerva* 1, no. 2 (1963): 159-171; H. Brooks, *The Government of Science* (Cambridge, MA: MIT Press, 1968), chapters 1 and 2.

[87] For instance, Intersociety Working Group, *AAAS Report XXVII: Research and Development FY 2004* (Washington, DC: AAAS, 2003).

[88] For instance, National Science Board, *Science and Engineering Indicators 2002* (Washington, DC: National Science Foundation, 2002).

[89] R. Weiss, "NIH braces for slower funding growth: President may apply brakes on 14% to 15% annual increase, and trim it to 2%," *Washington Post* (Feb. 2, 2003): A14.

[90] For instance, Carnegie Commission on Science, Technology, and Government, *Enabling the Future: Linking Science and*

Technology to Societal Goals (New York, NY: Carnegie Corporation, 1992); Institute of Medicine, *Scientific Opportunities and Public Needs: Improving Priority Setting and Public Input at the National Institutes of Health* (Washington, DC: National Academies Press, 1998).

[91] For instance, J. C. Petersen, *Citizen Participation in Science Policy* (Amherst, MA: University of Massachusetts Press, 1984); P. Kitcher, *Science, Truth, and Democracy* (New York, NY: Oxford University Press, 2001).

[92] For instance, B. H. Lerner, *The Breast Cancer Wars* (New York, NY: Oxford University Press, 2001); S. Epstein, *Impure Science: AIDS, Activism, and the Politics of Knowledge* (Berkeley, CA: University of California Press, 1996).

[93] G. E. Brown Jr., "Past and prologue: Why I am optimistic about the future," in *1999 AAAS Science and Technology Policy Yearbook* (Washington, DC: AAAS, 1999), chapter 3.

6

PUBLIC VALUE MAPPING AND SCIENCE POLICY EVALUATION[*]

Barry Bozeman and Daniel Sarewitz

Science policy did not become the focus of serious intellectual inquiry until the early 1960s. Previously, debates raged in both England and the United States about the extent to which science could be directed toward societal aims, but such disagreements (exemplified in England by the 1930s debates between J.D. Bernal and Michael Polanyi,[1] and in the United States by the policy debates that pitted Vannevar Bush against Harley Kilgore shortly after World War II[2]) were little informed by robust theory and even less by data. In large part, *Minerva*, first published in 1962, was created to help fill this intellectual and research vacuum. "Improved understanding of the relations between government and systematic and disciplined inquiry in science and scholarship was taken as the subject matter

---

[*] Originally published as B. Bozeman and D. Sarewitz, "Public Value Mapping and Science Policy Evaluation," *Minerva* 49, no. 1 (2011): 1-23. Reprinted with permission from Springer.

of *Minerva*," wrote its first editor, Edward Shils.[3] Shils's explicit hope was that such understanding would "make scientific and academic policy more reasonable and realistic."[4]

From the beginning, the central problem in science policy was recognized by workers in the field as the problem of choice. In a world of finite resources, how should policymakers choose among the many competing scientific disciplines, projects, and programs in making public investments? *Minerva* published three early, seminal papers on this problem,[5] and many others that contributed to setting the terms of the problem. As the philosopher Stephen Toulmin noted, the choice problem was both "difficult and inescapable."[6] Difficult not only because the problem itself was poorly specified, but also "because we are sheerly ignorant about many of the relevant factors and relationships" between scientific advance and societal "repercussion."[7]

Toulmin's discussion of the choice problem remains particularly apt for two reasons. First, he identified the two important poles that still represent the organizing dichotomy of work in the subsequent four-plus decades: the "economist's view, according to which science is basically deserving of support because it is the handmaid of industrial growth; and a scientist's view, representing technology as a kind of scientific roulette in which those who plunge deepest tend to win the biggest prize."[8] Second, he recognized that the problem of choice was significantly a "chalk-and-cheese" problem, where diverse activities categorized as science (much as chalk and cheese might both be categorized as "crumbly white-ish materials") were in fact constituted by a multitude of activities that were in many ways incommensurable, so that, for example, "the choice between particle physics and cancer research becomes a decision whether to allocate more funds (a) to the patronage of the intellect or (b) to improving the nation's health. *This is not a technical choice, but a political one.*"[9]

Toulmin's identification of science policy's economic and scientific poles, and his recognition of the chalk-and-cheese problem, help to explain why, despite three decades' progress in the ability to conceptualize, measure, and evaluate research impacts, a gaping hole remains in research evaluation methods and technique: the ability to evaluate the social and public value impacts of research. Indeed, such impacts have been defined out of the problem as at once irrelevant (they are not encompassed in the science-economy dimension) and inaccessible (they simply add to the already intractable problem of incommensurability of choices).

Thus, professional researchers have developed powerful economic tools to measure economic impacts of research, sophisticated bibliometric tools to measure the impacts of research outputs on scientific fields and the course of science and technology, and improved peer review techniques for assessing projects, programs and proposals. But there has been remarkably little progress in the ability to measure directly, systematically, and validly the impacts of research on social change. Many scientists have extolled the communal and cultural value of scientific knowledge.[10] However, without rejecting compelling arguments for the intrinsic value of research in intellectual, cultural, and aesthetic terms,[11] most policymakers and citizens seem to agree that the chief purpose for public funding of research is to improve the quality of life.[12] And most scientists justify it as such.

As Toulmin and his colleagues well understood,[13] the critical problem of choice is not that the chalk-and-cheese problem is at heart a political one, but that we have no satisfactory analytical tools for characterizing the social impacts of chalk or of cheese—for understanding, that is, causal impact and magnitude of effects of research activities on social change. This gap is not surprising when one considers the difficulty of the task and the adolescent stage in the development of research evaluation. Yet, part of the problem is self-imposed: if science policy research in the past forty years had focused as energetically on the problem of social values and social impacts as it did on assessing scientific and economic impacts, we might have made considerably more progress on resolving the problem of choice. This counterfactual suggestion is not mere philosophizing, as we hope to demonstrate by the case studies that follow this paper. Not only are the diverse public values that are invariably deployed to justify scientific choices ascertainable, so are the relations among such values, and, to an extent, the capacity to advance them. With this in mind, and to provide a theoretical and methodological framework for the subsequent case studies, in this paper we will consider: (1) why new approaches and alternatives to research evaluation are needed and how they relate to extant approaches; (2) special difficulties or challenges of developing such approaches; and (3) a specific methodological framework that can be employed, which we here term "public value mapping of science outcomes." Importantly, the work described in this paper and the cases that follow were supported by the U.S. National Science Foundation program on the "Science of Science and Innovation Policy," a program that in turn responds to the observation by a former U.S. presidential science advisor that "the nascent field of the social science of science policy needs to grow up, and quickly."[14]

Growing Up Quickly: Bringing Public Values to Science Policy Processes

U.S. science policy since World War II has to a large extent centered on three inter-related clusters of values. The value cluster we label "Scientific Productivity" includes concerns about the quality and quantity of U.S. research output, perceived or measured world leadership in science, human resources issues, including not only the "pipeline" but also the capacity of scientific fields, and, of course, funding issues, usually framed as "why we need more money for science." These values occupy Toulmin's "science" pole. The second value cluster, corresponding to Toulmin's economic pole, is a continual and pervasive concern with economic productivity, which includes concerns about innovation, technological advance, economic growth, and, in some instances, an implication that economic benefits, widely shared, will advance social goals and quality of life. A third value cluster, "Defense and National Security," includes concerns with weapons superiority, developing non-weapons technology to support the military, and generally using science and technology to enhance military strength expressed regionally and globally.

Obviously there are other core values associated with publicly funded science, and it is certainly the case that U.S. science policy continues to add new values and attendant missions. The 1970s witnessed the emergence of values clusters pertaining to energy and environment. The vast expansion in the 1980s of the National Institutes of Health was rationalized largely on the basis of improved health and well-being. Yet for all four broad areas of research — military, energy, environment, and health — the public values served by such priorities have been significantly subsumed by the demand for scientific excellence in the pursuit of enhanced economic productivity.[15] (For example, the military rationale has been largely subsumed by the core values of science[16] and economic growth.[17]) The result is that the breadth of values expressed in U.S. science policy is significantly wider than the breadth of values directly pursued or assessed. In particular, and as documented in each of our case studies, even where broader public and social values are expressed in science policy development, they are often subverted, reinterpreted, and subjugated to the science-economy axis. The result is a winnowing of values brought to science policy and, overall, a decrement in public values. Thus, our goal in this paper is both to discuss why public values are so easily deflected in science policy, and also to suggest an approach to tracking public values and monitoring and evaluating their influence on science policy.

Before discussing the reasons why we feel it is especially difficult to infuse and maintain public values in science policy, we consider the meaning of "public values." We use this definition:

> *A society's "public values" are those providing normative consensus about (1) the rights, benefits, and prerogatives to which citizens should (and should not) be entitled; (2) the obligations of citizens to society, the state, and one another; (3) and the principles on which governments and policies should be based.*[18]

Our focus on public values requires at present no more precise definition, but we note these implications of the above definition: (1) public values are not static and immutable, there is no "natural law" or "natural rights" meaning to our concept of public value; (2) economic values may in some instances qualify as public values; (3) in some instances and for some policy controversies, there may be insufficient consensus to identify public values (however, this is rare); (4) public values may conflict (e.g., liberty and security, privacy and transparency); (5) public values may or may not be interdependent.

We aim to increase the public values component of science policy, essentially expanding science policies' dominant value sets, by making it possible to consider diverse values using methods and criteria comparable to those already widely accepted and used for scientific and economic values. This goal immediately raises a practical concern: Where can public values be found? A nation's more fundamental laws and, if there is one, its constitution, provide good starting points for identifying public values, though public laws and public policies are best viewed as reflecting and expressing public values rather than establishing them. If policies do not necessarily tap the roots of public values, they often can be taken as surrogates. For example, laws or policies may be justified (e.g., in legislative language or agency strategic plans) on the basis of a public value such as "improvements in public health and longevity," or "decreased infant deaths," or "cleaner air." One can expect disagreements on the need for and desirability of additional increments in any of these values, but few would find the public values themselves to be objectionable.

Another obvious and time-tested approach to tapping citizens' values is by public opinion survey.[19] There is abundant information about such issues as trust in government, division of responsibility between federal and state governments, political ideology, and responsiveness of government.[20] Careful study of general views and values of citizens — studies performed apart from any specific decision — may be useful for making specific choices, such as whether government or the private sector should manage the state prison. This suggestion is not unlike the widespread practice, used especially in local governance, and, recently, in conjunction with new internet and telecommunications technology,[21] of citizen polling.[22] It is simply polling citizens about their most fundamental values.

Third, some recent studies[23] seeking to apply public values criteria have employed a posited model,[24] one that has the value of being explicit and of providing criteria not dissimilar to those from ubiquitously applied market failure models. We discuss the posited model below. Finally, we note that public policy statements can in many instances be taken as de facto public values and that a valuable activity of policy analysts is to track the evolution of those values as policies evolve from ideas premised on diverse and deep values to practical, front-line policies that may be far removed from the values summoned initially to articulate or defend policy ideas. A recent study has applied public value mapping in just this manner to the field of nanoscale science and engineering.[25]

In short, the answer to the question "Where can public values be found?" is that they are located in a great many places: formal scholarly literature, cultural artifacts and traditions, government documents, even some opinion polls (ones receiving valid and representative responses to questions about core values). Toben Jorgensen and Barry Bozeman sought to develop an inventory of public values from such sources, as well as from the public documents and literature on public values, public interest, and governance.[26] Civil societies are necessarily permeated by public values since it is these that provide much of the structure of civil societies to begin with. And, crucially, specific public values are selected to justify science policy and other government actions. A greater problem than identifying public values is understanding them in some analytically useful form.

The Need for Public Values in Science Policy

Many major science policy initiatives are premised on values one might take to be "public values." It is not difficult to find values statements supporting research for environmental protection or health, for example. Why do we feel there is an under-emphasis in public values in science policy? In the first place, public values are more likely to contain as their content the end state outcomes ultimately important to most people. For example, few care about economic growth per se. Economic growth often is taken as a surrogate for well-being or even happiness, but in fact economic growth is by most accounts an instrumental value, a way of achieving broader public values such as family health, leisure, safety, clean air, education and job attainment, and career satisfaction. But why begin with surrogate values? Is it not more sensible to premise policies on the outcomes they should achieve rather than the instruments presumed (perhaps erroneously) to enable those outcomes?

Second, public science is supported by tax dollars, under a tax system that is designed (however inadequately) to be progressive and promote equity. One reason to infuse public values in science policy is that they are by definition broader values and by implication ones more likely to affect all or most citizens. Yet it is by no means clear that the dominant values of scientific excellence and economic productivity are sufficient to account for the broad range of values that the public hopes to gain from science. Most obviously, even the idea of the linear model of science policy, science leading to technology leading to goods and services leading to economic growth, has been thoroughly repudiated by economists of innovation.[27] But even if it were true, the idea that all will benefit from the economic growth ends of science and technology, even though widely asserted, has little plausibility.[28]

Third, one must be vigilant about public values in science policy because they are so easily subverted. This point is subtler than the previous two. We can say that science policy values, and indeed all values expressed in all major policies, are dynamic, and that they evolve in stages, albeit not always in a straightforward fashion and not always sequentially. In most instances, stages include (1) agenda setting, (2) policy design(s), (3) policy choice, (4) policy implementation, and (usually but not always) (5) policy assessment or even systematic evaluation.

Values are important at every stage, but they are volatile. In some cases values change as a result of learning, in some cases they atrophy for lack of advocacy, and in still others they fall under the weight of new values infused by self-interested parties (i.e. politics).

Different types of values are privileged at different stages.[29] In particular, broad public and social values fare well at the very outset when policy rhetoric and ideals are articulated and advocates seek support for policies. At that stage, before policymakers and other parties have settled to the business of making difficult choices and having to mount rationales or even evidence for those choices, it is easy enough to speak broadly about public values. Once the dust settles, and policy options are winnowed, public values are often shunted to the background as advocates and disputants begin to negotiate, usually on a narrower basis. The public values remain as justifications for policies, sometimes even tacked on as rhetorical cover to sub-optimal or patched-together policies that accommodate a great many conflicting values, including many private ones or ones advanced by narrow coalitions.

But public values usually are not advanced during choice processes, for three related reasons. First, science values and economic values are available as accepted and dominant surrogates for all other values. Second, public values are supported by no coherent set of conceptual tools to aid in choice. Third, and in contrast, many such tools are available for science and economic values. In particular, the market failure model is easily available, widely known, anchored in theory assumptions consonant with much of U.S. policymaking, and, thus, it often plays a role in framing choices and in the policy choices themselves. The market failure model also directly links the core science value of knowledge creation to the economic rationale via the discredited yet ever-present linear model. Availability is everything and there is no corresponding model of public values or public interest to compete with market failure and similar decision models based loosely on microeconomics.

After their initial use as rationales or rhetorical devices, public values tend to stay at the rear throughout the remainder of the research and development (R&D) policy process until such a time as public officials or other interested parties began to question whether the policy has had desired results. In some such instances public values make a return appearance, but usually not for long. The reason they are again set to the side is that one quickly finds that both the analytical tools at evaluators' disposal usually have little to do with public values — but mesh quite well with Economic Productivity or Scientific Productivity values sets. One sees this process at work in many public value mapping case studies. For example, the application of nanotechnology to cancer has been justified for its potential to contribute to equitable health outcomes, but in the end is assessed in terms of the broader economic goals of nanotechnology innovation;[30] research on hurricane tracking is supported for its capacity to improve preparedness but continues to displace other, perhaps more vital, lines of research on the basis of claims of scientific excellence and opportunity.[31]

To reiterate our most fundamental point, while there are many reasons to expect that public values will often be displaced in science policy, there are two key problems that can be addressed and remediated. First, the lack of adequate conceptual apparatuses to compete against market failure and other economics-based models means that advocates for public values have limited analytical support. We have begun to address this issue elsewhere[32] by providing a "public values failure" model that is a rough equivalent of the market failure model, and which is adopted in all the following case studies. Second, approaches to evaluating science and technology outcomes have been dominated by techniques and methods anchored either in microeconomics (e.g., cost benefit analysis), supporting the economic productivity value set, or bibliometrics (e.g., citation analysis, co-citation networks) supporting the academic productivity value set. As we will show, however, a competing approach rooted in public value assessment is not merely practicable, but revealing.

Bearing in mind this relationship between public values infusion in science policy and the difficulty of bringing public values to bear in evaluation, we consider in the next section the evolution of research evaluation and, particularly, reasons why public values have been conspicuously absent in both formal evaluations and indicators-based assessments. We focus particularly on the economics origins of research evaluation because most research evaluation remains centered on economics and because bibliometric approaches tend to be less general in their purview and less often in competition with public values concerns.

Economics Bases of Research Evaluation

For present purposes, we mean by "research evaluation" any systematic, data-based (including qualitative data) analysis that seeks as its objective to determine or to forecast the social or economic impacts of research and attendant technical activity.[33] In post hoc research evaluation, the focus is generally on some set of discrete scientific or technological outputs such as publications, patents, or some other expression of intellectual property. Importantly, formal research evaluation always involves some such discrete commodity, either singly or aggregated. Rarely does it begin explicitly with the goals, objectives, or values of the program and then trace back to various outputs and impacts.

Formal research evaluation is a recent invention and its origins tell us much about why it remains dominated by economic analysis and economic values, with public values having made little headway. As late as the 1980s, research evaluation was a field with few practitioners, mostly focused on economic evaluation of industrial firms' internal rate of return.[34] Whereas the Canadian government[35] and some European nations[36] had begun systematic evaluation of publicly funded research, in the United States and many other nations, evaluation of public research impacts was not a field at all, but rather an agglomeration of fragmented, largely isolated works, many unpublished.

To understand the roots of research evaluation one can consider the state-of-the-art as reported in one the earliest reviews focusing specifically on studies of the evaluation of publicly funded research. John Salasin, Lowell Hattery, and Thomas Ramsay's *The Evaluation of Federal Research Programs*[37] stated intention was to "identify useful approaches for evaluating R&D programs conducted and sponsored by the federal government,"[38] and in pursuit of that objective they interviewed more than two hundred experts in evaluation generally or research evaluation specifically, most of them based in industry. The resulting monograph cited 49 papers, including exactly one journal article[39] and one book[40] focusing explicitly on systematic evaluation of government-sponsored research. The monograph identified four problems endemic to evaluating government research impacts, including (1) lack of a straightforward definition of effectiveness; (2) multiple and competing objectives; (3) problems in aggregating products and results, especially across programs; and (4) reconciling political and scientific measures of success—a list that would work just as well today.

Since then, studies and methods of R&D evaluation have greatly proliferated.[41] But most of the problems identified nearly three decades ago in Salasin, Hattery, and Ramsay's pioneering monograph still exist, particularly the problems associated with a focus on discrete R&D outputs. This is especially inimical to public-values-based research evaluations inasmuch as discrete outputs in most cases can hardly begin to provide an adequate gauge for the social change sought from research programs.

Economics Bases for Research Impacts Evaluation

Economic assessments of research and technology generally fall into two basic categories, one of which is most relevant to practical research evaluation. Less relevant to practical evaluation, but influential to broad science policy decision making and rationalization—not to mention the core rhetoric of national politics—are aggregate-level production function analyses,[42] typically focusing on the contribution of technology to national or regional economic growth. More useful for research evaluation are those economic studies seeking social rates of return,[43] that is, approaches that use indicators of marginal economic benefit as a surrogate for estimating the social utility of research and technology. The implication is that wealth can be used to obtain socially desirable outcomes and, thus, increments in wealth can be taken as indicators of social benefit. Among social rate of return approaches, benefit-cost analysis has been most common and most prominent in project- and program-level evaluations of research.[44] Aside from the possibility that one may not wish to assume that economic benefits, measured in monetary terms, fully express or stand in for public values, there is also the issue that very few such studies even begin to consider equity issues in the distribution of benefits. This is not because the evaluators do not recognize the distributional issues in play in science and technology outcomes, but rather because the methods and techniques employed cannot in most instances accommodate distributional variables.[45]

Because economics approaches to research evaluation focus on discrete technological outputs such as patents and articles, they are useful for those who wish to aggregate outputs and consider them in connection with, for example, the performance of technology transfer programs and regional commercialization efforts. The utility of these approaches should be obvious even to skeptics. While the benefits of economics-based approaches to evaluation are explored in more detail elsewhere,[46] we can for present purposes summarize them as follows:

1. Evaluation rooted in neoclassical economics seems to hold forth promise of "harder" more rigorous analysis and, thus, matches well the policymaker's need for metrics to justify expenditures. Typically, these approaches yield numerical assessments of such factors as increments in patents or job creation or firm partnerships.[47]

2. Whereas most approaches to research evaluation are either atheoretical and exclusively tool-oriented, or based on poorly developed theory, economics approaches can draw from decades of development of relatively strong (for the social sciences) theories of the firm, rational choice, and economic growth.

3. While economists recognize that there are values that cannot be well accounted for by monetized units, many have been quite creative in developing quasi-economic techniques based on preference functions and units that mimic rational economic choice (e.g., contingent value analysis[48]).

4. Economic development and growth is a driving impetus for policy and politics throughout the world, and as we have emphasized, science and technology policies are strongly rationalized in terms of pursuit of economic growth. It is not surprising that economics-based approaches to research evaluation underpin economics-rationalized science and technology policy.

Despite their many advantages, economics-based approaches to research evaluation have many limitations, especially if one is interested in gauging the impact of research on public values and social change.

1. As already mentioned, most economic approaches to research evaluation focus on the discrete products of research. While this is methodologically sensible, in that it

promotes measurement, it also promotes a narrowness of view. For example, if one is interested in the long-range capability to produce innovation, then simply counting the results of discrete products may not provide a good insight into the health and viability of scientific fields or a nation's innovation systems. If one is interested in the capacity to produce innovation, rather than just the innovation products themselves, then a focus on "scientific and technical human capital" — the integrated social networks and aggregate skills of scientists[49] — and other, non-economic, approaches to evaluation are required. As well, a focus on particular products and projects works best when there are crisp boundaries (e.g., a single R&D project), while most social objectives do not have easily discernible boundaries and are influenced by myriad causal factors. An approach focused on assessing the capacity to achieve non-economic public values requires methods permitting soft boundaries.

2. Despite efforts to consider implications of future streams of benefit, economics-based evaluations tend to be static. They rarely take into consideration the mutability of the "products" evaluated, much less the changes in the persons and institutions producing them. Thus, an economic analysis of the impacts of a mechanical heart valve innovation would have great difficulty taking into account broad secondary effects such as the implications for a longer-lived population or for equity of health care access, and would also have difficulty tracing the differential impacts of successive generations of the technology.

3. Product-oriented and output-focused evaluations tend to give short shrift to the generation of capacity in science and technology, and to the ability to produce sustained knowledge and innovations.

4. Most important and obvious for present purposes, there are just some things that money can't buy: many social benefits and costs of research are not well or even validly accounted for in monetary units. For example, while economics does a good job of precisely measuring the value of a human life, the question of whether such measures as lifetime earnings capabilities are also accurate indicators is utterly laden with values that are non-economic. Indeed, as the subsequent case studies document, research is generally justified on non-monetary values and, thus, the evaluation of research in purely monetary terms amounts to a sort of bait-and-switch, where public policy intent becomes transformed by subjecting it to the available theories and evaluation methods, as if one went to a doctor for a health examination and ended up with an assessment of one's earning potential.

It is this latter limitation, the inadequacy of economics-based approaches for measuring and providing understanding about the social impacts of research, that is our chief concern here. To be sure, economics approaches are not unique in their inadequacy for this task. Currently, no satisfactory method (except, perhaps, case studies that are very context specific and rarely generalizable) has been developed to validly assess the impacts of research on social change.

Social Impacts of Research: Challenges to Theory and Method

A methodological problem in all approaches to research evaluation is that research is often only one factor in determining social outcomes and is rarely the most important one. The science advisor to President Obama has identified a series of "challenges" for U.S. science and technology that include "better [healthcare] outcomes for all at lower cost," "poverty eradication," "transforming the global energy system," and "reducing risks from biological and nuclear weapons,"[50] but of course when research plays any significant role in achieving such desirable social outcomes it is in concert with a great many other social, economic, and natural determinants. The outcomes, that is, are highly overdetermined. In such circumstances, it is virtually impossible to parse out the contribution of research; this is what Toulmin meant when he observed that "we are sheerly ignorant about many of the relevant factors and relationships" connecting science to outcomes.[51] Our ability to trace these links is not much better now than it was in 1964. Whether one employs standard economics-based approaches such as cost-benefit analysis, social indicators monitoring, and social accounting, or even in-depth case studies, causal attribution for complex social impacts is always fraught with great difficulty.

A related problem pertains to the "dependent variables." Determining causation is difficult enough, but often the effects are themselves interwoven in ways that are difficult to understand or unravel. Social outcomes occur in clusters. For example, in the case of automobile safety, research has shown that safety innovations such as disk brakes or even seat belt laws can actually result in more accidents as drivers' behavior becomes more risky as a result of technologies providing an increased sense of security.[52] Similarly, many of the social and public health gains that have been realized by smoking cessation programs are offset by the fact that reductions of smoking have contributed in some degree to the increase in obesity rates. Case studies demonstrate these complex and contradictory effects: technology transfer programs may lead both to increased wealth and to greater inequities;[53] advances in nanotechnology-based cancer treatments appear likely to increase health inequities that are already significant in the United States.[54] In short, in modeling social outcomes from research one has difficulty not only tracing cause to effect, but also setting boundaries on effects. This is one of the reasons why we have adopted an open, "mapping" approach to evaluating public values. We are not seeking a deterministic model, but rather an approach that can enhance insight, debate, and expectations — and thus improve decision outcomes.

A related complication to developing public values theory in general and public values in science policy in particular is that not all values are public values, and means of demarcating values are hardly clear-cut. Consider this general definition of "value":

> *A value is a complex and broad-based assessment of an object or set of objects (where the objects may be concrete, psychological, socially constructed, or a combination of all three) characterized by both cognitive and emotive elements, arrived at after some deliberation, and, because a value is part of the individual's definition of self, it is not easily changed and it has the potential to elicit action.*[55]

Given this not unfamiliar description of value and the previous definition of "public value," it is perhaps apparent that the distance traveled from one to the next is considerable. From the standpoint of empirical social science, the fact that values held by individuals are not agent-neutral provides limits in values analysis. However, if the role of social science is limited with respect to such private values, it is virtually unbounded (though poorly developed) with respect to *public* values, because public values are typically instrumental, or employed instrumentally.

In seeking public values and their application, public value theory embraces empirical social science.[56] We begin with the assumption that all instrumental values, public, economic, or private, can be viewed as causal hypotheses that are, in principle, subject to empirical tests. From here it becomes possible to seek and even test public values statements found in broadly held articulations of desirable states toward which progress can be assessed ("decreased infant deaths"; "cleaner air"). We are not after prediction or proof, we are after plausibility, which seems to us a desirable, reasonable and achievable expectation for science policymaking (or any policymaking, for that matter). Ryan Meyer (in the next chapter) shows, for example, that the internal logic of the climate science policy process in the United States is completely incoherent, and for that reason alone can have little capacity to achieve the goals that justify and motivate the program. What makes this analysis possible is the recognition of the public values embedded in the process, and the logical relations (or lack thereof) among these public values.

Getting on With It: A Sober and Humble Rationale for Evaluation of Social Impacts of Research

The foregoing section identifies formidable obstacles to assessing the social impacts of research and, unfortunately, the list above is not exhaustive.[57] Yet, whether or not fully adequate analytical tools are available, policymakers will continue to make choices about research funding. These choices will continue to be premised on a causal logic. As we have discussed, and as the cases document in greater detail, in making decisions about investments in research, policymakers make assumptions about the effects of those investments on such social outcomes as public health, transportation systems, education, and wealth creation. In most instances those choices will, perforce, be based on limited information provided by interested parties. Any evidence that can be brought to bear on those choices, even when fraught with known methodological limitations, is likely an improvement over intuition, habit, rough-hewn ideology, political self-interest, powerful myths about how the world works, and other such biases that so typically guide investments in research aimed at solving social problems. If nothing else, new approaches can contribute to: (a) disciplined discussion, healthy skepticism, and reflection; and (b) openness to other, clearer, non-scientific options. It is in that spirit that we began to fashion the approach we refer to as "public value mapping."

Public Value Mapping and Its Lineage

Put simply, public value mapping (PVM) is an approach to identifying the public value premises of public policy and then tracking their evolution and impacts on policies and, ultimately, social outcomes. The primary rationales for the public value mapping of science are that (1) the focus of science policy should be on social goals and public values, and (2) current research evaluation and science policy analysis methods and techniques are not sufficient for analysis of the impacts of research on public values and fundamental social goals.

From the outset, public value mapping, an approach aspiring to practical application, has been rooted in public value theory. While we do not have space or great need to go into the details of public value theory, it is perhaps useful to provide a modest introduction.

A PVM taproot is new theoretical thinking about the value of knowledge and its assessment.[58] To a large extent, recent work on the value of knowledge is a response to limitations of economic theory in understanding knowledge value.[59] Economists have never made much headway valuing scientific knowledge.[60] Scientific knowledge, in economic terms, is generally considered a pure public good, and thus an example of pricing inefficiency. In the world of public finance economics, theory loses its power in instances where markets do not work in a straightforward fashion and where efficient pricing is impossible. However, it is generally in these realms that public values and, for that matter, governments and policies operate. Thus, stretching economic theory to the breaking point, rather than developing theories of public and social value, seems a poor route forward.

Philosopher Elizabeth Anderson presents an especially interesting analysis of economic value and value theory as it pertains to economics.[61] Anderson's position, one that would perhaps seem radical to many social scientists, is that economic values are inherently monistic. Because of the fundamental structure of assumptions built into economic values, they cannot accommodate pluralistic approaches to values. To put it another way, an analysis valuing exchanges, commodities, and services on the basis of market standards pre-empts simultaneous, comparable reference to other standards.[62] These assertions have direct implications for models of innovation and the impacts of scientific and technical knowledge.

In addition to philosophy of values, public value theory draws from the field of public administration.[63] In public administration, a useful theory is a theory in practice.[64] Perhaps for that reason, much theory that underpins analysis of public values is anchored in various aspects of pragmatism[65] and especially developing communitarian and procedural approaches suitable for the identification of and support of public values. Public administration literature[66] has begun to move from philosophical discussion of the public interest to a concern with identifying aspects of publicness or public values. Case studies focus on how public values are infused (or not) in public decisions.[67] To a large extent, cases such as Meyer's in the next chapter have that intent: to demonstrate and assess the extent of public values in public policies and to trace their roles and impacts.

Public value mapping can best be thought of as an analytical confederation. It is not a unified method nor does it aspire to closure. Indeed, it is not a method, per se. It is better viewed as a loose set of heuristics for developing analyses of public values. Public value mapping begins with a set of core assumptions but these are not inviolable. Box 1[68] provides these core assumptions. The cases following this paper, diverse as they are, strive to conform to these assumptions.

Box 1. Core Assumptions of Public Value Mapping

1. PVM is prospective (analyzing planned or projected research activities), "formative" (analyzing such activities as they are occurring), or "summative" (evaluating activities and their impacts after they have occurred).

2. It seeks to take into account the highest order impacts of activities (i.e. broad social aggregates) and, thus, focuses on social indices and social indicators.

3. It is multilevel in its analysis, seeking to show linkages among particular program activities of an agency or institution, activities of other agencies or institutions, relationships — either intended or not — among various institutional actors and their activities.

4. Related to number three, PVM is concerned with understanding the environmental context for research and related programmatic activities, locating the activities and their institutional actors in terms of other actors in the environment, the constraints, opportunities and resources presented in the environment.

5. Research in any field by any method is embedded in a social context; in PVM, analysis of the social context of the research (i.e. characteristics of research performers, their attributes and social relations) is a part of the analysis.

6. PVM is guided by a "public value model of science outcomes" rather than a market-based or market failure model. PVM explicitly rejects evaluation and assessment based on commodification of research values and outcomes. Market prices are viewed as weak partial in-

---

dicators of the social value of research and research outcomes. Even as a partial indicator, market value is considered in terms of not only magnitude but also distribution and equity criteria.

7. Since market value is eschewed in PVM and since social values are not interpersonally transmissible, PVM anchors its outcomes values in a wide range of criteria derived from diverse sources including: (1) official, legitimated statements of policy goals; (2) goals implicit in poorly articulated policy statements; (3) government agencies' goal statements in strategic plans; (4) aggregated statements of value represented in opinion polls; (5) official policy statements by government actors; and (6) official policy statements by relevant NGOs.

8. PVM analyzes (maps) the causal logic relating goals statements (any of the above) to science and research activities, impacts, and outcomes, both measured and hypothesized. When possible, this analysis begins with the causal logic articulated by responsible officials. The causal logics, explicit or implicit, that are the basis of science and research activities are then considered in relation to various plausible alternative hypotheses and alternative causal logics invented by the analyst.

9. PVM is not an analytical technique or even a set of analytical techniques, but a model that includes a guiding theoretical framework (public value theory), a set of assumptions and procedures. Research techniques employed in PVM depend upon the needs and possibilities afforded by the context of its application. The only technical approach used in all applications of PVM is the case study method.

10. After gathering data to test hypotheses about causal logics and outcomes, appropriate analysis (selected depending upon specific analytical techniques used) is employed to test hypotheses and, at the same time,

measure impacts and outcomes. Results of analysis focus on interrelationships among the causal logic, the environmental context and measured impacts and outcomes.

11. PVM concludes with a linkage of impact and outcome measures back to aggregate social indicators or other appropriately broad-based, trans-institutional, trans-research program measures of social well-being.

12. PVM concludes with analysis and recommendations focusing on possible changes (in research or program activity, causal logic, or implementation) that seem likely to lead to improved social outcomes.

Public Value Mapping Criteria Model

Just as important as the core assumptions of PVM are the analytical heuristics it brings to bear. Among these, we have found the public value mapping criteria model is useful for structuring analysis and assessment. These PVM criteria begin with a set of general criteria developed for judging public values failure,[69] but there is no claim that the criteria are canonical or exhaustive. Indeed, as presented in several of the cases that follow, the PVM approach encourages the further articulation of the criteria developed previously as well as the stipulation and justification of new criteria.

Public value criteria serve as heuristics for deliberation. Discussion and argumentation about public values and their measurement proves less troubling in those instances when there is a clear starting point, when one has at one's disposal public value criteria. Even when debates rage about choices of public value, concepts of public value, and the relevance of public values to particular states-of-affairs, one has hope of making headway if there are recognized public value criteria structuring arguments. Perhaps more important, the lack of public values criteria explains in part why economic frameworks such as market failure have often held sway, even in cases where they seem poorly adapted to the problem at hand.

Initial criteria for judging public values failure emerged in large measure as a conceptual parallel to traditional market failure criteria. While these public value criteria were set as companions to market failure criteria, initially they were posited rather than derived empirically. However, the criteria were subsequently submitted to test in various case studies, including cases pertaining to genetic modification,[70] public health issues in influenza vaccine,[71] and nanoscale science,[72] among others.

Public value failure is not a conceptual alternative to market failure. Rather, *public values failure occurs when neither the market nor public sector provides goods and services required to achieve public values.* This implies that public values can be realized (or can fail) under any set of market conditions. The chief point of PVM criteria is to expand the discussion of public policy and management by assuming that government (and market organizations as well) need be more than a means of ensuring market successes and technical efficiency in pricing structures. A fundamental assumption of the PVM model is that, contrary to current political dogma and academic thinking, market failure actually tells us little about whether government should "intervene." With PVM, the key policy question becomes: "Whether or not the market is efficient is there nonetheless a failure to provide an essential public value?" The PVM criteria model provides multiple lenses for viewing this question. It is not a precise decision-making tool (à la benefit-cost analysis), but a framework to (1) promote deliberation about public value (and its relation to economic value), and (2) provide guideposts for analysis and evaluation, within the context of public value mapping.

The PVM criteria themselves (Table 6.1[73]) are not, then, actual public values but, rather, a set of diagnostics applicable to questions of science policy[74] and research evaluation. Since science policy, as is the case with nearly all legitimate public policies, seeks ultimately to produce positive social change, it is subject to many of the same public and social values as other policies and, thus, the same values criteria prove useful. Case studies should employ the PVM criteria model in their analysis and different aspects are relevant in different cases.

Table 6.1: Public Failure and Public Policy: A General Diagnostic Model

Public Failure Criterion	Failure Definition	Science Policy Example
Mechanisms for values articulation and aggregation	Political processes and social cohesion insufficient to ensure effective communication and processing of public values.	Peer review, the favored means of making decisions of individual-level projects, is appropriated for decisions about huge scientific programs, resulting in the displacement of social goals for more easily resolved technical goals.
Imperfect monopolies	Private provision of goods and services permitted even though government monopoly deemed in the public interest.	When public authorities abrogate their responsibility for overseeing public safety in clinical trials for medical research, there is potential for violation of public trust and public value.
Scarcity of providers	Despite the recognition of a public value and agreement on the public provision of goods and services, they are not provided because of the unavailability of providers.	The premature privatization of the Landsat program shows that a scarcity of providers can create a public failure potentially remediable by government action.

213

Short time horizon	A short-term time horizon is employed when a longer term view shows that a set of actions is counter to public value.	Policy for energy R&D, by considering the short term, fails to fully capture the costs of global climate change on future generations.
Substitutability vs. conservation of resources	Policies focus on either substitutability or indemnification even in cases when there is no satisfactory substitute.	"No-net-loss" policies fail to take into account the non-substitutability of many natural organisms ranging from wetlands protection to prohibiting the sale of human organs on the open market.
Benefit hoarding	Public commodities and services have been captured by individuals or groups, limiting distribution to the population.	A prime technical success of genetic engineering, the "terminator gene," proves an excellent means of enhancing the efficiency of agricultural markets, potentially to the detriment of millions of subsistence farmers throughout the world.

Developing and Applying PVM

While considerable conceptual work has already been undertaken to provide building blocks for public value mapping, efforts thus far have been incremental. The goal of this paper and the cases cited is to begin to create a viable approach that can generate practical analytical tools and insights about public values in science policy. It is also to inspire others working in the field of science policy research to critique, adopt, transform, and apply public value mapping to what remains the central unresolved challenge of science policy practice: the development of evaluative methods that can help us make progress—theoretical, methodological, and most important, practical—on the problem of choice.

All PVM approaches begin as case study analyses. The cases should strive to implement the following four steps (though they vary in the extent to which each is emphasized). At this point in the development of the model we consider these steps to be the procedural core of PVM:

1. A search for "public values" pertaining to the case: We have discussed several approaches to identifying public values, including (a) surrogate public values (government mission statements, strategic plans, and broad policies, statutes); (b) distillation of public values from relevant academic literatures; and (c) public values as expressed in public opinion polls and public statements.

2. Application of the PVM criteria: Each case study examines the course of public values in light of the criteria presented in the PVM criteria model, using these criteria as a means of assessing possible failures in achieving public values. Not only do analysts apply useful and appropriate PVM criteria, but they are encouraged to identify criteria that do not fit their case and to begin to develop new PVM criteria that may be useful for their case and may be generalizable to others. There is an explicit expectation that the PVM criteria model will expand and refine its criteria, not to such an extent that highly idiosyncratic criteria will be included but to include criteria that have some potential for use in multiple cases and analyses.

3. Developing value analysis chains: Among the many reasons why public value analysis of science policy has made little headway is that values analysis itself is remarkably underdeveloped. One of the difficulties of values analysis[75] is that analysts sometimes fail to consider interrelationships among values, including such features as values hierarchies, conditional relations

among values, logical structures of multiple and related values, and ends-means relations.[76] One of the key objectives of the public value mapping is thus to develop the ability to clarify relationships among values, and assess how those relations influence the links between the conduct of research and the pursuit of particular desired outcomes.

4. Graphically display the relations between market failure/success and public values failure/success, using the public values failure grid.[77] The grid provides a qualitative, synoptic view of the results of the public value mapping, and thus helps with both communication and comparison. (For reasons of space, we do not illustrate the grid here; it can be seen used in the next chapter.)

In addition to adopting these four steps to ensure some intercomparability of both method and result, cases should also (1) perform the traditional case study role of "thick description"; (2) provide a context for the application of a variety of analytical approaches, including logic models and value chain analysis; (3) help determine the extent to which it is possible to distill public values in a satisfactory manner; (4) extend the theories upon which PVM is premised; and (5) point the way for further development of analytical tools.

Finally, PVM case studies should implicitly adopt one or more analytical lenses to guide their development. The analytical lenses can be thought of as essentially master hypotheses about possible determinants of the public value outcomes for the cases. We articulate the lenses in terms of the following contextual factors that affect the social impacts of research and science and technology policy.

a. *Characteristics of the knowledge that the research produces.* In some instances knowledge creation processes, innovation, and, ultimately, social impacts are very much governed by inherent characteristics of the science or technology (e.g., "technology push"), for example, conventional chemistry often uses stoichiometric reagents as a basis for creating desired products because they are convenient, economical, and traditional. But they are also wasteful and polluting. In contrast, "green" chemistry, which includes as an explicit public value the reduction of chemical pollution and toxicity, focuses on using catalysts to achieve the same economic and public values as conventional chemistry, but with much less waste.[78]

b. *Institutional arrangements and management affecting knowledge production and use.* This lens pertains to the configuration of producers and users of scientific and technical knowledge, the ways in which they interact, their internal and network management. In the case of climate change research, for example, institutional networks developed largely in support of values associated with ensuring high quality science, a situation that has proven very hard to alter despite a growing awareness that the current arrangements are not serving a range of public values that justify the investment in climate science.[79] Catherine Slade shows that, in research on nanotechnology-based cancer treatments, insufficient attention to questions of diversity and inclusiveness in both basic and clinical research potentially undermines the capacity of the research to reduce health disparities.[80]

c. *Policy and political domains of knowledge production and use.* This analytical lens examines the political, legal, public policy, and normative factors that determine research choices, utilization, and impact (e.g., characteristics of intellectual property policy or structures of budgets for research). Walter Valdivia shows, for example, that although congressional debates over technology transfer policy in the early 1980s did indeed show attention to a broad range of public values, the legislative and regulatory processes ended up neglecting such values for a much narrower focus on economic efficiency and wealth creation.[81]

Conclusion

We began this paper with Stephen Toulmin's chalk-and-cheese metaphor pertaining to incommensurate activities grouped together under the category "science." His metaphor speaks to specious aggregation, a difficulty that in turn conceals a still greater problem: omission. We may recognize that biochemistry cannot easily be played off against subatomic particle physics, but in its focus on the outputs of science qua science, research evaluation elides the deeper policy question: on what basis can we decide the extent to which either is worth doing? In publicly funded science, public values are often displaced, minimized, misrepresented, or altogether missing. A common scenario (we hope not the most common) is "bait and switch." During the agenda-setting phase of public policy, tax dollars spent on science and research are rationalized in terms of explicit and invariably lofty public values (everything is worth doing). After securing a place in the policy agenda, science policies fall prey to the same interest group politics and forces of institutional inertia that characterize most policy domains, often leading to incremental changes in the status quo. Scientists find ways to rationalize just how the research they have always been doing fits perfectly with the new goals and public value rhetoric. We could refer to this as the "phrenology problem": were the government to provide a billion dollars for phrenology research, many scientists would find ways to call themselves phrenologists. Institutions are no less indefatigable in their adaptation. Bureaucratic sinkholes serve as burial ground for public values. By the time research policy plays itself out at the level of individual choice (that is to say, the same scientists conducting science in the same institutional settings in which they have always worked), we can only hope for some remnants of public value. At this point, any public values that may have been prominent at the outset of research policies are likely only to be resurrected to justify the next increment of funding.

This is, of course, a pessimistic view, perhaps even a bit extreme, but generally descriptive of most instances of large-scale policy choice in science, where high minded beginnings translate into claims of progress measured by publications, citations, or patents and justified in terms of "scientific excellence" or contributions to "innovation" or economic growth. One role of evaluation, including research policy evaluation, is to hold feet to the fire. In the cases where the pessimistic scenario described above is also a most accurate one, should we not expect research evaluators to play a role as truthsayers, or if that is too ambitious a term, an alternative voice? By this point, research evaluation has developed serious methods and techniques, and even if the term "science of science policy" remains more aspiration than reality, evaluation has made great strides. However, those strides have been in three directions, none leading directly to the amelioration of what we may refer to, with apologies to Toulmin, as the chalk-cheese-choice problem. The oldest form of systematic evaluation, peer review, while changed, remains recognizable to peer reviewers of decades ago. Would we expect peer reviewers, when "peer" is defined in terms of technical expertise, to provide insight into bait and switch or the displacement of public values? Greater strides have been made in the application of economics to research evaluation. While there is some potential for adapting microeconomics and cost-benefit analysis to research evaluation, most any economist will readily declare that the discipline does very well with questions of efficiency and is generally unsuited to questions of equity. To the extent that public values in science questions are efficiency questions, then economics has much to contribute. Perhaps the greatest strides in research evaluation have been in the area of bibliometrics. In less than thirty years, the field has gone from citation counts to all manner of sophisticated analyses of academic productivity and collaboration networks. That is to say, bibliometrics can tell us much about the input side of science and quite a bit about the output side, but, as we have said, the impact focus remains narrow: productivity and collaboration.

Public value mapping is not as venerable as peer review, not as precise as economics-based evaluation, and not as ruthlessly objective as bibliometrics. However, through detailed exploration of cases (such as the chapter by Meyer in this book, as well as other cases we have cited) using the PVM lens we have outlined here, it is possible to directly address the science policy elephant in the room: the public value of publicly funded science. We recognize that these are tentative steps, but at least they are looking in the right direction, rather than under the proverbial lamp post that shines its bright light on what we can already do—assess scientific excellence and economic productivity—while leaving the rest in abject obscurity. We believe PVM case studies (such as Meyer's in the next chapter) represent progress toward addressing the chalk-cheese-choice problem but, even if they do not, we hope they will stimulate others to give more thought to the formidable challenge of expanding the domain of exploration to address and assess what is surely the core claim of science policy: that science outcomes should serve and advance public values.

Notes

[1] E.g., see C. Freeman, *The Economics of Hope: Essays on Technical Change, Economic Growth and the Environment* (London, UK: Thompson Learning, 1992).

[2] E.g., D. Kevles, *The Physicists: The History of a Scientific Community in Modern America* (Cambridge, MA: Harvard University Press, 1995).

3 E. Shils, "Introduction," in *Criteria for Scientific Development: Public Policy and National Goals*, E. Shils, ed. (Cambridge, MA: MIT Press, 1968), xiv.

4 Ibid.

5 M. Polanyi, "The Republic of Science: It's Political and Economic Theory," *Minerva* 1, no. 1 (1962): 54-73; A. Weinberg, "Criteria for Scientific Choice," *Minerva* 1, no. 2 (1963): 159-171, and S. Toulmin, "The Complexity of Scientific Choice: A Stocktaking," *Minerva* 2, no. 3 (1964): 343-359.

6 S. Toulmin, "The Complexity of Scientific Choice: A Stocktaking," *Minerva* 2, no. 3 (1964): 343-359.

7 Ibid., 343.

8 Ibid., 348.

9 Ibid., 357.

10 E.g., J. Ziman, *Public Knowledge: The Social Dimensions of Science* (Cambridge, UK: Cambridge University Press, 1968).

11 E. P. Fischer, *Beauty and the Beast: The Aesthetic Moment in Science*, trans. E. Oehlkers (New York, NY: Plenum Trade, 1997).

12 H. G. Johnson, "Federal Support of Basic Research: Some Economic Issues," *Minerva* 3, no. 4 (1965): 500-514.

13 S. Toulmin, "The Complexity of Scientific Choice: A Stocktaking," *Minerva* 2, no. 3 (1964): 343-359.

14 J. Marburger, Speech at the 30th Annual AAAS Forum on Science and Technology Policy in Washington, DC (Apr. 21, 2005).

15 E.g., D. Sarewitz, *Frontiers of Illusion: Science, Technology, and the Politics of Progress* (Philadelphia, PA: Temple University Press, 1996).

16 I.e., via the crucial role of the U.S. Department of Defense in building academic science programs, e.g., see S. W. Leslie, *The Cold War and American Science* (New York, NY: Columbia University Press, 1993).

[17] E.g., "dual use technology" and "spin-offs," e.g., see V. Ruttan, *Is War Necessary for Economic Growth?* (New York, NY: Oxford University Press, 2006).

[18] B. Bozeman, *Public Values and Public Interest: Counterbalancing Economic Individualism* (Washington, DC: Georgetown University Press, 2007): 37.

[19] A distinction should be made between public opinion and public values: Whereas public opinion is highly volatile, both in its concerns and its directions, public values are much more stable. New public values may enter and old ones may exit but generally only after great social change and the passing of generations.

[20] See J. Nye, "In Government We Don't Trust," *Foreign Policy* 108, no. 2 (1997): 99-111.

[21] E.g., J. Budd and L. Connaway, "University Faculty and Networked Information: Results of a Survey," *Journal of the American Society for Information Science* 48, no. 9 (1997): 843-852.

[22] E.g., T. van Houten and H. Hatry, *How to Conduct a Citizen Survey* (Washington, DC: American Planning Association, 1987).

[23] B. Bozeman and D. Sarewitz, "Public Values and Public Failure in U.S. Science Policy," *Science and Public Policy* 32, no. 2 (2005): 119-136; M. Feeney and B. Bozeman, "The 2004-2005 Influenza Episode as a Case of Public Failure," *Journal of Public Integrity* 9, no. 2 (2007): 179-195.

[24] B. Bozeman, J. Dietz, and M. Gaughan, "Scientific and technical human capital: An alternative model for research evaluation, *International Journal of Technology Management* 22, nos. 7-8 (2001): 716-740.

[25] E. Fisher, C. Slade, D. Anderson, and B. Bozeman, "The Public Value of Nanotechnology?" *Scientometrics* 85, no. 1 (2010): 29-39.

[26] T. B. Jorgensen and B. Bozeman, "Public values: An Inventory," *Administration & Society* 39, no. 3 (2007): 354-381.

[27] E.g., N. Rosenberg, "How Exogenous is Science?" in *Inside the Black Box* (New York, NY: Cambridge University Press, 1982), 141-159.

[28] E.g., E. Woodhouse and D. Sarewitz, "Science Policies for Reducing Societal Inequities," *Science and Public Policy* 34, no. 2 (2007): 139-150.

[29] F. R. Baumgartner and B. D. Jones, "Agenda Dynamics and Policy Subsystems," *Journal of Politics* 53, no. 4 (1991): 1044-1074.

[30] C. P. Slade, "Public Value Mapping of Equity in Emerging Nanomedicine," *Minerva* 49, no. 1 (2011): 71-86.

[31] G. E. Maricle, "Prediction as an Impediment to Preparedness: Lessons from the U.S. Hurricane and Earthquake Research Enterprises," *Minerva* 49, no. 1 (2011): 87-111.

[32] B. Bozeman, J. Dietz, and M. Gaughan, "Scientific and technical human capital: An alternative model for research evaluation, *International Journal of Technology Management* 22, nos. 7-8 (2001): 716-740; B. Bozeman and D. Sarewitz, "Public Values and Public Failure in U.S. Science Policy," *Science and Public Policy* 32, no. 2 (2005): 119-136.

[33] By "research assessment," not our focus in this paper, we mean an investigation with similar objectives but not necessarily including data and perhaps premised on indicators but with no formal analysis. (For a more detailed but similar definition, see T. Luukkonen-Gronow, "Scientific Research Evaluation: A Review of Methods and Various Contexts of their Application," *R&D Management* 17, no. 3 (2007): 207-221.

[34] During the history of modern science and technology policy and research evaluation, the most prominent approach to assessment has been peer review. While recognizing that peer review is crucially important, the present study focuses on systematic and potentially quantitative or mixed-method approaches and, thus, does not discuss peer review approaches to research evaluation. Similarly, this paper does not deal with the many and increasingly useful bibliometic approaches to research evaluation.

[35] For a history of government mandated research evaluation in Canada, including research evaluation, see Auditor General, *Program Evaluation in the Federal Government*, *Treasury Board of Canada: The Case for Program Evaluation* (1993). For a history of research evaluation activities in Canada, see A. Barbarie, "Evaluating Federal R&D in Canada," in *Evaluating R&D Impacts: Methods*

and Practice, B. Bozeman and J. Melkers, eds. (Norwell, MA: Kluwer, 1993), 155-162.

[36] Several publications provide synoptic reviews of the history and methods of research evaluation in European nations; see, for example, T. Luukkonen, "Research evaluation in Europe: State of the art," *Research Evaluation* 11, no. 2 (2002): 81-84.

[37] J. Salasin, L. Hattery, and T. Ramsay, "The Evaluation of Federal Research Programs," MITRE Technical Report MTR-80W123 (June 1980).

[38] Ibid., 1.

[39] A. Rubenstein, "Effectiveness of Federal Civilian-Oriented R&D Programs," *Policy Studies Journal* 5, no. 2 (1976): 217-227.

[40] F. M. Andrews, *Scientific Productivity: The Effectiveness of Research Groups in Six Countries* (Ann Arbor, MI: University of Michigan Press, 1979).

[41] For an overview of approaches and methods for research evaluation, see B. Bozeman and J. Melkers, eds., *Evaluating R&D Impacts: Methods and Practice* (Boston, MA: Kluwer, 1993); OECD, *The Evaluation of Scientific Research: Selected Experiences* (Paris, France: OECD, Committee for Scientific and Technological Policy, Document OECD/GD (97)194, 1997); and OECD, *Enhancing Public Research Performance through Evaluation, Impact   Assessment and Priority Setting* (Paris, France: OECD, Directorate for Science, Technology, and Industry).

[42] E.g., R. M. Solow, "Technical change and the aggregate production function," *Review of Economics and Statistics* 39, no. 3 (1957): 312-320.

[43] E.g., C. I. Jones and J. C. Williams, "Measuring the Social Return to R&D," *Quarterly Journal of Economics* 113, no. 4 (1998): 1119-1135.

[44] See, for example, A. N. Link, "Economic Performance Measures for Evaluating Government Sponsored Research," *Scientometrics* 36, no. 3 (1996): 325-342; A. N. Link, *Evaluating Public Sector Research & Development* (New York, NY: Greenwood, 1996); R. Ruegg, "Guidelines for Economic Evaluation of the Advanced Technology Program," NIST Internal Report 5896 (1996); D. B. Audretsch, B. Bozeman, K. Combs, M. Feldman, A. Link, D.

Siegel, P. Stephan, G. Tassey, and C. Wessner, "The Economics of Science and Technology," *Journal of Technology Transfer* 27, no. 2 (2002): 155-203.

[45] K. Martens, *Equity Concerns and Cost-Benefit Analysis: Opening the Black Box* (Washington, DC: Transportation Research Board, Paper #09-0586, 2009).

[46] A. N. Link, *Evaluating Public Sector Research & Development* (New York, NY: Greenwood, 1996).

[47] R. Kostoff, "The Metrics of Science and Technology," *Scientometrics* 50, no. 2 (2001): 353-361; J. P. Holdren, "Science and Technology Policy in the Obama Administration," remarks for the Business Higher Education Forum, Washington, DC (Jun. 16, 2009).

[48] R. Cummings and L. Taylor, "Unbiased Value Estimates for Environmental Goods: A Cheap Talk Design for the Contingent Valuation Method," *American Economic Review* 89, no. 3 (1999): 649-665.

[49] B. Bozeman, J. Dietz, and M. Gaughan, "Scientific and technical human capital: An alternative model for research evaluation, *International Journal of Technology Management* 22, nos. 7-8 (2001): 716-740.

[50] J. P. Holdren, "Science and Technology Policy in the Obama Administration," remarks for the Business Higher Education Forum, Washington, DC (Jun. 16, 2009).

[51] S. Toulmin, "The Complexity of Scientific Choice: A Stocktaking," *Minerva* 2, no. 3 (1964): 343.

[52] E.g., G. B. Adams, "Enthralled with Modernity: The Historical Context of Knowledge and Theory Development in Public Administration," *Public Administration Review* 52, no. 4 (1992): 363-373.

[53] W. Valdivia, "The Stakes in Bayh-Dole: Public Values Beyond the Pace of Innovation," *Minerva* 49, no. 1 (2011): 25-46.

[54] C. P. Slade, "Public Value Mapping of Equity in Emerging Nanomedicine," *Minerva* 49, no. 1 (2011): 71-86.

[55] Adapted from G. F. Gaus, *Value and Justification: The Foundations of Liberal Theory* (New York, NY: Cambridge University Press, 1990).

[56] B. Bozeman, "Public Value Failure and Market Failure," *Public Administration Review* 62, no. 2 (2002): 145-161; B. Bozeman, *Public Values and Public Interest: Counterbalancing Economic Individualism* (Washington, DC: Georgetown University Press, 2007).

[57] For a more detailed discussion of problems in tracing social and public value impacts, see B. Bozeman, *Public Values and Public Interest: Counterbalancing Economic Individualism* (Washington, DC: Georgetown University Press, 2007).

[58] See B. Bozeman, *Public Values and Public Interest: Counterbalancing Economic Individualism* (Washington, DC: Georgetown University Press, 2007) for a summary.

[59] E.g., B. Bozeman and J. R. Rogers, "A Churn Model of Scientific Knowledge Value: Internet Researchers as a Knowledge Value Collective," *Research Policy* 31, no. 5 (2002): 769-794.

[60] See F. Machlup, *The Production and Distribution of Knowledge in the United States* (Princeton, NJ: Princeton University Press, 1962).

[61] E. Anderson, *Value in Ethics and Economics* (Cambridge, MA: Harvard University Press, 1993).

[62] See E. Marmolo, "A Constitutional Theory of Public Goods," *Journal of Economic Behavior & Organization* 38, no. 1 (1999): 27-42; E. Anderson, *Value in Ethics and Economics* (Cambridge, MA: Harvard University Press, 1993).

[63] E.g., J. W. van Deth, and E. Scarbrough, *The Impact of Values* (Oxford, UK: Oxford University, 1995); J. Kirlin, "What Government Must Do Well: Creating Value for Society," *Journal of Public Administration Theory and Research* 6, no. 1 (1996): 161-185; B. Bozeman, *Public Values and Public Interest: Counterbalancing Economic Individualism* (Washington, DC: Georgetown University Press, 2007).

[64] G. B. Adams, "Enthralled with Modernity: The Historical Context of Knowledge and Theory Development in Public Administration," *Public Administration Review* 52, no. 4 (1992): 363-373.

[65] E.g., P. M. Shields, "Pragmatism: Exploring Public Administration's Policy Imprint," *Administration and Society* 28, no. 3 (1996): 390-411; J. Garrison, "Pragmatism and Public Administration," *Administration and Society* 32, no. 4 (2000): 458-478; B. Bozeman, *Public Values and Public Interest: Counterbalancing Economic Individualism* (Washington, DC: Georgetown University Press, 2007).

[66] E.g., J. W. van Deth, and E. Scarbrough, *The Impact of Values* (Oxford, UK: Oxford University, 1995); J. Kirlin, "What Government Must Do Well: Creating Value for Society," *Journal of Public Administration Theory and Research* 6, no. 1 (1996): 161-185.

[67] E.g., T. B. Jorgensen and B. Bozeman, "Public values: An Inventory," *Administration & Society* 39, no. 3 (2007): 354-381.

[68] B. Bozeman, "Public Value Mapping of Science Outcomes: Theory and Method," in *Knowledge Flows & Knowledge Collectives: Understanding the Role of Science & Technology Policies in Development*, vol. 1 (Washington, DC: Center for Science, Policy & Outcomes, 2003).

[69] B. Bozeman, "Public Value Failure and Market Failure," *Public Administration Review* 62, no. 2 (2002): 145-161; B. Bozeman and D. Sarewitz, "Public Values and Public Failure in U.S. Science Policy," *Science and Public Policy* 32, no. 2 (2005): 119-136.

[70] B. Bozeman, "Public Value Failure and Market Failure," *Public Administration Review* 62, no. 2 (2002): 145-161; B. Bozeman, *Public Values and Public Interest: Counterbalancing Economic Individualism* (Washington, DC: Georgetown University Press, 2007).

[71] M. Feeney and B. Bozeman, "The 2004-2005 Influenza Episode as a Case of Public Failure," *Journal of Public Integrity* 9, no. 2 (2007): 179-195.

[72] E. Fisher, C. Slade, D. Anderson, and B. Bozeman, "The Public Value of Nanotechnology?" *Scientometrics* 85, no. 1 (2010): 29-39.

[73] Adapted from B. Bozeman, *Public Values and Public Interest: Counterbalancing Economic Individualism* (Washington, DC: Georgetown University Press, 2007), and B. Bozeman and D. Sarewitz, "Public Values and Public Failure in U.S. Science Policy," *Science and Public Policy* 32, no. 2 (2005): 119-136.

[74] See B. Bozeman and D. Sarewitz, "Public Values and Public Failure in U.S. Science Policy," *Science and Public Policy* 32, no. 2 (2005): 119-136.

[75] G. F. Gaus, *Value and Justification: The Foundations of Liberal Theory* (New York, NY: Cambridge University Press, 1990).

[76] D. Braybrooke and C. E. Lindblom, *A Strategy of Decision: Policy Evaluation as a Social Process* (New York, NY: Free Press, 1963).

[77] B. Bozeman, "Public Value Failure and Market Failure," *Public Administration Review* 62, no. 2 (2002): 145-161; B. Bozeman and D. Sarewitz, "Public Values and Public Failure in U.S. Science Policy," *Science and Public Policy* 32, no. 2 (2005): 119-136.

[78] N. Logar, "Chemistry, Green Chemistry, and the Instrumental Valuation of Sustainability," *Minerva* 49, no. 1 (2011): 113-136.

[79] R. Meyer, "The Public Values Failure of Climate Science in the U.S.," *Minerva* 49, no. 1 (2011): 47-70.

[80] C. P. Slade, "Public Value Mapping of Equity in Emerging Nanomedicine," *Minerva* 49, no. 1 (2011): 71-86.

[81] W. Valdivia, "The Stakes in Bayh-Dole: Public Values Beyond the Pace of Innovation," *Minerva* 49, no. 1 (2011): 25-46.

7

THE PUBLIC VALUES FAILURE OF CLIMATE SCIENCE IN THE UNITED STATES[*]

Ryan Meyer

Introduction

In the United States, a large "global change research" community investigates climate change through research on the complex interrelations of natural processes, as well the role of humans in impacting and reacting to these forces. Atmospheric scientists, hydrologists, ecologists, paleobiologists, oceanographers, agronomists, statisticians, epidemiologists, glaciologists, and many others seek resources from U.S. climate science funding. They launch hundred million dollar satellites, which orbit the earth looking back at us. They assemble massive numerical mod-

---

[*] Originally published as R. Meyer, "The Public Values Failure of Climate Science in the U.S.," *Minerva* 49, no. 1 (2011): 47-70. Reprinted with permission from Springer.

els to run on the world's largest computers. They send research vessels throughout the world's oceans, and construct elaborate facilities to run experiments measuring ecological change.

Climate science[1] engages a wide range of disciplines and institutions: thirteen federal agencies fund work in this area. But this structural complexity exists under a single mission, vision, and framework set out in law by the Global Change Research Act of 1990, and maintained through an interagency coordination process. Since that time, more than $30 billion has gone to global change research.

A recent National Research Council (NRC) evaluation of U.S. climate science found that, while the program has significantly advanced understanding of climate change, "progress in synthesizing research results or supporting decision making and risk management has been inadequate."[2] This observation highlights an important fact: the Global Change Research Act (GCRA), like most science policies, has a broader purpose — it constructs an aspirational link between science and some form of social progress.

The GCRA stipulates funding for research in order to "produce information readily usable by policymakers." Nearly two decades later, the NRC finds that the great volume of knowledge resulting from global change research has failed to fulfill this mandate. In fact, from the very beginning, outside evaluators have highlighted the failure of the interagency program to make significant progress on this task.[3] In this paper, I use a public value mapping[4] to investigate the link between climate science and the broader social purpose of climate science policies to show how this has happened.

I assess the fulfillment of public values by examining policies, institutions, and the mental models of individual decision makers associated with U.S. climate science. As individuals and institutions coordinate, manage, and make specific choices about how to spend money on climate science, what drives their decisions? Do the incentives embedded in the system uphold the public values that motivate funding for climate science in the first place? Although the importance of such questions was highlighted in *Minerva* by Stephen Toulmin in 1964,[5] to this day they seldom receive adequate attention as the nation's research and development (R&D) system expands.

I begin by briefly outlining the public value mapping framework.[6] I then identify and describe the key public values that emerge from program documents, external documents such as National Research Council (NRC) reports, and interviews I conducted with more than fifty program officials who work for science agencies and participate in interagency climate science activities. A juxtaposition of these values with the dynamics of decision making and management within the climate science program provides the basis for a public values failure assessment. This assessment reveals widespread and ill-founded assumptions about the connections between knowledge advancement and difficult social problems like climate change, and provides important insight, both for climate science and for science policy in general.

Public Values Analysis

Barry Bozeman defines the public values of a society as: "Those providing a normative consensus about (a) the rights, benefits, and prerogatives to which citizens should (and should not) be entitled; (b) the obligations of citizens to society, the state, and one another; and (c) the principles on which governments and policies should be based."[7]

The term "normative consensus" does not imply universal agreement. It simply means that public values are widely recognized across a given society, and can serve as a basis for collective action. Public values also do not pre-scribe specific policy action. Thus, broad agreement on par-ticular public values such as air quality, public health, or human dignity (in other words, agreement that these are good, desirable things) by no means precludes deep con-flict over the way in which they might be achieved, or over their importance relative to one another. Public values fail-ures occur when "neither the market nor the public sector provides goods and services required to achieve public val-ues."[8]

Public values analyses are motivated by the conclusion that the economic outcome of a policy (e.g., profit, effi-ciency, growth of industry, GDP) is not necessarily an ap-propriate indicator of whether that policy is successful. For example, if a clean energy policy gives a substantial finan-cial boost to corn farmers selling their crops for biofuel, we may reserve judgment as to whether the policy has suc-ceeded in reducing emissions of pollutants as originally in-tended.

One can apply this argument to public investments in science as well. Barry Bozeman and Daniel Sarewitz (in chapter 5) argue against the common assumption that mar-ket success (or failure) correlates directly with public val-ues success (or failure) when it comes to the funding of re-search and development.[9] Medical research provides a particularly compelling example: massive investments by the U.S. government have fueled major advances in medi-cine, around which an enormous industry has grown. Yet health in the United States remains mediocre in compari-son to other developed nations even while its costs con-tinue to skyrocket: market success, public failure.[10]

Following this logic, one may view climate science as a market failure (funding is provided through the public sec-tor), and, in light of critiques by the NRC mentioned above, as a public values failure. The grid in Figure 7.1 below il-lustrates this.

Useful information, though important and prominent, is not the only public value associated with the climate science enterprise. In the next section, I present a list of five prominent public values that underpin U.S. climate science, and discuss each of these values in the context of individual decision making and institutional structures. The last two decades have seen considerable continuity in the general purpose of coordinating climate science among agencies, even if the language used to express that purpose and the means of achieving it have evolved. So far, under the Obama administration, the U.S. Climate Change Science Program (CCSP, as it was known under the Bush administration) remains largely intact, except that it has reverted to its pre-Bush administration name of "Global Change Research Program." For the sake of consistency, I will use CCSP as a reference to the federal interagency program in general.

Figure 7.1: Climate Science in the Context of Public Values and Market Values

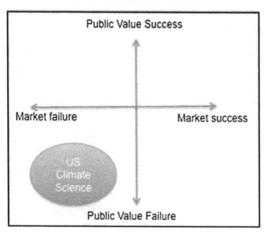

Public Values in Interagency Climate Science

A variety of sources can provide information about public values, including public law, a government's founding documents, the results of surveys and public polls, or the missions and visions of public institutions.[11] Such sources often articulate aspirations that link, through some internal logic, particular activities (such as scientific research) to the achievement of positive outcomes for society. Claims of social benefit might be utterly political and insincere, advanced merely for personal gain, or preservation of the status quo. This should not discourage their use as expressions of public value. Sincere or not, if offered as a policy goal, they may justifiably be used in evaluating the outcomes of that policy. Revealing divergences in public values and actual intent is precisely the point of public value mapping.

The list in Table 7.1 below focuses on the most commonly expressed, broadly agreed-upon principles and goals of the program drawn from a variety of documents. It is not hierarchical, and there is no clear consensus on how the values relate to one another, or should be balanced.

In discussing each of these values, I reference the concepts of instrumental and intrinsic values. Bozeman describes intrinsic values as representing a desired end state, while an instrumental value is adopted as a means to achieving an intrinsic value.[12] The distinction between these two types of values is not always clear, and some public values may be framed as one or the other. Indeed, as I argue later, in some cases this malleability can be at the heart of public value failure.

The example statements in Table 7.1 demonstrate the consistency with which these values have been expressed in the years since the passage of the GCRA in 1990. Below I discuss each public value in more detail, drawing on interviews and official documents.

Value 1: Useful Information

In 1979, Charles E. Lindblom and David K. Cohen observed that the complexities of the lay community are perhaps as great as or greater than the complexities associated with knowledge production.[13] A variety of more recent studies examining how lay communities make use of climate information have borne this out. Such studies highlight the importance of the social, physical, institutional, and political context of decision makers, and generally refute the common assumption that more information necessarily leads to better decision making or increased information use.[14] Scientific programs aimed at generating immediately useful knowledge must take this reality into account, and involve potential knowledge users throughout the research process.[15]

To develop useful information is the most obvious, prominent, and challenging intrinsic public value of interagency climate science, and it has become a subject of study for social scientists focused on climate issues.[16] In thinking about CCSP's relationship to the challenge of developing useful information, one may ask: (1) what users are targeted and why; (2) how is useful information defined; and (3) how could one guide or structure a research program to be responsive to questions one and two? In the case of U.S. climate science, the answers to these questions are not straightforward.

Who Is Targeted? Early discussions and wording of the GCRA seem to indicate that the program should generate information useful specifically to decision makers in Congress.[17] The CCSP has adopted a much wider view of the potential users who should benefit from the results of climate science. The CCSP *Strategic Plan for the U.S. Climate Change Science Program* and subsequent documentation tend to identify three categories of decisions that the program will inform: policy decisions, adaptive management decisions, and decisions related to the evolution of the science research agenda.[18] However, the program does not describe a plan for delivering useful information to these groups.

Table 7.1 Statements Associated with Public Values Underlying Interagency Climate Science

1. Useful information

- "Interagency climate science should 'produce information readily usable by policymakers.'"[19]

- CCSP vision: A nation and the global community, empowered with the science based knowledge to manage the risks and opportunities of change in the climate and related environmental systems.[20]

- CCSP mission: Facilitate the creation and application of knowledge of the earth's global environment through research, observations, decision support, and communication.[21]

2. High-quality science

- "Development of effective policies to abate, mitigate, and cope with global change will rely on greatly improved scientific understanding of global environmental processes and on our ability to distinguish human-induced from natural global change."[22]

- "[The strategic plan] reflects a commitment by its authors to high-quality science, which requires openness to review and criticism by the wider scientific community."[23]

- "CCSP remains committed to basic, ongoing research to understand climate processes and the forcing factors that cause changes in climate and related systems."[24]

- "It is therefore essential for society to be equipped with the best possible knowledge of climate variability and change so that we may exercise responsible stewardship for the environment, lessen the potential for negative climate impacts, and take advantage of opportunities where they exist."[25]

3. Coordination and collaboration

- "Although significant Federal global change research efforts are underway, an effective Federal research program will require efficient interagency coordination, and coordination with the research activities of State, private, and international entities."[26]

- "CCSP adds value to federal agency efforts in climate change research and related activities by providing a structure and coordination mechanism that leverages individual agency efforts through increased cooperation, collaboration, and the joint development of research priorities."[27]

4. Transparency and communication

- "The purpose of the [interagency] Office shall be to disseminate to foreign governments, businesses, and institutions, as well as the citizens of foreign countries, scientific research information available in the United States which would be useful in preventing, mitigating, or adapting to the effects of global change."[28]

- "CCSP has a major responsibility to communicate with interested partners in the United States and throughout the world, and to learn from these partners on a continuing basis."[29]

- "CCSP undertakes the significant responsibility of enhancing the quality of discussion by stressing openness and transparency in its findings and reports."[30]

5. Stakeholder participation and support

- "[The Program] shall consult with actual and potential users of the results of the Program to ensure that such results are useful in developing national and international policy responses to global change."[31]

- "The program will improve approaches for sustained interactions with stakeholders that consider needs for information from a 'user perspective.'"[32]

- "Programs must respond to needs for scientific information and enhance informed discussion by all relevant stakeholders."[33]

What Is Useful Information? CCSP's definition of "useful" is not always clear, but the program aims to do more than produce information that is merely relevant to decision-making issues. The strategic plan defines decision support resources as: "The set of observations, analyses, interdisciplinary research products, communication mechanisms, and operational services that provide timely and useful information to address questions confronting policymakers, resource managers, and other users."[34] Consistent with the findings and recommendations of those who have worked in this area,[35] this definition implies a proactive stance, responsive to the needs and limitations of those served by the program.

In general, ideas about what it takes to produce useful information in scientific research have evolved since the first decade of the program, when a major focus was the reduction of uncertainty. Many have pointed out that most decisions do not (indeed, they cannot) rely upon the eradication of uncertainty;[36] that scientific uncertainty can be a political tool used to win additional funds for science, or to delay a decision indefinitely;[37] and that a great deal of our uncertainty about the behavior of the climate and related systems is irreducible.[38] Reduction of uncertainty offers neither a sensible metric by which to judge progress in climate science, nor a reasonable surrogate for the goal of generating useful information.[39]

Consistent with this view, very few of those I interviewed saw reduction of uncertainty as a crucial goal for climate science. Instead, they described uncertainty as a matter of appropriate characterization, communication, and management. Despite this evolved notion of uncertainty, predictive capability is almost universally viewed as essential to generating useful climate science. As one official said, "How else will you know how high to build the sea wall?" Many take it for granted that deterministic predictive capability should be the main goal of climate science, because they truly believe that this is the kind of information necessary to deal with climate change effectively. In other words, these individuals presume a causal connection between a particular kind of knowledge advance (improved predictions) and the fulfillment of public values.[40]

The few program managers and agency officials I interviewed who rejected this mainstream view of prediction did so based on practical experience working with decision makers in various contexts. They described situations in which deterministic predictions were found to be unnecessary in helping communities, resource managers, local governments, and others to increase their resilience or better understand their options in the face of environmental change. These individuals do not view predictive models as totally irrelevant, but neither do they view them as "obligatory passage points"[41] for making climate science useful.

How Is the CCSP Managing Research Agendas to Produce Useful Information? Many CCSP documents focus on the need for useful information, but usually without any discussion of how specifically the research agenda needs to change in order to support that goal. Both the CCSP and the NRC, in their analyses and recommendations for climate science, tend to ignore the organizational and institutional components of science funding (i.e., the question of how to influence the direction of research and the composition of research portfolios). Simply identifying the gaps in knowledge or practice does not explain how to fill them using existing or new structures to advance desired public values.

One exception to this is the example of social science or "human dimensions" research, which is often cited as a crucial but under-represented and under-supported area. The example of human dimensions research and its relative presence in the interagency program over the last two decades illustrates a general inability or unwillingness on the part of CCSP to exert control over the makeup of the climate science portfolio.

In 1990, the NRC called human dimensions the most critically underfunded element of the USGCRP, a sentiment it has repeatedly echoed in the intervening 18 years.[42] A 1992 report recommended that annual funding for this area of research be increased to $40–50 million, an amount that would have represented about 4–5% of the overall program at the time. In 2007, the NRC found that "the level of investment ($25 million to $30 million) remains substantially lower than the level of investment in the other research elements, and funding is atomized across many agency programs."[43] This represents about 1.5% of the total budget.

As I discuss in a later section (see "Values in the Structure and Implementation ..."), the CCSP does not have a coherent or realistic approach to determining a research portfolio that will fulfill its mandate to develop useful information. Yet even in cases where a clear need for change has long been asserted by outside evaluators, as in this example of human dimensions research, the CCSP and participating agencies have not implemented change in this direction.

Value 2: High Quality Science

The need to maintain a thriving and robust scientific enterprise is emphasized throughout CCSP documentation, as well as by individuals involved with the program.[44] On its face, such an assertion seems both obvious and uncontroversial: it is, after all, a science program. But in the context of interagency climate science, a focus on maintaining high quality science is a political act which sends clear signals about the priorities of the program and the mental model that informs its behavior.

Sometimes high quality science functions as an instrumental value—a necessary element in achieving the program's underpinning goals and public values. For example, the CCSP's "Revised Research Plan" states that "substantive progress in CCSP Strategic Goals 1 through 3 is a required component of progress in many areas associated with Goals 4 and 5 ..."[45] (see goals in Table 7.3 below). This claim reflects a common but false assumption (discussed further in a later section) that advances in fundamental understanding necessarily precede work on applied problems.

In other cases (and sometimes in reaction to such criticisms), high quality research is expressed as an intrinsic public value. Many believe that maintaining capacity in the core areas of research that have contributed to interagency climate science in recent decades is an important goal in and of itself. One program manager linked the fundamental work her scientists are doing to the idea of a "strong America." Another manager felt that shifting to a more applied focus denigrates the enterprise as a whole, making it less attractive to future scholars. Many view science as an independent, curiosity driven activity, in which the research proceeds in a bottom-up fashion. Though these individuals may understand the political or practical necessity striving toward useful information, they view this as a compromise which cuts against the intrinsic value of basic science—against the science values that underpin much of their decision making.

Whether functioning as an intrinsic or instrumental value, high quality science is a political tool. In many instances, a reference to the maintenance of high quality science does not just mean ensuring rigorous research; it implies a commitment to what has come before. It is a signal to those with a vested interest in climate science that there is still a place for them in the evolving program.

Value 3: Coordination and Collaboration

The need to coordinate and collaborate across agencies, programs, and disciplines relates strongly to the idea of an efficient government. It also comports with the notion of the "super discipline" of earth system science, which strives to fully integrate human and natural systems to generate comprehensive understanding of global processes.[46] Even without the formal structure of the CCSP, coordination across agencies would be a common occurrence, as indeed it was prior to 1990.

Successful collaboration also emerged as a strongly held value among those I interviewed. When asked to describe a project which they had found personally rewarding, almost every person told a story in which they viewed the building of relationships across boundaries as one of the positive outcomes. Every story had a collaborative component.

Coordination and collaboration represent the biggest source of positive sentiment regarding the CCSP. Most interviewees agreed that CCSP, in convening interagency groups at various levels of government, serves a useful purpose in building a network of climate science managers and encouraging collaboration. Even among those whose general opinions of the CCSP are strongly negative—for example, because it distracts from important scientific work, or is cumbersome and ineffectual—this function of the program was commonly seen as valuable, and perhaps the sole reason that they continued to participate.

Value 4: Transparency and Communication

As is evident from the examples in Table 7.1, this value is related to ensuring high quality science, but also functions as a public value instrumental in making science useful and realizing its benefits. These two conceptions emerged in interviews as well. It is widely accepted in the CCSP that making the processes and results of science open and available will enhance the quality of the scientific enterprise. It follows, then, that any research program (or any effort to coordinate and advance research) should strive toward openness and transparency simply as a matter of ensuring the health of the scientific enterprise.

But many also describe openness as an essential part of achieving the broader aims of the CCSP. The 2003 strategic plan devotes a chapter to this goal, and the interagency coordination office devotes a considerable amount of time and resources to publicizing and explaining the synthesis and assessment reports it releases. Public events organized by CCSP at scientific meetings and other venues often combine an element of stakeholder feedback with a communications component in which staff explain what CCSP does in the broader landscape of climate science funding agencies.

Figure 7.2: Research Funding Allocated to CCSP Goals as a Proportion of the Overall CCSP Budget (Goals are Listed in Table 7.3)

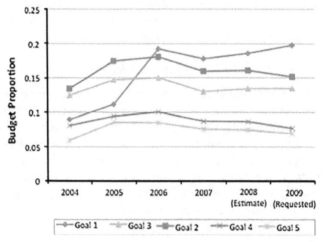

Note that the overall budget includes both research and observations, which is why the five goals do not add up to 100%.

Reporting progress to Congress is another important part of the communications effort. Almost every year since the passage of the Global Change Research Act, the interagency coordinating office has submitted an "Our Changing Planet" (OCP) report to Congress.[47] In general, the document provides research highlights from the previous year, a sampling of plans for the coming year, and budget tables documenting resources allocated to climate science from each participating agency.

The budget tables in OCP demonstrate the ambiguity of the CCSP's role in advancing federal climate science. With no consistency across agency budget reporting, and no direct link between agency activities and CCSP priorities, it is virtually impossible to track changes in climate science over time within the framework of values and priorities established by the CCSP. Beginning with its FY2006 report, the CCSP began to group agency budget allocations under particular CCSP goals.[48] This affords one snapshot of how the program has prioritized its funds over the last five years (Figure 7.2), but the ambiguity of the goals (discussed further below), subverts any attempt to monitor via budgets changes in priorities for U.S. climate science.

Value 5: Stakeholder Participation and Support

The term "stakeholder," along with variants involving communities and users, is one of the most important buzzwords in interagency climate science. These concepts appear in all but one of the 16 chapters in the CCSP *Strategic Plan for the U.S. Climate Change Science Program*,[49] and are similarly pervasive in the more recent "Revised Research Plan."[50] However, involving stakeholders in the processes associated with research and research policy requires managing, incentivizing, and carrying out research in different ways.[51]

The CCSP is pulled in many different directions with respect to who it is serving, and how it aims to interact with a wide variety of groups, both within the scientific community, and the broader public. Given the program's limited resources, and limited role in establishing research programs, it is not clear how the CCSP can systematically: (1) identify appropriate groups that should be involved; (2) work to understand the decision-making needs and other challenges faced by those groups; (3) reconcile those needs with climate research agenda; and (4) help to translate research results into usable forms for appropriate groups. Yet all of these functions are stated or at least implied by the CCSP.

The CCSP lacks the resources for a sustained effort to work with all of the groups of stakeholders that might make use of climate science knowledge. However, as a prominent public face of climate science in the United States tasked with meeting the requirements of the GCRA, politically the CCSP must be seen as ensuring that this is happening. One program manager told me, "I don't think the funding has been adequate in the program for that kind of work, but yet the program has been sold on that."

Another program manager involved in administering basic science activities conjectured: "I would guess that CCSP has not had any successes at any of that—the notion of helping the decision makers and policy people do things. As an organization, it's just muddied the waters. It has not clarified anything." In addition to its derision, the quotation is noteworthy for the subject's distance and unfamiliarity with such issues. Though he makes science policy decisions in his capacity as a manager, the program's success in leveraging that very process to achieve social benefit is of little concern to him. There is wide agreement among those I interviewed and outside evaluators[52] that the CCSP as an institution and climate science in general have not fulfilled this public value.

The scientific community's role as a stakeholder in agency funding programs further complicates matters. Scientists have traditionally had the loudest voices in the debate over what should be funded and how. As one program manager explained: "I think of [scientists] as stakeholders, because if I step back, and look at the way they interact with the CCSP, they have all the characteristics of stakeholders. They're fully vested. They have needs. They have very strong ideas about where the science needs to go."

Many of the program managers I interviewed rely on the scientific community to guide them, whether through informal networks of colleagues, scientific advisory boards, peer review panels, or conversations at the many science meetings they attend. This kind of proximity with the scientific community is obviously a crucial element of effective science management. Yet such interactions tend to reinforce the status quo and work against prioritization based on criteria related to public values other than those internal to the science itself. As one program manager noted, "the scientists, who are CCSP's traditional major stakeholder group, are watching to make sure that you're not selling them down the river."

This dynamic raises questions about whether a manager is working to support a discipline for the sake of itself, or trying to fund the work most likely to support outcomes consistent with the public values of the program. Undoubtedly the solution to such a conflict would be different for each agency, and in all cases it would involve striking an appropriate balance. However, in the current system, tensions between discipline-driven science and needs-driven science are rarely acknowledged.

Some programs or agencies within the departments that participate in the CCSP, such as Interior, Commerce, Agriculture, Defense, and Transportation, have extensive capacity and experience with decision support in very well-defined communities. These elements of the federal government could themselves be seen as stakeholders for U.S. global change research. They could use the interagency process as a forum to argue for the climate science information needs of their respective stakeholders. But federal programs with decision support capacity (but which do not fund research) are generally absent from the decision-making processes of the CCSP, which explicitly involves programs focused on basic science.[53] One program manager noted that "if the mission is to empower decision makers, then decision-making agencies ... should definitely be at the table. Some of them are, but they have really small [climate science] budgets."

Public Values Failure in Interagency Climate Science

Having identified and described a set of public values underpinning U.S. climate science, we can now look more closely at the ways in which the system is failing to deliver them. I draw on Bozeman's "public values failure criteria,"[54] as a starting point for diagnosing public values failures. In Table 7.2, I list public values failure criteria from Bozeman that apply to this case, as well as two additional entries, "Public Values Displacement" and "Inadequate or Inappropriate Institutions," which I have added as a result of the public values inventory described above. The right-hand column in the table gives examples and explanations of how each criterion applies to U.S. climate science. It is important to note that a wide variety of sources (such as program manager perspectives, public law, and budget reports) have contributed to this assessment of public values failure, each providing a different perspective.

Table 7.2 demonstrates the complexity of the interagency climate science landscape, and the variety of points at which the system lacks the structural and conceptual elements needed to link climate science more concretely to public values. The public value failures listed in Table 7.2 are not inevitable. Rather the CCSP strategy, framework, and processes *accommodate* them. This identification of public values failures serves as a critique of the general framework linking knowledge production to societal benefit, not a predictive or deterministic account. For example, in applying the "Inadequate Institutions" criterion, we find that managers are not incentivized to pursue CCSP goals within their own programs. However, this does not prevent a dedicated individual from doing so, or from directing his or her staff of program managers to do so. Interagency climate science is a product of both individuals and organizations, of institutional incentives conditioning behavior, and of leadership that challenges and reshapes existing rules. The following section explores these dynamics in greater depth.

Table 7.2: Public Values Failure Criteria and Potential Public Values Failures of Interagency Climate Science[55]

PV Failure Criterion	Definition	Explanation/Examples of the Potential Failure in Climate Science
Mechanisms for values articulation and aggregation	Political processes and social cohesion should be sufficient to ensure effective communication and processing of public values.	• CCSP criteria for prioritization are too broad and vague to provide real guidance. No connection between science priorities and desired outcomes or public values. • Agency priorities trump interagency (CCSP) priorities. • Stakeholders too widely or ambiguously defined for meaningful, sustained interaction.
Imperfect public information	Similar to the market failure criterion, public values may be thwarted when transparency is insufficient to permit citizens to make informed judgments.	• Budget reporting inconsistent across agencies and generally opaque; detailed information not readily available.
Distribution of benefits	Public commodities and services should, ceteris paribus, be freely and equitably distributed. When "equity goods" have been captured by individuals or groups, "benefit hoarding" occurs in violation of public value.	• Particular kinds of climate science (particularly related to prediction) dominate the budget. Human dimensions research has not grown, despite recognized need.
Provider availability	When there is a legitimated recognition about the necessity of providing scarce goods and services, providers need to be	• Priorities tend to favor natural science over social science, and science-driven research

	available. When a vital good or service is not provided because of the unavailability of providers or because providers prefer to ignore public value goods, there is a public values failure due to unavailable providers.	over needs-oriented research despite recognized need.
**Implausible and/or incomplete value chains	Pursuit of a proximate goal with ambiguous or unrealistic link to public values.	• Managers may assume that supporting the needs of the scientific community will achieve broader public values. • Managers judge program success based on scientific outputs, and not the impact or use of those products. • Five overarching goals of CCSP strategic plan assumed to lead to specified public value, but the link is neither explained, nor backed by an organizational structure that can establish that connection.
**Inadequate or inappropriate institutions	The structure or culture of an institution disincentivizes the achievement of its motivating public values.	• Inadequate resources for decision support and communications (approaches 3 and 4). • Incentive structures built into science management emphasize science values. • Managers not incentivized to work toward interagency goals in building their programs.

Values in the Structure and Implementation of U.S. Climate Science

The most recent strategic plan published by the CCSP[56] provides a useful entry point for understanding the way in which assumptions linking knowledge advance to public values can influence the decision making and overall structure of U.S. climate science policy. Table 7.3 lists the main elements included in the strategic plan. Its basic structure prescribes four different "approaches" to be used in pursuit of five goals, which ostensibly support the mission and vision of the program, evincing the following structure:

approaches → goals → mission → vision

But the plan does *not* describe how achievement of the goals (which all relate to advancement of knowledge) would actually support the mission and vision (which relate to the beneficial use of knowledge). Indeed each of the links in the structure is implicit, and taken for granted.

The two elements of the plan that indicate something beyond supporting research and expanding knowledge are the third and fourth "approaches": Decision Support and Communications. Decision support and communications, in turn, may be crucial to the mission and vision of CCSP, but they are not necessary for achieving the five over-arching goals of the strategic plan, which are research goals. Many involved with CCSP view goals one, two, and three as pertaining to "basic science" activities, with goals four and five constituting the more applied, or "decision support" work. But in reality, all five of the goals are flexible and overlapping, and all are concerned with expanding knowledge, not with developing capacity to apply it.[57] Thus, efforts to achieve identified goals (i.e., via research) can ignore completely the broader values that motivate global change research (i.e., supporting decision making to reduce negative social outcomes), even as they are consistent with the logic expressed in the plan.

Table 7.3: Major Components of CCSP's Strategic Plan[58]

Vision
A nation and the global community, empowered with the science based knowledge to manage the risks and opportunities of change in the climate and related environmental systems.

Mission
Facilitate the creation and application of knowledge of the Earth's global environment through *research, observations, decision support,* and *communication.*

Approaches	Goals	Research Areas
1. Scientific *Research*: Plan, sponsor, and conduct research on changes in climate and related systems. 2. *Observations*: Enhance observations and data management systems to generate a comprehensive set of variables needed for climate-related research. 3. *Decision Support*: Develop improved science-based resources to aid in decision making. 4. *Communications*: Communicate results to domestic and international scientific stakeholders, stressing openness and transparency.	1. Improve knowledge of the earth's past and present climate and environment, including its natural variability and improve understanding of the causes of observed variability and change. 2. Improve quantification of the forces bringing about changes in the earth's climate and related systems. 3. Reduce uncertainty in projections of how the earth's climate and related systems may change in the future. 4. Understand the sensitivity and adaptability of different natural and managed ecosystems and human systems to climate and related global changes. 5. Explore the uses and identify the limits of evolving knowledge to manage risks and opportunities related to climate variability and change.	Atmospheric Composition Climate Variability and Change Water Cycle Land-Use/Land-Cover Change Carbon Cycle Ecosystems Human Contributions and Responses to Environmental Change

Another important element of the plan is its list of "Criteria for Prioritization":[59] scientific or technical quality; relevance to reducing uncertainties and improving decision support tools in priority areas; track record of consistently good past performance and identified metrics for evaluating future progress; and cost and value. It would be difficult for any single research effort to satisfy all of these criteria, but the list is broad enough that anything currently underway at participating agencies will probably satisfy at least one or two. Thus, instead of providing concrete direction for those wishing to make funding decisions with CCSP priorities in mind, the plan offers complete flexibility within the normal limits of science funding.

The strategic plan designates "Interagency Working Groups" (IWGs) in key research areas, with members drawn from across participating federal agencies. As program managers with budget authority within their own agencies,[60] IWG members are in an ideal position to translate the goals of interagency climate science into requests for proposals, funding decisions, and the general management of climate science.

However, the circularity of this arrangement (specifying priorities that they themselves will carry out and subsequently report on) combined with a lack of authority and resources on the part of the CCSP, leaves little incentive for program managers to initiate anything beyond, or at odds with, the expectations of their home agencies. Thus, if asked to specify a priority relevant to CCSP goals for the coming year, the easiest answer for an IWG member would be whatever he or she had planned to fund anyway.

As one program manager put it:

We get asked every year how much money are we spending on _____, so, I'll come back and say, well, do you want a large number or small? Because I can go through my proposals and there's some of them that have some relevance …

so do you want me to say "half of that's _____ money?" If you want me to, sure, fine, I don't care. If you want to say "none of it,"' that's okay, too. (Blanks inserted to preserve anonymity.)

This account highlights structural issues and incentives that tend to discourage interagency climate science from moving in new directions, creating considerable inertia in the research portfolio.

Observers and participants in the CCSP, including the NRC on multiple occasions (2005, 2007, 2009), and many of the people I interviewed, have pointed out that the inter-agency process has very little authority when it comes to influencing the research agenda for climate science. In that sense, it promises more than it can deliver (as the example of budgets for human dimensions research demonstrates). Even so, it is not at all clear what the CCSP is trying to de-liver. In other words, the CCSP has not offered a clear ac-count of what kinds of scientific advance would help to sat-isfy the public values that motivate the program to begin with. Under the current structure, any good science is good enough. This logic works because of the influence of intrin-sic values related to the conduct of science itself, what I term "science values."

Science Values and Public Values

Whereas other cases have revealed the pitfalls of the "profit as progress" assumption,[61] the systemic problems in U.S. climate science stem from an equally problematic "knowledge as progress" assumption. Indeed, much of sci-ence policy is based on this rationale analogous to, but en-tirely separate from, the market failure model.[62] In this sec-tion, I describe a "science values" framework, which often motivates science policies and their implementation, and which helps to explain the public values failures described above. I then show how science values have led to the current structure of interagency climate science.

The Linear Model

The "linear model of science"[63] is a simplistic conception of scientific and technical advance that nonetheless remains an influential driver of science policy. According to the linear model, innovation happens in the following way: basic or fundamental research contributes to a general pool of knowledge; that pool of knowledge provides a resource for engineers or other innovators, who then apply it to create products that increase productivity, drive economic growth, enhance military power, and otherwise enrich lives and benefit society. This model assumes that advances in knowledge are by and large beneficial to society, and that the benefits are both automatic and unpredictable. It also assumes a unidirectional flow of knowledge that privileges basic research above applied as the originator of all scientific benefit.[64]

Daniel Sarewitz documents the implications of the linear model in a description of the myths that form a basis for science policy in the United States,[65] the first three of which are particularly relevant here:

1. The myth of infinite benefit: More science and more technology will lead to more public good.
2. The myth of unfettered research: Any scientifically reasonable line of research into fundamental natural processes is as likely to yield societal benefit as any other.
3. The myth of accountability: Peer review, reproducibility of results, and other controls on the quality of scientific research embody the principal ethical responsibilities of the research system.

These assumptions about the nature of scientific progress have shaped, over many decades, what Simon Shackley and Brian Wynne call "the tacit commitments and assumptions which underpin a prevailing common culture of science and policy."[66]

The most important elements of the linear model as it relates to the fulfillment of public values are the assumptions of automatic benefit and unpredictability. Taken together, the three myths suggest that more basic research is an unquestionably, if unpredictably, good thing. Few would deny that public investments in basic science have the potential to bring great benefit to society, often in unpredictable ways. However, these assumptions — when driving policy decisions — can compromise public values. For example, the unpredictability of outcomes renders nonsensical any attempt at reasoned choice among scientific activities. As Michael Polanyi wrote, "You can kill or mutilate the advance of science, you cannot shape it,"[67] and the sentiment remains strong to this day. It emerges, for example, in outrage over attempts to limit certain areas of science (e.g., stem cell research).

But the history of government-driven innovation in the United States shows that we can make sensible decisions about research investments in order to address particular problems. We would not, for example, fund seismologists in the hope that their work might one day lead to an AIDS vaccine, and it is not only reasonable to expect that we might make even finer-grained choices with some success,[68] but historically clear that this has been the case.[69] Furthermore, reasoned attempts to direct research toward the solution of particular problems compromise neither the quality of research nor its potential to yield unexpected breakthroughs.

Debate over how science should be funded, governed, and evaluated has a long history in the United States[70] and continues to spark controversy as issues such as stem cell research, climate change, and nanotechnology capture the public eye. The appropriate technology movement,[71] the rise of the congressional Office of Technology Assessment,[72] passage of the Government Performance and Results Act (GPRA),[73] and calls by President George W. Bush's science advisor for a new research program on the "science of science and innovation policy"[74] are all examples of a trend toward increased expectations of accountability in science since the 1970s.[75]

Beyond the problem of choosing among potential lines of research, the linear model also creates problems for the assessment of that choice. If the benefits of science are at once automatic yet unpredictable, then public investments in science need not be evaluated beyond the general expectation that they meet the requirements of "good" science in the sense of academic rigor and allegiance to the ideals of objectivity and independence. This syllogism raises a crucial concern regarding science and public values: under the linear model, it is not economic productivity that serves as a surrogate for social benefit, but scientific productivity. In other words, knowledge equals progress.

There are two problems with this logical step. First, it is obvious that not all advances in knowledge are inherently good.[76] Indeed, judging the "goodness" of knowledge is impossible without consideration of the use of that knowledge—its function in a broader context.[77] Second, if we accept the advancement of knowledge as an index to progress, then a complex *social* problem with many political and social facets, such as climate change or disease, is easily reduced to a *science funding* problem, wherein the solution is simply to fund more research, with little concern for the broader social context.[78] Put differently, linear model thinking ignores the fact that, even if a particular advance in knowledge can be said to be "good," beneficial use of that knowledge is not guaranteed.

The linear model and its accompanying science policy myths add context to claims by mainstream institutions such as the NRC that U.S. climate science has greatly advanced knowledge while failing to achieve its broader purpose. Yet, it also helps clarify why appropriate solutions are rarely articulated or adopted. These very institutions exist to embody and protect science values as *intrinsic* public values. Figure 7.3 illustrates this problem by replacing the "market" axis of the grid in Figure 7.1 with an axis representing "science values." The right side of this axis indicates a decision making environment in which "knowledge advance" is taken as a reasonable and appropriate equivalent for public values. The left side indicates an approach to science policy that acknowledges the contingent and contextual aspects of scientific advance.

Figure 7.3: Climate Science in the Context of Public Values and Science Values

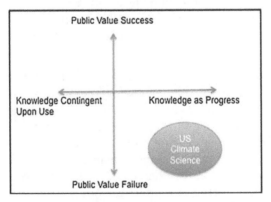

As with market values in Figure 7.1, the key point of Figure 7.3 is that science values may or may not be consistent with the public values that motivate a policy or program. The outcome depends a great deal upon how different values are prioritized, and on how institutions and individuals contribute to the implementation of science policies. Examining how different sets of values impact policy implementation helps to reveal why public values failures occur.

Recommendations

There is no simple hierarchy of values within U.S. climate science, and the relationships among values are complex, but the preceding analysis leads to two general observations. First, although decision making based on science values often seems to subvert public values, there are also many points of compatibility. Public values 3 and 4 (coordination and collaboration; transparency and communication) are also important *science* values. And high quality science (value 2) is necessary (though not sufficient) for developing useful information. Moreover, given the logical incoherence of the CCSP structure itself, there can be no way to connect the program's public values to its organization. In other words, CCSP reflects incoherence both in its organizing structure and in the relations among its public values. More careful thinking about how the program's public values can relate to one another could provide a valuable framework for reconsidering program structure.

The role of high quality science leads to the second point about value chains and public failures: high quality science and useful information are compatible as values; it is the flexibility and ambiguity of their relationship that leads to public values failure. When functioning as an intrinsic value, high quality science reinforces the linear model and subverts public values because advancement of knowledge serves as an end, rather than a means (i.e. an instrumental value). The interagency program should adopt language and institutional processes promoting high quality science that *also* contributes useful information. Without a structure that clearly identifies high quality science as a necessary (though not sufficient) step in generating useful information, potential for public values failure will remain.

Strengthening and clarifying value chains is a matter of individual leadership and institutional change. As long as program managers continue to view the public failures of

CCSP as unrelated to their own work (as in a quotation offered previously), they may continue to operate under linear model assumptions, and on-the-ground implementation of science policies will remain divorced from public values. Any changes in this direction are likely to result from leadership at multiple levels, both within science agencies, and in those parts of government charged with oversight of the interagency program (e.g., Congress, the interagency coordination office, and the president's Office of Science and Technology Policy).

The ambiguity and weakness of CCSP's value chains contribute to public values failure, but they are an advantage to the organization in other ways. To survive politically, CCSP needs to be able to show progress over time, despite a lack of control over the activities it must report on. Put in this light, the program's goals (see Table 7.3) are quite convenient. They are a general prediction of what the collective agencies will accomplish over time as they pursue *science values*, rather than a reflection of what needs to be done to achieve *public values*. The CCSP should pursue public values by setting goals for *science policy* (e.g., measures such as budget allocation, breadth and depth of decision support activities, or the generation of useful information), rather than goals for science. However, given CCSP's limited authority and resources, such goals might be unachievable, and thus politically untenable. Seen in this light, public values serve the program as political cover, rather than as a firm basis for guiding both policy and practice.

It is not clear that the United States currently has the institutional capacity to achieve the public values promised from climate science. Probably no one knows exactly how an effective program should be structured. However, it is fairly clear that the current system has proven inadequate in several important ways. This failure can be attributed, in large part, to the prevailing assumption that "knowledge equals progress" — that any advance in understanding justifies the initial investment of research dollars. This is analogous to other public values analyses which trace the implications of the assumption, "economic growth (or efficiency) equals social progress." Both cases may lead to or mask public failure.

To enhance the achievement of public values, the CCSP and its successors need to reject science values assumptions and instead ask what *kinds* of knowledge would lead to desired progress toward public values. What kinds of institutions are needed to facilitate that progress? CCSP must strengthen its value chains and make them more explicit. Even more crucially, it should differentiate its own priorities from those of participating agencies, and draw a distinction between goals that merely support science, and goals that *connect* science to public values.

In its 2003 strategic plan (see Table 7.3), the CCSP tried to fit the whole of U.S. climate science into a single, unified framework, which resulted in an incoherent internal logic. Instead, the CCSP should identify the concrete areas of climate science in which it can make progress toward its own public values-based goals, and focus on those. This would mean thinking small. For example, CCSP could set a goal of incentivizing and supporting program managers who fund research that responds to stakeholder needs. This might mean providing additional funding for programs that qualify; convening workshops in which managers learn about ways of incorporating public values into their program solicitations, evaluations of proposals, and progress reports; and lobbying agencies and the Office of Management and Budget to give additional recognition to such programs in the course of assessment and evaluation. This would not amount to a complete overhaul of the climate science enterprise, but it could have a visible impact in an important, but neglected area, and create conditions for further evolution away from science policy based on the linear model.

The CCSP might take on the role of a boundary organization specializing in communicating between normally disparate policy and disciplinary worlds,[79] with a goal of strengthening the connections between science programs and regulatory or service programs that have particular information needs. With this approach, the CCSP could begin with federal agencies and programs that already have representation in various CCSP committees, such as the Environmental Protection Agency, the Department of Transportation, or the Forest Service, and work to ensure that the relevant *research* programs become more responsive to their needs. Such an effort, if successful, could grow to include state and local groups as well.

Either one of the two suggestions above would allow incremental progress in addressing some of the public value failures of U.S. climate science over the last two decades. A key aspect of both examples is an approach grounded in public values—and the relations among such values—as a basis for planning, action, and assessment. At present, such values tend to serve simply as political cover for business as usual.

Notes

[1] As is common in many policy documents related to federal climate research, I use "climate science" and "global change research" interchangeably.

[2] National Research Council, *Evaluating Progress of the U.S. Climate Change Science Program: Methods and Preliminary Results* (Washington, DC: National Academies Press, 2007), 3.

[3] R. A. Pielke Jr., "Policy history of the U.S. global change research program: Part I. Administrative development," *Global Environmental Change* 10, no. 1 (2000): 9-25; National Research

Council, *Thinking Strategically: The Appropriate Use of Metrics for the Climate Change Science Program* (Washington, DC: National Academies Press, 2005); National Research Council *Evaluating Progress of the U.S. Climate Change Science Program: Methods and Preliminary Results* (Washington, DC: National Academies Press, 2007); R. Byerly Jr., "The policy dynamics of global change," *Earthquest* 3, no. 1 (1989): 11-14.

[4] B. Bozeman and D. Sarewitz, "Public value mapping and science policy evaluation," *Minerva* 49, no. 1 (2011): 1-23.

[5] See also P. Kitcher, "What kinds of science *should* be done?" on *Living with the Genie: Essays on Technology and the Quest for Human Mastery*, A. P. Lightman, D. R. Sarewitz, and C. Desser, eds. (London, UK: Island Press, 2003); B. Bozeman and D. Sarewitz, "Public value mapping and science policy evaluation," *Minerva* 49, no. 1 (2011): 1-23.

[6] See B. Bozeman and D. Sarewitz, "Public value mapping and science policy evaluation," *Minerva* 49, no. 1 (2011): 1-23, for a more detailed account of public value mapping in science policy.

[7] B. Bozeman, *Public Values and Public Interest: Counterbalancing Economic Individualism* (Washington, DC: Georgetown University Press, 2007), 13.

[8] Ibid., 16.

[9] B. Bozeman and D. Sarewitz, "Public values and public failure in U.S. science policy," *Science and Public Policy* 32, no. 2 (2005): 119-136.

[10] M. Gaughan, "Public value mapping breast cancer case studies," in *Knowledge Flows and Knowledge Collectives: Understanding the Role of Science and Technology Policies in Development*, D. Sarewitz, ed. (Washington, DC: Consortium for Science, Policy & Outcomes, 2002); A. Gawande, "The cost conundrum: What a Texas town can teach us about health care," *New Yorker* (June 1, 2009); C. P. Slade, "Public value mapping of equity in emerging nanomedicine," *Minerva* 49, no. 1 (2011): 71-86.

[11] See B. Bozeman, *Public Values and Public Interest: Counterbalancing Economic Individualism* (Washington, DC: Georgetown

University Press, 2007), and B. Bozeman and D. Sarewitz, "Public value mapping and science policy evaluation," *Minerva* 49, no. 1 (2011): 1-23, for more on this.

[12] B. Bozeman, *Public Values and Public Interest: Counterbalancing Economic Individualism* (Washington, DC: Georgetown University Press, 2007).

[13] C. E. Lindblom and D. K. Cohen, *Usable Knowledge: Social Science and Social Problem Solving* (New Haven, CT: Yale University Press, 1979).

[14] E.g., D. Lach, H. Ingram, and S. Rayner, "Maintaining the status quo: How institutional norms and practices create conservative water organizations," *Texas Law Review* 83, no. 7 (2005): 2027-2053; D. Lach, S. Rayner, and H. Ingram, "Taming the waters: Strategies to domesticate the wicked problems of water resource management," *International Journal of Water* 3, no. 1 (2005): 1-17; S. Rayner, D. Lach, and H. Ingram, "Weather forecasts are for wimps: Why water resource managers do not use climate forecasts," *Climatic Change* 69, no. 2 (2005): 197-227; M. Lahsen and C. A. Nobre, "Challenges of connecting international science and local level sustainability efforts: The case of the large-scale biosphere atmosphere experiment in Amazonia," *Environmental Science and Policy* 10, no. 1 (2007): 62-74; N. J. Logar and R. T. Conant, "Reconciling the supply of and demand for carbon cycle science in the U.S. agricultural sector," *Environmental Science and Policy* 10, no. 1 (2007): 75-84; E. C. McNie, "Reconciling the supply of scientific information with user demands: An analysis of the problem and review of the literature," *Environmental Science and Policy* 10, no. 1 (2007): 17-38; D. Sarewitz and R. A. Pielke Jr., "The neglected heart of science policy: Reconciling supply of and demand for science," *Environmental Science and Policy* 10, no. 1 (2007): 5-16; R. A. Pielke Jr., "Usable information for policy: An appraisal of the U.S. global change research program," *Policy Sciences* 28, no. 1 (1995): 39-77.

[15] D. W. Cash, J. C. Borck, and A. G. Patt, "Countering the loading-dock approach to linking science and decision making: Comparative analysis of El Nino/Southern oscillation (ENSO) forecasting systems," *Science, Technology, & Human Values* 31, no. 4 (2006): 465-494; K. Jacobs, G. Garfin, and M. Lenart, "More than just talk: Connecting science and decision making," *Environment*

47, no. 9 (2005): 6-21; H. Meinke, R. Nelson, P. Kokic, R. Stone, R. Selvaraju, and W. Baethgen, "Actionable climate knowledge: From analysis to synthesis," *Climate Research* 33, no. 1 (2006): 101-110; R. Nelson, M. Howden, and M. S. Smith, "Using adaptive governance to rethink the way science supports Australian drought policy," *Environmental Science and Policy* 11, no. 7 (2008): 588-601.

[16] C.f. R. A. Pielke Jr., "Policy history of the U.S. global change research program: Part I. Administrative development," *Global Environmental Change* 10, no. 1 (2000): 9-25; S. Agrawala, K. Broad, and D. H. Guston, "Integrating climate forecasts and societal decision making: Challenges to an emergent boundary organization," *Science, Technology, & Human Values* 26, no. 4 (2001): 454-477; D. W. Cash, J. C. Borck, and A. G. Patt, "Countering the loading-dock approach to linking science and decision making: Comparative analysis of El Nino/Southern oscillation (ENSO) forecasting systems," *Science, Technology, & Human Values* 31, no. 4 (2006): 465-494; National Research Council *Evaluating Progress of the U.S. Climate Change Science Program: Methods and Preliminary Results* (Washington, DC: National Academies Press, 2007); D. Sarewitz and R. A. Pielke Jr., "The neglected heart of science policy: Reconciling supply of and demand for science," *Environmental Science and Policy* 10, no. 1 (2007): 5-16; K. Jacobs, G. Garfin, and M. Lenart, "More than just talk: Connecting science and decision making," *Environment* 47, no. 9 (2005): 6-21; R. A. Pielke Jr., "Policy history of the U.S. global change research program: Part I. Administrative development," *Global Environmental Change* 10, no. 1 (2000): 9-25; National Research Council, "Informing decisions in a changing climate," in *Panel on Strategies and Methods for Climate-Related Decision Support* (Washington, DC: National Research Council, Committee on Human Dimensions of Global Change, 2009).

[17] R. A. Pielke Jr., "Policy history of the U.S. global change research program: Part I. Administrative development," *Global Environmental Change* 10, no. 1 (2000): 9-25; R. A. Pielke Jr., "Policy history of the U.S. global change research program: Part II. Legislative process," *Global Environmental Change* 10, no. 2 (2000): 133-144.

[18] See CCSP, *Strategic Plan for the U.S. Climate Change Science Program: U.S. Climate Change Science Program* (Washington, DC:

Climate Change Science Program and Subcommittee on Global Change Research, 2003), 112.

[19] Global Change Research Act of 1990, Public Law 101-606, 104 Stat. 3096-3104 (1990).

[20] CCSP, *Strategic Plan for the U.S. Climate Change Science Program: U.S. Climate Change Science Program* (Washington, DC: Climate Change Science Program and Subcommittee on Global Change Research, 2003); CCSP, *Our Changing Planet: The U.S. Climate Change Science Program for Fiscal Year 2008* (Washington, DC: Climate Change Science Program and Subcommittee on Global Change Research, 2008).

[21] Ibid.

[22] Global Change Research Act of 1990, Public Law 101-606, 104 Stat. 3096-3104 (1990).

[23] CCSP, *Strategic Plan for the U.S. Climate Change Science Program: U.S. Climate Change Science Program* (Washington, DC: Climate Change Science Program and Subcommittee on Global Change Research, 2003), 1.

[24] CCSP, *Revised Research Plan for the U.S. Climate Change Science Program* (Washington, DC: Climate Change Science Program and Subcommittee on Global Change Research, 2008), ii.

[25] CCSP, *Our Changing Planet: The U.S. Climate Change Science Program for Fiscal Year 2008* (Washington, DC: Climate Change Science Program and Subcommittee on Global Change Research, 2008).

[26] Global Change Research Act of 1990, Public Law 101-606, 104 Stat. 3096-3104 (1990).

[27] CCSP, *Our Changing Planet: The U.S. Climate Change Science Program for Fiscal Year 2008* (Washington, DC: Climate Change Science Program and Subcommittee on Global Change Research, 2008), ii.

[28] Global Change Research Act of 1990, Public Law 101-606, 104 Stat. 3096-3104 (1990).

[29] CCSP, *Strategic Plan for the U.S. Climate Change Science Program: U.S. Climate Change Science Program* (Washington, DC: Climate Change Science Program and Subcommittee on Global Change Research, 2003), 7.

[30] Ibid.

[31] Global Change Research Act of 1990, Public Law 101-606, 104 Stat. 3096-3104 (1990).

[32] CCSP, *Strategic Plan for the U.S. Climate Change Science Program: U.S. Climate Change Science Program* (Washington, DC: Climate Change Science Program and Subcommittee on Global Change Research, 2003), 7.

[33] Ibid., 8.

[34] Ibid., 2.

[35] E.g., D. W. Cash, J. C. Borck, and A. G. Patt, "Countering the loading-dock approach to linking science and decision making: Comparative analysis of El Nino/Southern oscillation (ENSO) forecasting systems," *Science, Technology, & Human Values* 31, no. 4 (2006): 465-494; K. Jacobs, G. Garfin, and M. Lenart, "More than just talk: Connecting science and decision making," *Environment* 47, no. 9 (2005): 6-21; H. Meinke, R. Nelson, P. Kokic, R. Stone, R. Selvaraju, and W. Baethgen, "Actionable climate knowledge: From analysis to synthesis," *Climate Research* 33, no. 1 (2006): 101-110.

[36] R. A. Pielke Jr., "Usable information for policy: An appraisal of the U.S. global change research program," *Policy Sciences* 28, no. 1 (1995): 39-77.

[37] S. Shackley and B. Wynne, "Representing uncertainty in global climate change science and policy: Boundary-ordering devices and authority," *Science, Technology, & Human Values* 21, no. 3 (1996): 275-302.

[38] S. Dessai and M. Hulme, "Does climate adaptation policy need probabilities," *Climate Policy* 4, no. 2 (2004): 107-128.

[39] National Research Council, *Thinking Strategically: The Appropriate Use of Metrics for the Climate Change Science Program* (Washington, DC: National Academies Press, 2005).

[40] The questions of where the "prediction imperative" in climate science has come from, and why it is so dominant a force in shaping the research agenda, are important and interesting, but require more space than I have here. G. Maricle, "Prediction as an impediment to preparedness: Lessons from the U.S. hurricane and earthquake research enterprises," *Minerva* 49, no. 1 (2011): 87-111, discusses these issues in a case study examining hazards research (earthquake and hurricane prediction).

[41] B. Latour, *Science in Action* (Cambridge, MA: Harvard University Press, 1987), cited in S. Shackley and B. Wynne, "Integrating knowledges for climate change: Pyramids, nets, and uncertainties," *Global Environmental Change* 5, no. 2 (1995): 113-126.

[42] C.f. National Research Council, *The U.S. Global Change Research Program: An Assessment of the FY 1991 Plans* (Washington, DC: National Research Council, Committee on Global Change, 1990); National Research Council, *Global Environmental Change: Understanding the Human Dimensions* (Washington, DC: National Research Council, 1992); National Research Council, *Global Environmental Change: Research Pathways for the Next Decade* (Washington, DC: National Research Council, 1999); National Research Council. *Climate Change Science: An Analysis of Some Key Questions* (Washington, DC: National Research Council, 2001); National Research Council, *Thinking Strategically: The Appropriate Use of Metrics for the Climate Change Science Program* (Washington, DC: National Academies Press, 2005); National Research Council *Evaluating Progress of the U.S. Climate Change Science Program: Methods and Preliminary Results* (Washington, DC: National Academies Press, 2007); National Research Council, "Informing decisions in a changing climate," in *Panel on Strategies and Methods for Climate-Related Decision Support* (Washington, DC: National Research Council, Committee on Human Dimensions of Global Change, 2009); National Research Council, "Restructuring federal climate research to meet challenges of climate change," prepublication version, in *Committee on Strategic Advice on the U.S. Climate Change Science Program* (Washington, DC: National Research Council, 2009). It is worth noting that many of these NRC reports were commissioned by the GCRP or CCSP for the specific purpose of providing guidance on these issues.

43 National Research Council, *Evaluating Progress of the U.S. Climate Change Science Program: Methods and Preliminary Results* (Washington, DC: National Academies Press, 2007), 4.

44 The CCSP does not offer a clear definition of "high quality science," though the examples in Table 7.1 do give some indication of what the term implies. This trope may function as a subtle, perhaps unconscious acknowledgement of the highly politicized nature of climate change debates, in which authority and expertise are routinely contested based on scientific credentials.

45 CCSP, *Revised Research Plan for the U.S. Climate Change Science Program* (Washington, DC: Climate Change Science Program and Subcommittee on Global Change Research, 2008), 10.

46 E. Lovbrand, J. Stripple, and B. Wiman, "Earth system governmentality: Reflections on science in the Anthropocene," *Global Environmental Change* 10, no. 1 (2009): 7-13.

47 To access these reports, visit http://www.usgcrp.gov/usgcrp/Library/default.htm#ocp.

48 However, the allocation of research to particular goals was done by the agencies, so the process is "black-boxed" and most likely based on inconsistent decision criteria.

49 The chapter on "Observing and Monitoring the Climate System" does not mention stakeholders but does mention decision support. It mentions users in reference to the science community.

50 CCSP, *Revised Research Plan for the U.S. Climate Change Science Program* (Washington, DC: Climate Change Science Program and Subcommittee on Global Change Research, 2008).

51 E.g., K. Jacobs, G. Garfin, and M. Lenart, "More than just talk: Connecting science and decision making," *Environment* 47, no. 9 (2005): 6-21; D. W. Cash and J. Buizer, "Knowledge-action systems for seasonal to interannual climate forecasting: Summary of a workshop," report to the Roundtable on Science and Technology for Sustainability, Policy, and Global Affairs (Washington, DC: National Academies Press, 2005).

52 National Research Council, *Evaluating Progress of the U.S. Climate Change Science Program: Methods and Preliminary Results* (Washington, DC: National Academies Press, 2007), 3.

[53] There are a few exceptions to this. NOAA and EPA both have small programs with decision support elements, and those program managers participate in the CCSP. Other departments with decision support capacity (such as Transportation, Interior, and Agriculture) do participate in the CCSP, but through their science programs, rather than their decision support programs.

[54] B. Bozeman, *Public Values and Public Interest: Counterbalancing Economic Individualism* (Washington, DC: Georgetown University Press, 2007), 16; see also B. Bozeman and D. Sarewitz, "Public value mapping and science policy evaluation," *Minerva* 49, no. 1 (2011): 1-23.

[55] Adapted from B. Bozeman, *Public Values and Public Interest: Counterbalancing Economic Individualism* (Washington, DC: Georgetown University Press, 2007).

[56] CCSP, *Strategic Plan for the U.S. Climate Change Science Program: U.S. Climate Change Science Program* (Washington, DC: Climate Change Science Program and Subcommittee on Global Change Research, 2003).

[57] There is an important distinction to be made here: research on how to apply climate science effectively, though quite necessary, does not in and of itself generate sustained capacity in that regard.

[58] CCSP, *Strategic Plan for the U.S. Climate Change Science Program: U.S. Climate Change Science Program* (Washington, DC: Climate Change Science Program and Subcommittee on Global Change Research, 2003).

[59] Ibid., 8.

[60] The strategic plan specifies that IWG participants should have budget authority within their own agencies. In practice this is not always the case. One IWG co-chair complained to me that he was the only person in the group with budget authority, making it quite difficult from them to implement new priorities, even if they wanted to.

[61] See B. Bozeman, *Public Values and Public Interest: Counterbalancing Economic Individualism* (Washington, DC: Georgetown University Press, 2007); other articles in *Minerva* 49, no. 1 (2011).

[62] Richard Nelson's account of basic science as a public good may describe an economic incentive for basic research investments in a general sense, but specific decisions to invest in, for example, biology, geology, or sociology may have a variety of drivers far removed from the logic of market failure. R. R. Nelson, "The simple economics of basic scientific research," *The Journal of Political Economy* 67, no. 3 (1959): 297-306.

[63] R. A. Pielke Jr. and R. Byerly Jr., "Beyond basic and applied," *Physics Today* 51, no. 2 (1998): 42-46.

[64] D. E. Stokes, *Pasteur's Quadrant: Basic Science and Technological Innovation* (Washington, DC: Brookings Institution Press, 1997).

[65] D. Sarewitz, *Frontiers of Illusion: Science, Technology, and the Politics of Progress* (Philadelphia, PA: Temple University Press, 1996), 10.

[66] S. Shackley and B. Wynne, "Integrating knowledges for climate change: Pyramids, nets and uncertainties," *Global Environmental Change* 5, no. 2 (1995): 113.

[67] M. Polanyi, "The republic of science: Its political and economic theory," *Minerva* 1 (1962): 62.

[68] See P. Kitcher, "What kinds of science *should* be done?" on *Living with the Genie: Essays on Technology and the Quest for Human Mastery*, A. P. Lightman, D. R. Sarewitz, and C. Desser, eds. (London, UK: Island Press, 2003); S. Toulmin, "The complexity of scientific choice: A stocktaking," *Minerva* 2, no. 3 (1964): 343-359.

[69] E.g., D. S. Greenberg, *The Politics of Pure Science* (Chicago, IL: University of Chicago Press, 1967); D. J. Kevles, *The Physicists: The History of a Scientific Community in Modern America* (New York, NY: Knopf, 1977); H. Brooks, "The evolution of U.S. science policy," in *Technology, R&D, and the Economy*, B. Smith and C. Barfield, eds. (Washington, DC: Brookings Institution, 1995).

[70] C.f. D. H. Guston, "Congressmen and scientists in the making of science policy: The Allison Commission, 1884–1886," *Minerva* 32, no. 1 (1994): 25-52; D. S. Greenberg, *Science, Money, and Politics* (Chicago, IL: University of Chicago Press, 2001); S. Toulmin, "The complexity of scientific choice: A stocktaking," *Mi-*

nerva 2, no. 3 (1964): 343-359; M. Polanyi, "The republic of science: Its political and economic theory," *Minerva* 1 (1962): 54-74; S. Jasanoff, *The Fifth Branch: Science Advisers as Policymakers* (Cambridge, MA: Harvard University Press, 1990).

71 E.g., L. Winner, *The Whale and the Reactor: A Search for Limits in an Age of High Technology* (Chicago, IL: University of Chicago Press, 1986).

72 B. A. Bimber, *The Politics of Expertise in Congress: The Rise and Fall of the Office of Technology Assessment* (Albany, NY: State University of New York Press, 1996).

73 E.g., S. E. Cozzens, "Assessment of fundamental science programs in the context of the government performance and results act (GPRA)," Critical Technologies Institute, RAND, MR-707.0-OSTP (1995).

74 J. Marburger, "Marburger defends U.S. R&D investment," American Association for the Advancement of Science (2005).

75 S. E. Cozzens, "Are new accountability rules bad for science?" *Issues in Science and Technology* 15, no. 4 (1999): 59-66; D. H. Guston, *Between Politics and Science: Assuring the Integrity and Productivity of Research* (Cambridge, UK: Cambridge University Press, 2000).

76 P. Kitcher, "What kinds of science *should* be done?" on *Living with the Genie: Essays on Technology and the Quest for Human Mastery*, A. P. Lightman, D. R. Sarewitz, and C. Desser, eds. (London, UK: Island Press, 2003).

77 B. Bozeman and J. D. Rogers, "A churn model of scientific knowledge value: Internet researchers as a knowledge value collective," *Research Policy* 31, no. 5 (2002): 769-794.

78 D. Sarewitz, "How science makes environmental controversies worse," *Environmental Science and Policy* 7 (2004): 385-403; D. Sarewitz, G. Foladori, N. Invernizzi, and M. Garfinkel, "Science policy in its social context," *Philosophy Today* 49 (2004): 67-83.

79 E.g., D. H. Guston, "Boundary organizations in environmental policy and science: An introduction," *Science, Technology, & Human Values* 26, no. 4 (2001): 399-408.

ACKNOWLEDGEMENTS

All of the articles collected here have been previously published in books, reports, or peer-reviewed journals. We are grateful to the authors for allowing us to republish their work, and to the original publishers for graciously providing permission to include these pieces and waiving their normal fees.

We would like especially to thank Island Press for permission to reprint "Decision Making and the Future of Nature: Understanding and Using Predictions," which was originally published in *Prediction: Science, Decision Making, and the Future of Nature* (2000). Guy Edwards at Oxford University Press gave us permission to use "Public Values and Public Failure in U.S. Science Policy," which was originally published in *Science and Public Policy*. Peter Weingart at *Minerva* and Lucy Fleet at Springer generously allowed us to use two articles from a special issue of *Minerva* (volume 49, no. 1, 2011): "Public Value Mapping and Science Policy Evaluation" and "The Public Values Failures of Climate Science in the United States." The other case studies in that issue would also be of great interest to anyone reading this collection. Thanks also to Lisa Dilling and the members of the SPARC project team at University of Colorado Boulder.

Thanks to Sonia Dermer for her tireless formatting efforts, and to Kimberly Quach and Leah Kaplan for copyediting assistance. Jason Lloyd spent nearly three years working on this volume—acquiring permissions, tracking down documents, editing the text, and formatting the book—and was essential to getting this important collection finally published. Finally, many thanks to series editor G. Pascal Zachary for his vision and support.

ABOUT THE CONTRIBUTORS

Marilyn Averill

Marilyn Averill is a senior fellow with the Getches-Wilkinson Center for Natural Resources, Energy, and the Environment at the University of Colorado Law School, and is affiliated with the Center for Science and Technology Policy Research at the University Colorado. Her research interests focus on international environmental governance, the politics of science, and the ethical implications of environmental issues, primarily in the context of global climate change.

Barry Bozeman

Barry Bozeman is the Arizona Centennial Professor of Public Management and Technology Policy at Arizona State University, and he is director of the Center for Organization Research and Design. He specializes in organization theory and science and technology policy.

Radford Byerly Jr.

Radford Byerly Jr. (1936-2016) spent more than twenty years on the staff of the U.S. House of Representatives Committee on Science and Technology. He served as staff director of the Space Subcommittee, and as chief of staff of the full committee. He also directed the Center for Space and Geosciences Policy at the University of Colorado Boulder. Originally trained as a physicist, he edited books and wrote articles on science policy and served on many science policy advisory committees.

Lisa Dilling

Lisa Dilling is associate professor of environmental studies and director of the Western Water Assessment team at the University of Colorado Boulder. Her scholarship focuses on decision making, the use of information, and science policy, to understand how we can best manage climate and weather risks.

J. Britt Holbrook

J. Britt Holbrook is an assistant professor in the Department of Humanities at the New Jersey Institute of Technology. His teaching and research explore the value of knowledge.

Nat Logar

Nat Logar is an Emmett/Frankel Fellow in Environmental Law and Policy at the University of California, Los Angeles, School of Law. His writing and research have explored energy innovation policy and science and public policy.

Genevieve Maricle

Genevieve Maricle is the Global Knowledge and Innovation Lead in the Climate and Energy Practice of the World Wildlife Fund. Previously, she was the senior policy advisor on climate and sustainable development to the U.S.

Ambassador to the United Nations, Samantha Power, and a policy advisor at USAID.

Elizabeth McNie

Elizabeth McNie is an assistant professor at the California State University Maritime Academy. She holds a United States Coast Guard license as a U.S. Merchant Marine 2nd Officer. Her research explores usable science, boundary organizations, and linking knowledge with action in the context of agroforestry, climate change, water resources, natural resource management, and shipping in the Arctic.

Ryan Meyer

Ryan Meyer is the executive director of the Center for Community and Citizen Science at the University of California, Davis, School of Education. He works on the connections among science, environment, and society.

Mark Neff

Mark Neff is an associate professor in the Environmental Studies Department at Western Washington University. He explores how society organizes and utilizes science to advance its interests.

Adam Parris

Adam Parris is the executive director at the Science and Resilience Institute at Jamaica Bay in New York City. He is passionate about positive change where people, waters, and diverse species converge at the coast, and about making science more relevant and useful.

Roger Pielke Jr.

Roger Pielke Jr. has been on the faculty of the University of Colorado Boulder since 2001. He is a professor of environmental studies. He is the author of *The Rightful Place of Science: Disasters & Climate Change*, 2nd ed. (2018), among many other books.

Daniel Sarewitz

Daniel Sarewitz is the co-director of the Consortium for Science, Policy & Outcomes and a professor of science and society at the School for the Future of Innovation in Society at Arizona State University. His work focuses on the connections between science policy decisions, scientific research, and social outcomes.

CPSIA information can be obtained
at www.ICGtesting.com
Printed in the USA
LVHW051013191221
706635LV00011B/1018

9 780999 587751